LITTLE ANTHONY

My Journey, My Destiny

MASCOT® BOOKS

Dedicated in loving memory to Elizabeth and Thomas Gourdine – my loving parents, Casey – my beautiful son. And to those in my life today: Linda Gourdine – my wife and soul mate, my children, grandchildren and great-grandchildren.

Requests for permission to make copies of any part of the work
should be submitted online at info@mascotbooks.com or mailed to
Mascot Books, 560 Herndon Parkway #120, Herndon, VA 20170.

ISBN-13: 9781620866931
CPSIA Code: PRB0714A

Printed in the United States

www.mascotbooks.com

LITTLE ANTHONY

My Journey, My Destiny

Arlene Krieger

FOREWORD

"I knew you before I formed you in your mother's womb. Before you were born I set you apart..." Jeremiah 1:5.

"Perhaps you are wondering why I'm quoting a verse from the Old Testament, but this is what I have come to believe. The Creator knew me before I was born and set me on my path to destiny. I believe in each of us lies a plan, our own destinies; you just have to open yourself up and listen. In this journey of life there are many obstacles thrown our way. What follows is the story of my journey, seeking the destiny that I believe has been preordained. Each one of us is unique, and each one of us is special. It doesn't matter what you do: a singer, a garbage collector, a candlestick maker, we all have a destiny and a purpose. I hope, as you read my story, you will find your own destiny, the destiny that is within each and every human soul."

CHAPTER 1

How do you measure a man's life? To explain one mortal soul whose existence is larger than the man himself? To go beyond the normal realm of thinking where one person is just one person, nothing more, nothing less: but yet, Jerome Anthony Gourdine is more than a person. The sum of his life doesn't belong to his own person, it belongs to the universe. His being embodies more than the one person he is, it embodies a multitude of lives and a multitude of souls. He has looked into the eyes of God and touched heaven's gate and he has steeped himself at the hands of the devil, to have those doors shut forever. It is his right and his calling to pay witness to a life so well-lived that it seeks a plateau of its own. Little Anthony has already earned his place in history, but his life's story supersedes his music and the man. His story is a life lived beyond all others, a life so blessed that no one thing can properly serve to define him. Redemption is how he explains his life: "I should have been dead, yet something always pulled me away. When I look back, it seems as though there was always something bigger than me that was keeping me alive. There is a God that has kept me living to tell this story of my life. He has brought me a group of people who have pushed me in a direction to live. Fifty-nine years of show business, beginning at the age of fourteen- how did I do that? Only God can answer that question. He wants me to live so I can tell my story and thank all of those people who have come with me as I eventually walk through the gates of heaven."

"My water just broke," screamed Elizabeth as she woke her sleepy husband in the middle of the night. "It's time." The couple kissed their three sons good-bye, waved to the cousin, who had been sitting the vigil, and flagged down the first cab in the dim of the early morning light. A few snowflakes floated in the bitter cold air as they were whisked to Metropolitan Hospital. The date was January 8, 1941, and the couple was hoping for a daughter. With three sons at home, they were sure this next child had to be a girl. Elizabeth had carried high and round, just like her cousins. It was meant to be; this time most certainly it was a girl's name they would be pondering in the maternity ward. When the obstetrician announced Elizabeth had given birth to a healthy son, they were shocked as they scrambled for a male name, one they never realized that would go down in history: Jerome Anthony Gourdine.

After the requisite week-long stay, they bundled up their son in a blue flannel blanket and brought him home to meet his three older brothers: Sonny, approaching twelve; Elliot, nine; and Donald, seven. Their youngest son would remain the youngest child – Elizabeth shut down shop turning out perfect baby boys. They simply gave up trying to bring home a baby wrapped in a pink blanket. Perhaps it would be unfair to confess that their youngest child stole the best of both parents. His cocoa colored skin was flawless, his cheekbones high like his mother's, his deep, dark, brown eyes set wide apart, and his bow-shaped mouth made him the cutest baby in the bunch.

When he smiled, his arched eyebrows made his entire face light up. He was a happy child who injected joy into the Gourdine household.

Like Anthony, his doting mom, Elizabeth, was the youngest in her family. At the age of ten she had lost her mother to cancer. Lying still in a dank humid room at the back of their tiny Savannah home, she and her sisters huddled around the bed watching their mother take her last breaths. Elizabeth was holding one hand, Bessie the other and when the last sigh reached their mother's lips, Elizabeth looked up and screamed, "Damn!" Shortly after, the three sisters packed up the household, bought tickets on a steamer, and moved from the hardships of Savannah's prejudice to the thriving world of New York City. By Southern Black standards, they had lived a comfortable life. With several acres of rich farmland the parents had carved out a decent living: sending the children to school, living in a substantial home, setting the dining room table with a bounty of fresh food every day. This life was torn away from them when the land was illegally taken by jealous white neighbors. The family was left destitute and when their mom became ill, there was no money for treatment. The sisters stood around helplessly and watched their beloved mother wither away.

It was a simple fact of life that if the oppressed Southern Blacks could muster enough money, they would hop on the cheapest form of transportation and move to the northern industrialized cities where jobs were attainable and they could make a decent living. The four sisters formed a tight family circle, abounding in companionship and enduring love and trust. It was all they needed as they struggled to make it in the city. Each sister shined in her own way: one a cook, another singer, a worker, and the last a disciplinarian, but as different as they were, their sisterly love was a tight knot no one could ever untwist. Elizabeth was coddled by her older sisters, but she needed the warmth and affection with a mother gone before Elizabeth reached her early teens. Undeniably attractive, with a small button nose, symmetrical face, and large round eyes, she was strikingly beautiful and she had a beautiful curvaceous body to match. Men were drawn to her and at the tender age of fifteen, she found herself pregnant and was very depressed. She had known Thomas for several months, and he stepped up to the plate, and to save her face and humiliation he asked her to marry him. A true child bride she went on to stamp out three boys before she reached twenty. Back-to-back babies left a gorgeous young woman exhausted, and thus she waited seven years before Anthony appeared on the scene.

The four boys in the household were raised by Elizabeth and her three sisters, with each taking an active role, contributing in the boys' lives while Thomas worked. Everyone thrived, became educated, obtained jobs, had comfortable roofs over their heads, food on the table, and clothing in their closets. Between Harlem and the projects in Brooklyn, the family lived happy, fulfilled lives. Life in the city was so much different than in Savannah. Every place was integrated. They weren't naïve enough to think that racism was negated once they crossed the Mason-Dixon Line, but at least in the North, there were no blatant signs of loathing. They lived side by side with people of all races and backgrounds. The local shops were filled with food, clothing and goods from around the world, and no one was sent away at the ice-cream counter because of the color of their skin. New York was a true melting pot of cultures where they shared and accepted differences.

The Upper West Side apartment soon became cramped with four energetic boys and two parents who needed privacy from time to time. One year later, the moving van arrived and transported the family to the Fort Greene Projects (Navy housing built in Brooklyn to take care of the workers at the Naval Yard). The four bedroom apartment was huge, with a large living room for playing and watching television, three bedrooms for the kids, and one slightly larger master bedroom and two full bathrooms. Although the kitchen was small, it was large in comparison to their last space. With an ice-box, they were in heaven as the six shared their lives together.

Thomas kissed his four sons good-bye as he left each morning to work as an electrician on the massive Navy ships docked at the harbor. His hair was slicked back in thick waves held by an elixir from the local barber shop, his curved thick eyebrows and eclipsed shaped mouth were always in a turned up smiling position. Clear and certain, he was a happy man who rarely, if ever, raised his voice and rarely, if ever, disciplined his offspring. Lanky and tall, his calloused hands gave away his trade: they were strong with a grip toughened by years of tireless manual labor.

Standing at the base of the Battleship Missouri, he was a proud man: he was working on the largest seaworthy ship in the Navy, which would have a history of its own as it plowed through ocean waves and fell into combat. Launched January 29, 1944, Thomas was steeped in pride as "Mighty Mo" slowly eased out of the shipyard and into the unexpectedly turbulent ocean waters. "I remember outings with my dad to the Naval Yard as we stood at the pier staring at the bow of the huge ship. Dad would tell me how he had laid the electrical lines and then point up to the lights flickering on inside the windows. He was gratified of the work he had done on that ship and the many ships to come, but mostly, he was proud to be an American. My dad was a happy and contented person. He made me feel that way when I was way too young to understand. His constant smile told me all I ever needed to know about my pa."

Yet Thomas' true passion, other than his love for Elizabeth, was music. In the evenings he would practice the saxophone by playing gigs with numerous famous swing bands. Many nights the four boys were lulled to sleep from the sweet sounds emanating from the brass horn. In dreams, the youngest child replayed those sounds over and over again – they soothed him, bringing him a sense of peace and joy. There were many other nights their dad left home performing with Duke Ellington, Buddy Johnson, and Count Basie, playing both alto and tenor sax. The bands were all-Black and they entertained at all-Black nightclubs, the two most well-known being the Cotton Club, and the Apollo Theater, still standing today.

"Please take me with you, Dad," pleaded the three-year-old, "I want to hear you play with a real band."

"Can you promise to be good, to sit still and listen?" Thomas questioned.

"Yes, I can do that. I want to hear you play." The look in Anthony's eyes was so sincere that Thomas grabbed his son's jacket, threw some snacks into a paper bag, and together they boarded the subway up to Harlem and the famed Apollo Theater. Thomas found a small chair and set it behind the red velvet curtains as close to the stage as possible so he could keep a watchful eye on his young son. Once the music began, Anthony's face lit up as he listened intently to the swing sounds of the orchestra. Although his dad had played music on the large vinyls at home, this was the first time he had heard the music live and he was in heaven. His tiny body moved to the rhythm of the drums and his feet tapped on the sides of the chair as he took in the melodies of the swing sounds. That night, two women sang fast jive sounds to an upbeat tempo and Anthony popped out of his seat swaying and humming to the music. When the show ended at midnight, Thomas zipped up his son's jacket, carried his sleeping body down the steps of the subway, up the steps of their apartment, and placed him lovingly in his crib. That night, Anthony witnessed his first live show, and somewhere deep inside his mind, it became his passion paving the road he would take for the rest of his life.

Since Elizabeth had closed up her baby producing days, she, too, took a job: at A&S, the finest department store in the heart of Brooklyn. Her was job was to man the information booth but on many occasions when the porters called in sick, she took charge of the elevators, whisking customers up and down the store. In her early thirties, her slim body showed few telltale signs of carrying four healthy babies to term. Her oval face was the color of bronzed seashells, her eyes were wide, her cheekbones high, and her mouth full – usually holding a smile. She had long legs and when dressed for work in strapping heels, they seemed to go on forever. Elizabeth was strikingly beautiful and she knew how to accentuate her beauty with the products that she shared with her cousins. Running the elevator, yelling out the floor numbers, sometimes she sang out the items at each level. Like her husband, she too performed, but it was as a singer with the Nazareth Baptist Gospel Singers who toured throughout the boroughs of New York City and the tri-state area. As Anthony looked back on his life, it might have been his parents who raised him, but it was the Nazareth Singers who fed him the fuel, and who made him infatuated with singing.

On any given day of the week, before Anthony had entered elementary school, if there was a performance by either parent, they took their youngest son to listen to the live shows, which were always filled with animation and intense emotion. The sounds of music became the heart and soul of his being, defining the world he would come to live in. Surprisingly his three older brothers never shared this passion, nor accompanied the parents to the shows; they preferred playing ball in the streets, or meeting up with their friends. Elizabeth knew her boys and the one thing she sensed about her youngest was that he could sing. At three years old, he would break out in song in his crib, keeping his brothers up late into the night. "The first song I ever remember singing was 'Lay That Pistol Down'. This was the beginning. It just came naturally; I have always sung, that's all I ever remember doing and that's all I ever wanted to do," reminisced Anthony, who was too young to realize that in fact, he was a child prodigy. "When I sang, people listened to me and they were drawn to me. When I opened up my voice, people paid attention. I made friends with my voice, something no one else could do. So I just kept singing and singing."

With four children and four jobs, when Saturday night rolled around, Thomas and Elizabeth took the train up to the base of Harlem and celebrated the weekend with her family. Bessie and Sarah were Elizabeth's sisters and they, along with Hilda made up the Gospel group and were in charge of the weekly weekend celebrations. Living on top of each other, the women took turns hosting the Saturday night parties. Opening up the front door, Anthony was fondly greeted by his aunts, godmother, and several other friends; he was the only child in the whole bunch. Taking off his jacket, he glanced up at the flocked wallpaper, and down at the oak-planked floor, a lot nicer and cleaner than his own home. From the perspective of a young child, his aunts were rich. The glass rectangular coffee table and dark red leather lounger had been turned sideways to make room for dancing. Anthony looked up into the large deep set brown eyes of Aunt Shortie and smiled. She was wearing a purple print jersey dress with shiny black buttons and a rhinestone clip in her dense curly hair caught up in a bun at the base of her neck. In every sense of the word, she was regal, like an

Amazon queen. She always had a look of determination on her face, especially when she sang with his mother. She believed every word she was singing and for those who sat and listened, she made them believe it too. He knew later that night she would be performing and he looked forward to that, but for the moment, he had to put up with her series of hugs and kisses. Breaking away, he ran into the kitchen, a shield from doting family members; in this room everyone was so busy scurrying about, no one noticed him.

The kitchen was illuminated brightly by overhead lighting. The yellow patterned linoleum matched the yellow metal drawers of the huge space and in the corner sat a black dial telephone with one of his uncles talking to someone about numbers. The smell of Southern cooking wafted through the air, and the alcohol was freely poured. The large 78s were pulled from their jackets and the music pulsated. After the potluck meal, someone would pluck the needle off the record player, break open a brass horn or two, sit down at the piano, and then the live family concert began. The soulful sounds of the Gospel music drowned out the smell of the food, replacing the atmosphere with revelry and pure, unadulterated joy. As the only child, Anthony bore witness to the supreme talent of not only his parents, but also his extended family. His aunts' voices were just as magnificent as his mother's – but when they sang as a unit, it was divine. Seated on an uncle's lap, he clapped to the music, soaking in the bounty and the essence of the sounds. Although quiet, he was engaged; he just wasn't ready to actively share in the overwhelming scene.

Thomas seemed to wake up from his dull work-week routine and radiated on those Saturday nights. He would shine his shoes, button up his finest white cotton shirt, pull on a freshly pressed pair of trousers, and steam the lint off his suit jacket. Then he would go into the bathroom, take great pains to slick back his hair, lightly dab cologne on his neck, and fold over his printed silk tie just so. It was as if he were paying homage to the music he was about to play. For him, the music was his church; it was what he believed in most, his place of reverence. This was what the youngest child witnessed as they locked the front door of the apartment and took the train up to Harlem.

Picking up his saxophone, Thomas would play it like he was making love. Caressing the polished metal, his fingers adeptly pressed in the spatula and side keys as the notes bellowed up the neck of the horn releasing the rich, sounds of soulful jazz. Each sound was more than a note as it gently rose, peaked, lingering just until the next phrase. It was about more than the keys, but also timing, an oscillating sound on the same pitch, all emanating from a passion so deep, only an artist could recreate these intense tones. Those were the memories that settled into Anthony's brain as he soaked in every note. Unlike his brothers, it became a huge part of who he would eventually become. It was his father's heart and soul melting into him, and as time progressed, he would be able to duplicate those soulful sounds, but in his own way. The party would continue for hours, sometimes until the first rays of daylight filtered through the curtains in the living room and then everyone would disband, preparing for Sunday church.

Being a religious family, no matter how hung over, or how late they arrived home, the entire family dressed and walked to the Baptist church. The pastor cared deeply for Elizabeth. Both she and three other women had made a name for his beloved church with their prominent Gospel group. It was a rare Sunday morning when all of the pews weren't filled, even in the worst of the Brooklyn winters. Although the pastor hoped it was his skilled rhetoric that kept the seats warm, in his heart he knew it was the sanguine voices of the choir and the Nazareth Gospel group that kept the worshipers returning.

The guaranteed time of the week when all the brothers would be together was always Sunday School at the church; but church wasn't just the morning services, it rambled on the entire day. There was the morning service, followed by lunch, an early afternoon service and an early evening service, and what did all these services have in common? Music, of course. Unlike his three older brothers who left church as soon as the first session was over, Anthony stayed the rest of the day savoring the music and the message it brought. Cute as a button, with his cherubic face, small nose, short cropped hair, and happy demeanor, the girls were drawn to Anthony like bees to honey. He loved the attention and he learned to love the girls.

As the years passed, and Anthony continued to accompany his parents to the Saturday night parties, he became more animated and less shy about opening up and joining in the entertainment. Everyone was jubilant: singing, dancing, clapping, or playing an instrument; it was like a private concert, every weekend. As a toddler, he had been quiet, had sat back listening and observing, but now his feet were tapping, his mouth moving to the melodies, and his body swaying to the beat. As the music coursed through his blood, Aunt Bessie yelled over to her nephew, "Anthony, get up and dance!" It was as if he had been waiting for permission to join the adults, and now, with his aunt's blessing, he got up off the chair and began dancing to the upbeat tempo tunes. Smiling, he flailed his thin arms in the air, bouncing up and down to the rhythm; he was happily enthralled and completely immersed in the music. When his uncle plucked the needle off the record and announced dinner was served, he was sorely disappointed, but he knew there was plenty of music to come before the night ended.

"Anthony, come over here and give me a kiss," demanded Shortie. Without hesitation, he leaped across the room and kissed his aunt on her cheek. She was the disciplinarian and all the boys stood at attention when Shortie was in their presence. Ironically, she was the tallest and largest sister in the family. Often demanding hugs, none of the boys could ever get their arms completely wrapped around her large girth. When she was young, a doctor had operated on her leg, leaving one shorter than the other and for the rest of her life, she walked with a limp, unable to properly exercise. Shortie became her nickname because of that shortened leg, but she graciously accepted her fate, making the best of the other traits she had been blessed with. Her head of thick brown curls and broad smile were always abundant whenever she was around the family and for Shortie, that was enough. Both sides of the family were rooted in the South, which was reflected in the abundance of Southern cooking. Mounds of fried chicken, bowls of potato salad, steamed collard greens, dirty rice, and biscuits oozing with melted butter and honey were arranged on the long oak dining room table and everyone helped themselves while one of the uncles played bartender. Him being the only child left at home, they always made sure Anthony's plate was filled and that he had a proper seat flanked by two hovering aunts. The dining room was fastidiously set with fine china, starched white linens, and crystal stemware. A series of candles lit the room with a soft peach glow, creating a warmth reflecting the loving family. Observing his uncles and aunts – smiling, laughing, raising their glasses to toast a series of boastful events – all Anthony ever took away from these Saturday nights was the happiness and love they felt for each other. There was never a squabble or bad vibrations. It was all about the love and joy in living.

Anthony would never say he had a perfect childhood, but it came pretty close. He was constantly surrounded by love and support. As he sat gobbling down the remains of his chicken leg, he was as content as any child could be.

The clanging of dirty dishes in the kitchen sink signaled dinner was over, and it was time to get to the heart of the evening: live music. Sensing the right moment had arrived, Aunt Bessie encouraged her nephew, "Sing, Anthony, sing." Accompanied by an uncle seated at the piano and aunts in the choir, he joined them, keeping perfectly in tune, all the while wearing a wide grin. He had found his niche, a place where he was completely happy.

Along his musical journey, Anthony attributed an appreciation of classical music to his elementary school teacher, Ethel Mannex, who introduced him to the sounds of Bach, Beethoven, Brahms, Mozart and Wagner. "I remember looking up above the chalkboard and starring into the photos of all those great composers. Friday was music appreciation day and the teacher would play all that beautiful music. I remember staring out the window, watching the birds fly by, the clouds moving slowly across the sky, all the while soaking in the sounds of the music. As lunchtime grew near, the teacher gave us kids a choice: we could either go outside and play ball, or go to the auditorium and watch *Bambi*. I was the only boy who chose *Bambi* and was teased by all the other boys as they left the lunchroom to play outside. I chose *Bambi* because I loved the music that Disney productions had put into every screenplay: it was warm, playful, and helped shaped my appreciation of songs and melody lines. Jiminy Cricket's "When You Wish Upon A Star" was my absolute favorite song. With its strong melody and hopeful lyrics, it opened up limitless possibilities: 'When you wish upon a star, makes no difference who you are…your dreams come true.'"

Anthony believed those lyrics, and believed in himself, but at eight, he just didn't know how far he could take his dreams.

"I loved school. PS 67, in the Fort Greene Projects was where I began my formal education, but as I reflect on that time, I have a disdain for the use and the purpose of the IQ tests. We all had to take them and based upon the results, they would put you in a category and once you were labeled, it was like a paper bag that you couldn't fight your way out of. It was one size fits all and that doesn't really work. They told me I had an IQ of 94; what a joke. Putting that seed of potential brain power into my mind was not geared to the benefit of the kids; it was to benefit the teachers. The test didn't look at your talent or creativity. It was just a confined little box that the teachers used to predetermine your potential. I guess they were wrong about me. I couldn't have cared less at the time. I just kept doing what I loved, and that saw me through." When spring rolled around and the days grew warmer and lighter, Aunt Bessie took Anthony under her wing, helping to shape and mold him into the man he was to become. One afternoon, she packed a picnic hamper filled with her Southern specialties and they ventured to a graveyard where several members of the family had been buried. She laid a large blanket in the middle of the cemetery, and they sat for hours singing, talking, and sharing lunch. She taught him to sing, "God is My Sunbeam," which was the very first song he performed in front of an audience – albeit a church audience that was very forgiving.

The next morning, the pastor called the seven-year-old, dressed somberly in a dark blue suit with a white shirt and striped tie, to the pulpit. The pastor nodded to the choir, and Anthony sang the psalm his Aunt Bessie had so patiently taught him, a cappella at the Nazareth Baptist Church. There was no applause – it was church, and singing was like saying prayer – but there was a strong chorus of hallelujahs echoing along throughout the church when he had finished. Smiling, he scampered off to the Sunday School classroom, joining the rest of his classmates as they colored pictures for the upcoming Thanksgiving holiday. After the successful performance, Bessie turned toward Elizabeth and told her that her youngest son was going to be a preacher, a singing preacher. "Just mark my words," she prognosticated, "Did you hear the way that boy of yours can sing? He is an angel. Did you know that just yesterday, I taught him how to sing that very song and today, how beautiful it sounded? My oh my, that little boy has got talent."

Reverend Milton kept the youngsters busy and out of trouble with his Sunday youth day activities; between early morning classes, lunch, recess, movies, singing, dancing, art, and snacks, the parishioner's children were safe and well cared for. When the church day finally ended, Aunt Bessie retrieved her nephew, walked him home and entertained him until her sister came to collect him. Never married and without children, Bessie showered Anthony not only with love, but imbued him with a sense of self-worth and a belief that he could do anything he set his mind to do. She, more than her sister, believed in his extraordinary talent, and supported him at every opportunity. If it wasn't in song, it was piano playing, or listening to the radio, or dancing, or teaching him to sing Gospel melodies.

In spite of all those long Sundays spent in the house of God, Anthony was a boy and boys will be boys. "Robert Leek, we all called him 'Popi' although I can't tell you why, lived three flights down from our apartment and we were friends. He never exactly could tell you who or what happened to his mother, but his grandmother raised him. He was a couple of years older than me and in my eyes, he knew the way of the world. I remember that Saturday like it was yesterday. Popi's grandma was getting on in years, and on that Saturday she was too sick to go out. She asked her grandson to do her a little favor. Handing him a brown bag she told him to take it to the pizza parlor a few blocks away, but what she failed to tell him was why. Back then, when people got older and there was no Social Security, running numbers for the local mafia was a way for retirees to make a few bucks and help pay the bills. I remember racing down the steps and yelling at Popi, who told me he was going on a walk, and since it was Saturday, and the weather was sunny, and I had nothing else better to do, I joined him. We started walking and I asked him what was in the brown bag. He looked at me with big sad eyes and explained his grandma told him to deliver the bag but not to look inside.

"'Not to look inside? Don't you want to know what's inside the bag? Well if you don't want to know what's inside I do, it could be anything.' I grabbed the bag and lifted it in the air, didn't weigh all that much, but Popi quickly grabbed it back, holding it close to his chest."

"'Come on,' I pestered, 'aren't you curious? Let's have a look, it can't do any harm, just to look.' So we stopped near a tree and together we opened the bag. Our hearts stopped: it was filled with money, lots of money, more than we had ever seen. I could tell that Popi was surprised and a little nervous, so I suggested that we take a small cut from the bag, convincing him that no one would ever know some of the money was gone. There was so much money in that bag that taking a tiny bit would surely go unnoticed. We both went a little crazy: first we got something to eat, and then we went to the toy store and bought a bunch of small toys, and then onto the candy store. We were having so much fun spending all that money.

"Finally Popi said we had better get going, and with full stomachs and bags of toys, we walked into the pizza parlor. I remember the place was empty except for a high school kid with his hands in flour and then this huge man comes out from the back and grabs the bag. He shakes it and then looks at the two of us, waves his hand, and tells us to leave.

"Two days later Mrs. Leeks gets an unhappy call from that very same man at the pizza store bitterly complaining that the numbers didn't jive and a lot of the loot was missing. He blamed the missing money on the two of us boys and told Popi's grandma in no uncertain terms that money better be returned or there would be hell to pay. It was no secret, everyone knew they were mafia and it was no secret what the mafia could do; they are unforgiving and they never forget. That night, Mrs. Leeks took the elevator to see my parents and explained what had happened, and that the money had to be returned, or else. It was the 'or else' that worried my parents the most, so we were punished. My dad, who never laid a hand on me, and rarely disciplined me at all, was so angry that he gave me a sound beating, and I was sent to my room. There were no movies or fun stuff for several Saturdays, and for Popi, it was the same.

"Between my parents and Mrs. Leek, the money was eventually paid back. The only good thing that came out of those Saturday afternoons was that, left alone with my ma, I learned how to play cards. She taught me all there was to know about poker."

CHAPTER 2

"Hurry up," shouted Elizabeth, as she extracted a sweet potato casserole from the oven. "It's time to go to Thanksgiving dinner." Wearing high heels and a soft, printed wool sheath, she was radiantly beautiful despite her harried state as she readied her four sons, scooting them out the front door. Thomas stood at the rear watching the boys cluster around their mom as he securely latched the door, and carted off the huge, hot casserole. "Sweetheart, from the weight of this, I think it will feed an army." And an army they were about to help feed as they entered Bessie and Shortie's home. Emerging from the subway, Sonny, the eldest brother, remarked he could smell the turkey cooking from a block away. Walking into the crowded apartment, the extended family of twenty-five was dressed in their Sunday best already singing, drinking, and nibbling on appetizers. Because the occasion was a bit more somber than the raucous of Saturday night parties, the atmosphere was a bit more subdued. Instead of contemporary, upbeat tunes, the three sisters gathered around the piano singing Gospel music, which held all the revelry of rock and roll, but with a reverent message. When the last silver platter had been set on the table, the family clasped hands, creating an unbroken ring around the huge dining table, said grace, and then sang grace. With the harmonies resounding off the walls and ceilings of the apartment, the true essence of the holiday was celebrated: the love of family.

There was such an abundance of food and drink, it was impossible to taste all the dishes, but Elizabeth took charge, filling up four plates for her sons, and then one for herself. No one fought over the turkey legs. Her sister Sarah had not only prepared three huge turkeys, but cooked several extra legs so every child could have their own, and for that, Elizabeth was forever grateful. The warmth of family and friendship permeated the room as the adults talked amongst themselves while keeping a watchful eye on the children's table. After stuffing themselves, the women cleared the table in preparation for dessert, while Thomas and the uncles tuned up their instruments, playing the softer sounds of jazz. Bessie yelled out from the kitchen, "Sing something, Anthony," and with no coaxing, an uncle began playing the piano, nodded, and waited for his nephew to join him as they sang their favorite psalm. At home it was okay to clap, and that they did when he had finished. He basked in the glow of his family, and every time Anthony sang, he grew stronger, happier, and more confident. This was the road he wanted to travel; music became the essence and the purpose of his life.

"If you are creative in one part of your life, you become creative in other parts of your life," said Anthony as he remembered his first cooking lessons with Aunt Sarah. Although his mom was a decent cook, with two jobs and a family of six to feed, she cooked expeditiously, rarely lingering over potted meats or convoluted recipes. But at his aunt's home, where she was fortunate enough to just sing in the Gospel group and care for only one perfect daughter, Bea, her cuisine was just short of gourmet. Unlike any other nephew or niece, Anthony would run into her kitchen and watch her cook while she explained not only the ingredients, but exactly how she was preparing each dish. The aromas drifting through her kitchen intoxicated his senses and being the curious soul that he was, he stood patiently, taking in the culinary lessons as if he were studying at Le Cordon Bleu. She taught him a plethora of Southern delicacies, the shrimp patties later bringing an award from Wine & Culinary. What his Aunt Sarah taught him was to understand and test the food for taste, making his palette discern the difference in flavors. Closing his eyes, she would spoon food into his mouth, discuss the flavors and how to improve, or simply leave the dish as it was. The teachings of his aunt have remained with him his entire life; the difference between a well-prepared dish and an ill-prepared one was akin to the difference of a well- or poorly-sung song. What his family gave him was the ability to make accurate judgments, whether it was in music, food, or behavior. They provided the foundation of his ethics, his talents, his values, and his future success, but above all, they taught him the essence of love.

"It's my favorite holiday, has always been, and will always be: Christmas, especially Christmas in New York City." It was the fragrant evergreen tree that their dad dragged home from the corner each year that marked the beginning of the holiday. It always had to be the biggest, tallest, fattest tree on the lot, and when it was finally assembled in the center of the living room, Thomas would grab his shears and trim it with the skill of a barber, making it perfectly symmetrical. Since he was an electrician, the lights were expertly hung, illumination flickering throughout the living room. Then he would ceremoniously remove the white star which lived stuffed inside a shoe box, and place it at the top of the tree. The tree appeared magical. When he was done, Thomas gathered the family, creating a circle around the evergreen, just to ensure that every limb had been perfectly trimmed. The boys hugged their dad, and told him it was the best most beautiful Christmas tree they had ever seen, although it sure looked exactly like the one he had trimmed the year before. The four boys stood thoughtfully, taking in the smell of the pine as they dreamed about the gifts Santa would be leaving on Christmas morning.

New York was the place to celebrate the holidays. All decked out with decorations, A&S was their first destination as Elizabeth held Anthony's hand in the biting cold, pointing out the different scenes depicted in each window. He sat on Santa's lap as the photographer snapped pictures, and then it was onto the toy section where his eyes grew big at the sight of rows upon rows of toys. Every wish any young child had at Christmastime could be found in the massive selection of toys. With both parents working, each year Santa was able to up the ante, sliding down the chimney with a more bountiful selection of gifts.

Being the consummate dreamer, Anthony never wanted to give up the idea of Santa Claus. On the playground during middle school, he was heckled by classmates that he still believed. Embarrassed, he refrained from responding, but when he returned home that evening he shared the incident with his dad. Being a parent was trying, especially when raising someone as quirky as Anthony. Mulling over the situation, Thomas and Elizabeth came to terms and decided on a plan that would break the news gently to their youngest child. That following Saturday morning, Thomas boarded the train to Sears with his youngest son. After again reviewing the holiday windows, they took the elevator to the top floor. At first Anthony ran to stand in line to see Santa, but Thomas sharply took his hand leading him to the huge room of toys.

"What would you like for Christmas this year?" asked his father.

"Dad, I can't tell you, I have to tell Santa."

"No, tell me what you would like. Would you like a train set?" Shaking his head yes, when that exact train set showed up underneath the tree, Anthony finally accepted the fact that Santa Claus was his dad. For a child so smart and discerning in other ways, there were dreams he simply didn't want to give up.

After early morning Christmas services, the family quickly returned home, where they grabbed bundles of brightly wrapped gifts and whatever casserole Elizabeth had prepared, and took the subway up to Aunt Sara's home for feasting and gift sharing. The house smelled different than at Thanksgiving: there were roasts in the over, garlic mixed with onions, and the sharp scent of cabbage. So many flavors and so many smells! The cousins played in Bea's room, while the adults popped open bottles of champagne and Johnnie Walker, toasting the holiday and giving thanks that they had made it through another season together. They said a prayer and blessed the food, and with a sharp slap of a knife slicing into the huge roast beef, the room came alive, as Sarah's husband announced, "Let's eat." The solemn pall quickly lifted as they dug into the rich food. Finally, the children were set free to open the sea of gifts lining the base of the tree. The sounds of laughter and music echoed throughout the home. They were safe, happy, and healthy. Life didn't get much better than that.

Saturday evening get-togethers with the family continued as the years passed and Anthony, still the only child, made his weekly appearances. Sandwiched in between his uncles and aunts, he would dance to whatever was on the record player as he gazed up at the taller adults. Now too big to be picked up, he received endless hugs and squeezes while he attentively observed the dance moves. When it came time for the live entertainment, the family gave Anthony more and more opportunities and support. Singing alone, with his aunts, or harmonizing with the jazz sounds, he learned and appreciated how to perform a wide range of songs.

"Not this Saturday," said Elizabeth, "Tonight we will go upstairs to Aunt Sarah's home, and you can play with Bea. Sweetheart, your Aunt Bessie doesn't feel that well so we will let her rest." Although he wouldn't quibble with his mom, he sensed something was wrong – but he was young and didn't give it another thought. That night the celebration continued, but when his mom and aunts got up to sing and Bessie was missing, he saw his mom shed rare tears. There was no cause for celebration. The following Saturday, the entire family found themselves at the cemetery, the very same cemetery that Bessie had taken Anthony earlier that spring. As the pastor said the obligatory prayers, Anthony stood mute, numb with pain. It was all so final. So young at thirty-two, it didn't seem fair. As they lowered the casket into the ground, Anthony could hear her say, "Dance, Anthony, dance; sing, Anthony, sing. You're going to be a preacher, I just know it, and I love you." He shed more tears at the funeral than he had his entire ten years of life. Crushed, he flung himself on the casket and fainted from heartbreak. The large circle of family and friends couldn't console him; he had loved his Aunt Bessie so much, and there was no one who could ever take her place. "I remember the scent of smelling salts under my nose as I woke up in a daze at Aunt Sarah's home. They told me I fainted, right on the casket. I don't remember that, all I could remember was the deep sense of pain I felt."

Life went on. Anthony watched his mom grieve for the loss of a sister while he took to the roof of the projects sharing his grief with the stars, the moon, and God. I Believe, made famous by the Frankie Laine, truly expressed all that he was feeling inside. From the top of the building he could see the lights of Manhattan, the skyline of Queens, and the inky blue waters of the Atlantic Ocean. "Who's up there?" he wondered. The view gave him peace, and a chance to heal the deep wounds left by the absence of Aunt Bessie. He was a dreamer and there was no place better on this earth than to do it from the top of the apartment building, the view was as limitless as his life was about to come.

Except for a mild bump or two in the road, Anthony's childhood was as perfect as anyone could hope for. The youngest of a bevy of brothers, he was doted on by uncles, aunts and older cousins, all who contributed to enriching and encouraging his talents. Although it was obvious from the Saturday night parties that their nephew was gifted, none of them foresaw the legend he would become. Nevertheless, this perfect life would be shattered by forces over which he had no control.

Thomas had a younger sister, Naomi, who became a member of the household. Coming from Charleston, South Carolina, her parents wanted their daughter to have a better education and a chance at better opportunities. Although the Gourdine household was already brimming with life, Thomas made room for his fourteen-year-old niece. She was another mouth to feed, another young child to clothe, but he loved his family, and when they asked favors, he always stepped up to the plate. It wasn't as if Naomi had a bad life; quite the contrary: for a Southern Black child, she lived well, but her mother, Eleanor, wanted more for her daughter. Naomi's grandmother had been a maid, Eleanora was a maid, and when Naomi looked into her crystal ball, all she could see for her life was to become a third generation maid. No, that was not the life she wanted nor what her parents wanted. Her mom worked as a maid inside the stately home of Chief Justice Earl Warren. On certain days when there was no babysitter in sight, Eleanor would bring Naomi along. Unlike every other maid, she knocked on the front door, and was allowed entrance by the servant on duty. Walking to the kitchen at the rear of the first floor, she wrapped a clean apron around her waist and began an unremarkable day of chores. On many occasions, Naomi would run into different sections of the mansion. One morning, she discovered the Justice's daughter, and they began playing together. Their friendship flourished, and became so strong that it was decided that Naomi would accompany the Justice's daughter to school. The only black child in a room filled with affluent white children, she kept up with the school work. Her mom knew at some point that the girls would have to part; there would simply be too much pressure from friends, peers, and family. Eleanora could almost feel the humiliation Naomi would face if a slip of the tongue occurred, and a classmate called her a nigger. So Eleanora made the call to Thomas, packed up a small suitcase, and sent her daughter to New York. When the day arrived and the bus door opened, Eleanora grabbed Naomi, kissed her, and then whispered into her ear, "No, sweetheart, you're not going to be a maid, you are going to be someone great."

The North provided those opportunities, and Naomi's parents were willing to give up watching her grow so that she could grow up in a richer, more promising life. Elizabeth made sure Naomi would have all that she needed for a successful life. Showered with love, and all the material items her own parents were unable to provide, it was a splendid day when Naomi walked down the aisle and accepted her high school diploma. She stayed until she was nineteen, and found the love of her life, Washington, married, and set out on an independent life. She never forgot Thomas or Elizabeth, the love and compassion they had given her, and the opportunities they provided that paved the way to her content and happy life.

CHAPTER 3

On Saturday morning Elizabeth and Anthony boarded the subway for a trip to downtown Brooklyn. The first stop was the bank where she deposited both paychecks and cashed just enough money to purchase a couple of birthday gifts and some new clothes for her growing son. The corner bank stood taller than the surrounding buildings, appearing regal in prewar architecture. The façade towered above Anthony's head, and his mother had business to attend to in this important place. "Stay outside, I'll be right back," Elizabeth admonished. Already jumping around the sidewalk, staring up at the top of the building, he remained happily in the crisp morning air. A couple of pigeons had landed on a nearby bench and he raced over to tease them away. Watching the three birds flap their wings and fly across the street, he laughed, and felt strong, powerful, and in charge. Another child was standing patiently near the edge of the bank door, also waiting for his mother and intently watched this unknown kid chasing the pigeons.

When his mother emerged from the bank, he yelled, "Hey, Mom, there's a nigger running around like a fool." Anthony stopped dead in his tracks, and felt an overwhelming sense of degradation. He had never heard that word, but his intuition told him it wasn't good.

Elizabeth emerged from the building, grasped Anthony's hand, and began walking toward the shops. The beauty of Montague Street had disintegrated. The beauty of all those thick oak trees lining the streets, all of those majestic Tudor homes dissipated, the only thing on his mind was the echo of the word "nigger" ringing in his ears. Did it matter that it was a young boy who had screamed the word? He needed to know. When they arrived home, Elizabeth tossed the packages on the kitchen table and Anthony took her arm, looked into her eyes and asked, "Mom, what's a nigger? A kid called me that today when you were in the bank. I think it's bad, but I did nothing to hurt him." A somber expression replaced Elizabeth's radiant glow. She pulled out two chairs, sat her son down and began a conversation that would be much more difficult than the birds and the bees. Explaining hate and bigotry was so daunting a task, she didn't know where to begin, but she knew this wasn't a topic to be brushed underneath the carpet: ignoring it didn't mean it didn't exist or that it would go away. Methodically, she explained hate, but kept her voice soft and steady. She wasn't about to pass this legacy onto the next generation, but Anthony had the right to understand.

"My neighborhood was completely integrated, a melting pot of first- and second-generation immigrants who all sought the same thing: a better life. It was the rainbow of cultures that made the projects a rich, safe, and interesting place to live.

"*Our Gang* was my favorite show; it was all about a bunch of kids having a great time together. The show could have been filmed right at our playground. We all grew up together, a mixed bag of races and cultures. We played and ate together, we were too busy to notice the differences, and our parents were too busy working to point out the differences. If it was Friday night, the Goldbergs ate chicken soup and said prayers over brass candlesticks, and if it was Ash

Wednesday, some of my friends had a black smudge on their foreheads. Our differences never overshadowed our love for each other, nor did we see those differences as barriers. We embraced and accepted our diversities. Unlike that kid at the corner of Montague Street, we saw ourselves as part of the community. I never wanted to be like that kid. That was one of the hardest days of my life and I knew it was hard on my mom. I never heard that word again until years later when I began my first tour with the Imperials, but I never ever forgot it."

Shiny, long, and black, the 1948 Packard was the biggest car Anthony had every laid eyes on. It smelled just so, a smell so unique that decades later when he attended an antique car show, that same scent remained. Perhaps it was the upholstery, or the memories of those long afternoon drives, but that smell never left his memory.

The owner of this car was Uncle Oliver, a tall and swarthy man, who loved his Aunty Shortie. They didn't live together, but back then, it was considered polite and deserved to call this man his uncle. He was the only person who owned a vehicle, so six adults and one young child piled into the spacious car and spent Saturdays and holidays motoring around the tri-state area. Memorial Day, the Gourdines celebrated with a picnic at a graveyard on Long Island, where several relatives had headstones. Anthony was jammed in the back seat between two aunts, and the trunk was filled with picnic baskets, blankets and beach chairs, all in preparation for a day of celebration on the grassy knolls of a cemetery. They stopped to pick up a huge watermelon, which Oliver placed inside the cooler and motored on. They knew they had arrived when the only activity for acres was the sound of the birds tweeting and the rustle of the limbs on the sturdy trees. Laying the blanket at the site of their grandparents' graves, they opened up the containers of food, and bottles of chilled sodas, said grace, and ate the beautifully prepared lunch. Surprising, then, that the only child among them was thin as a rail while the aunts kept adding food to his plate. Cool breezes swept above their heads while Aunt Sara and Aunt Shortie talked and sang endlessly. Anthony hummed along, he had perfect pitch. The sounds were lifted up and carried along the winds. Sitting in the middle of death, surrounded by family, Anthony never felt more alive; he was as content as any child could ever be, and was too young to appreciate the irony of the moment.

Other people entered the cemetery, laid down fresh flowers, stood silently, shed a few tears, placed small tokens on top of the stones, and left, but not the Gourdines. This was cause for celebration and they spent the entire afternoon under a huge elm, talking, and eating, and drinking in the vitality of life. Anthony observed pensively. He knew he was different and today proved his family was a little off the beaten track: they knew how to make each day a cause for celebration. They held a constant reverence and appreciation for the gift of life.

The adventures continued as Uncle Oliver escorted the family to upstate New Jersey, into the greenery of the lush forests, and then onto Coney Island and the excitement of the rides and consumption of hot dogs from Nathan's. "I loved that car, the way the doors all opened outward, the running board, the large whitewall tires, and the spacious back seat, unobstructed by seatbelts and dividers. Back then, there were no laws about how many passengers one car could carry, so each weekend, we would squeeze at least six adults into the car and off we'd go."

One weekend the expedition led them to the foot of Manhattan, where Oliver drove the family onto the Staten Island Ferry. Quietly, the wheels of the Packard pulled into line; once the ferry was filled, the fence was slammed shut and the ferry eased out from the dock. Anthony ran to the top of the stairs, gazed out to the harbor, and dreamed he was riding the tides of the sea. He saw foreign shores, wild animals, sandy beaches and rocky mountains; his imagination was afire with ideas while he continued to survey the surroundings. As the winds roughed up his ears, he swore he could hear the fish talking while birds circled around the edges of the ferry. There was a certain smell, a taste of saltiness that caught in his throat, a sense of unbridled freedom that he would never forget. Standing at the edge of the railing, he saw the Statue of Liberty in all her glory, with her arm reaching toward the sky. What he saw was exactly how he felt: he was reaching with her; he, too, would seek the heavens, and aspire toward greatness.

Upon returning home, Elizabeth notified the children they were moving to another apartment just a few blocks away, but that nothing would change besides their address. Diligently packing up their possessions into cardboard boxes, the family made a swift move. With the war winding down, the Naval yards had laid off hundreds of workers, and Thomas was among the many who fell into that category. He had skills, and quickly landed a job in the center of Manhattan in the heart of the fur district as the handyman of a large prewar building. It had always been his dream to go to Greece, and he got second best when he discovered that most of the workers were from Greece and they began teaching him the language. By the time he retired, Thomas was fluent in Greek, but never realized his dream of actually visiting the country. On school holidays he would take Anthony's hand and they would travel to the city, where Anthony would spend the day playing and learning from his dad. Thomas taught him how to operate a freight elevator, fix broken pipes and windows, repair plumbing, and speak a few words of Greek. When lunchtime rolled around, they walked down the dark cement steps to the belly of the building, opened up a gray metal locker, and ate sitting next to the boiler room, which was raging hot in the summertime.

If Anthony could pick his favorite moments with his dad, it would surely be the trips on Thanksgiving morning when they would take the crowded train to the center of Manhattan, stake out a place, and watch the Macy's Thanksgiving Day Parade. Television could not do justice to observing the yearly extravaganza in person. Placed on his father's burly shoulders, Anthony's view was unobstructed. Seeing the crowd wince with fear as a gust of wind would sweep underneath one of the gigantic balloons and make it impossible for the army of handlers to keep control, or listening to the sounds of the synchronized feet pounding the pavement as the marching bands played Christmas songs, or seeing the real Santa Claus wave at the end of the parade was unforgettable. The vivid sights, the marching band music, and the aroma from the street vendors selling roasted chestnuts, were encapsulated in his memory. Despite the cold, it was all so invigorating that he never wanted it to end. Purchasing two large cups of hot cocoa, father and son reentered the subway just in time to prepare for the family tradition: dinner at Elizabeth's sister's home, with a guaranteed crowd of at least two dozen relatives.

The smell of food sailed through the darkened hallways as father and son trekked up the four flights of stairs. "Don't take your coats off," said Elizabeth. "We're already late and we need to leave for my sister's house. She will be angry if we are late, especially since I made a few appetizers which she plans to serve first." After making a quick pit stop in the bathroom, the three took the train to the base of Harlem. Holding the warm dishes, they collected a series of smiles from passengers whose empty stomachs were also anticipating a holiday meal. Before they emerged from the station, Elizabeth had given out her recipes to several passengers, all wanting to emulate the smells of her freshly prepared appetizers. "Friendly and safe, that was how it was back then riding the subways of New York."

The threesome was met with an open door and a multitude of strongly planted kisses and warm bear hugs. "There he is," said his aunt, who lovingly nicknamed her nephew "Ferdinand the Bull," the child who preferred to stop and smell the flowers rather than wrestle his way out of a bull ring. "Just keep dreaming," she encouraged, "and one day all that dreaming will add up to a life of fulfillment."

Sometimes on Saturday afternoons, a friend of Elizabeth's would drop by for coffee and an hour or two of chatting and catching up on the latest gossip. "Who is Anthony playing with? I can hear at least three voices coming from his room," she asked.

Startled, Elizabeth explained that there was no one in the room but her son; all those voices were coming from one child. "He likes to talk and play by himself, and create things in his mind," she answered unapologetically. By modern-day standards, many parents would have rushed their kid off to the closest psychologist, but his mother knew better; she truly understood him. It was his method of creativity: he was preparing to become an actor and what they were observing was natural talent manifesting itself. At home, safe in his bedroom, looking out the window, Anthony felt completely free to dream and experiment. His parents not only accepted him for whatever he was, but encouraged him to expand his mind. With an unabashed belief in their son, he had a sense of being able to conquer the world. Once he set his mind to do something, he had faith he could do it.

This philosophy came in very handy when Anthony, one of the

smallest eighth graders in the elementary school play yard, was tormented by Earl Washington. One overcast lunch period, when most of the girls opted for the movie, he joined the boys in a game of stickball. Calvin, a tall, heavyset classmate, saw this as an opportunity to pop the shortest guy in the face, thinking the punch would never be returned. But Earl, Anthony's nemesis, cried out mockingly, "Fight back, Anthony, don't let that kid get the best of you." Hell-bent on showing Earl he could weather any storm, Anthony summoned up all of his courage, put all his energy into his fists, and soundly beat the crap out of Earl. "That's when I realized I could fight and I realized I could do anything I set my mind to do." After that, Earl befriended him, never tormented him again. When the prize fighter returned home with a black eye, Anthony's parents didn't quite see it that way, although secretly, Thomas was happy as a clam: at least in some ways, their youngest was just the average kid.

The next year when Christmas rolled around, money was tight, tighter than it had ever been in the household. Anthony was too young to understand about money; all he knew was that every Christmas, Santa (even though he now realized who he really was) laid a bounty of presents under the tree for him and his brothers. This year, the tree seemed a lot smaller, and as the season approached, his mom baked fewer cookies. Late one night a few days before Christmas Eve, he heard his father crying. That was the second time he had ever known his father to shed tears: once for his mother's death, and now something was terribly wrong, but whatever it was, the youngest child in the family would have to live with the mystery.

When Christmas morning arrived, Anthony bounded from his bed and ran into the living room, but all that was underneath the tree was one brightly wrapped gift. He tore it open. It was a jet plane. Then he began searching the rest of the living room for all the other presents Santa had left, but there were none to be found. Clutching the single gift, he was gravely disappointed as he somberly walked back to his room. Traditionally, all of his friends would meet early in the afternoon displaying the wondrous gifts they had received but Anthony was so sad, he didn't leave his room until Elizabeth reminded him to get dressed for Aunt Bessie and Sara's dinner. He had spent the morning pushing that single jet plane over the wooden floor, admiring the sparks flashing out the sides of the turbo engines. He cried; he just couldn't understand what terrible deeds he must have done that year to be on the outs with Santa, and his father. As he pushed the plane he searched his memory for all his bad behavior but came up empty. When it was time to leave, Thomas took his hand and held it all the way to Harlem. The sad expression on his dad's face matched the sadness in his young heart. He was still just too young to realize the heartbreak; sometimes love wasn't enough and for his father that was certainly the case: money would have made all the difference in the joy of his son's heart, but he couldn't give what he didn't have. The year-end bonuses were never dispersed, things were tough all over. Thomas just felt lucky to have a job and never complained.

The Christmas dinner didn't disappoint, with the aunts showering love, hugs, kisses, and small gifts upon the youngest child. When the Gourdines took the train home, smiles had replaced frowns and they were reminded what the holidays and family were all about: love. Love was truly the only thing that mattered and the only thing that made them happy. That night as Anthony stood staring out of his bedroom window into the endless starlit night, he recited a poem his Aunt Bessie had taught him, "Star light, star bright…" When he was finished, he cast his eyes towards the moon and asked God for a bike. But a bike cost thirty-eight dollars, and there was no way his wish would be granted. When he finally fell asleep, for some odd reason the number 227 kept recurring in his mind. To this day he couldn't explain it, but when he awoke the next morning, that number was still clearly on his mind.

Elizabeth, like everyone in the neighborhood, played the numbers. "Good morning, sleepyhead," she said as she ran her hands through his curly brown hair. "I hope you slept well. I was reading this book about dreams; it interprets your thoughts. What do you think about that?"

"It sounds weird, but I do remember dreaming about the number 227. I don't know why. I was wishing for a bicycle and in the middle of a dream about searching for the bike, I kept seeing that same number popping up on storefronts. When I woke up this morning, I still remembered it. What do you think that means?"

Elizabeth was superstitious and so she played that number. Handing the runner a dollar bill with the number 227 written on an envelope she was shocked when the runner returned that night with forty dollars! Grabbing Anthony she hugged and kissed him. The very next morning they boarded a bus, got off at Sears, and she bought him that bike. In both their hearts that Christmas, Santa was arriving a little later in the form of an illegal bet and had fulfilled Anthony's dream; at least, that was what Elizabeth insisted. He was the happiest kid alive as he walked his shiny new bike into the subway and walked home with his mom. Anthony set the bike inside the storage bin; first, he had to learn how to ride it, and training wheels were out of the question, more money than the numbers allowed. Weeks later, with an inspired sense of determination, Anthony begged his dad to take out the bike he had received from Santa but was afraid to ride. Thomas shrugged his shoulders, and they trotted down to the garage storage bins, his dad pulled out the two-wheeler, Anthony hopped onto the seat and took off as if he had been riding for years. The adrenaline pulsed through every cell in his body as he experienced the rush of the wind pedaling through the city streets. Thomas shook his head incredulously: without so much as a lesson, his son had figured the whole thing out on the first try. Watching him race up and down the streets without an inkling of falling, he was filled with pride: his son was riding the bike. Yes, the kid who could do anything.

"Ah, the faith of a child," thought Elizabeth as she looked out the kitchen window and saw her youngest son disappear down the street. Extracting a handkerchief from her apron, she wiped away tears of joy. She was able to give her son what Santa could not. She made a vow to pester Anthony about future dreams. Apparently he was a good luck charm and there was no telling what fortunes lay ahead.

CHAPTER 4

They were headed to a small village on the southern shores of Long Island. Passing the airport, the busy suburban towns, and expansive farm lands, the train stopped in West Hampton. It was bucolic, quiet, nothing to interfere with the panoramic view of the cloudless sky. The only sounds were made by the animals and mother nature; such silence was a novelty, since Anthony had grown up in the city where noise was norm.

Sonny, his oldest brother, had married and moved his wife into his parent's home for the first year of their marriage, and later, when they were both making a decent income, moved into a modest one bedroom apartment. In the summer the couple would spend the weekends at a sprawling home which sat on several acres of rich farmland, owned by Sonny's mother-in-law.

Rushing to the front door, Sonny ran to greet his family, showering them with kisses; it seemed forever since he had hugged his parents. Greeting the in-laws, the parents ushered Thomas and Elizabeth to their beautifully appointed bedrooms and asked them to join the celebration in the parlor where cocktails and lavish hors d'oeuvres were being served. There was no doubt that Sonny had married well, and that he was happy and financially secure. After a few moments of bonding, Anthony left the adults and joined a few kids playing at the back of the house.

Sonny was the oldest brother and the one whom Anthony most admired. A handsome and smart kid, at the tender age of sixteen, Sonny left home, obtained a false birth certificate, and joined the military. After the requisite training, he landed in Guam for a few tough years of training and combat. Ten years younger, Anthony felt like Sonny had been away forever, but when he finally walked through the front door, Sonny was ready to move on with his life. Although he remained in the military, he was the first person in the family to receive a college degree. He scouted out the most beautiful coed and sat behind her. At the end of the first period, he gently tapped Billie on the shoulder and asked her if she would like to study with him. He had been out of academia for years while serving his country and he needed a few pointers. Sonny was impossible to resist; they had but one study date, and a year later, the young couple married.

Sonny had relentlessly complained that he was treated differently than the other three boys, but he could never put his finger on exactly why. All he knew was that his dad seemed to favor the other boys, especially Anthony, the youngest. It wasn't until decades later that Sonny would discover Elizabeth had become pregnant at fourteen and never married his biological father. When she gave birth to Sonny, Thomas had made an honest woman out of her, in the full knowledge that the child was not his own. There was bountiful love in the household, he knew that and when Sonny finally found out the truth, his respect for Thomas – who was actually his stepfather – was full of admiration and a rekindling of love.

"Mom," bellyached Sonny, "why isn't Anthony throwing out the trash or doing any chores? I'm sick of him always being pampered and getting away with murder."

"Now, now, Sonny, age has its privileges. Look at you, the firstborn and the smartest and most handsome of all my sons. So don't go complaining about the youngest, he gets what's left over from the rest of you," Elizabeth said diplomatically. Kissing him on the cheek, she suggested they take Anthony out to the movies; he just loved to see all those stars on the big screen. Taking Billie's hand, they trotted down the hall and invited the youngest to go see the show.

"Wow, you would take me with you and Billie?"

"Sure," Sonny answered. "How about 'Singin' In the Rain'?" Before Sonny could get the title out of his mouth, his youngest brother began a rapid dissertation about the movie, describing in detail the plot, characters, and even singing some of the music. "Well, Anthony, if you have seen the movie before then maybe you don't want to see it again."

"Sure I do," he yelled back, "I've never seen it!"

"But how could you know all about the story, every word, the music, the characters?" "Because I made it up, all of it."

Sonny and Billie shook their heads incredulously and were thinking that Anthony's wild imagination was probably better than the actual show. Luckily when they finished the last kernel of popcorn, the true movie had won out, it was better than they had all imagined. As for Anthony, he was completely mesmerized, and the movie left a permanent impact in his creative soul.

Puppy love happened at Sonny's new home. There was this girl, she was cute, and when she looked into Anthony's eyes, his heart melted for the very first time. Could this preteen, with dark brown braided hair, oval eyes, bronzed and sun-kissed skin, be his first love? Walking towards her on the rural gravel road, he was about to find out. "Hi," he said with a broad smile. But she didn't want to be bothered. Being as cruel as children could be, she told him that he was the ugliest kid she ever saw, that his face resembled the man in the moon. Devastated, he quickly turned his head so she couldn't see his disappointment, and he ran back to the house, throwing himself on the bed. No one had ever called him ugly, no one had ever been so cruel, for the first time, he had faced rejection and it felt awful.

He stayed in the room until dinner was ready and then reluctantly joined the family, remaining unusually quiet. After the sumptuous meal of veal chops, served with garden greens, potatoes au gratin, and French pastries, they gathered in the living room. Billie, Sonny's wife, sat down, asking Anthony to sing whatever came to mind, which turned out to be a ballad of lost love. Surprised, she picked up on the melody as his voice lamented with the morose lyrics. Searching the eyes of his brother and extended family, Anthony noticed that they were riveted and when he had finished, the sound of clapping filled the entire room. "People ignored me unless I sang. I became so shy that I thought that not only girls but everyone thought I was ugly. When I sang and everyone paid attention, I didn't think I was ugly, so I just kept on singing." He was short, but truly, he was as comely as a young preteen could get; his broad forehead was covered with thick ringlets, his eyes set wide and deep, his mouth shaped like a cupid's bow, and his body thin but strong. The telltale effects of his first puppy love had wreaked havoc on his self-image and it would take him years to recover. It was those intense feelings that would later be put to song, and become one of the most-played tunes in the history of music: "Tears on My Pillow."

It was rare not going to church on Sunday, but the family stayed for the weekend, boarding the Sunday afternoon train back to Brooklyn. "Anthony," asked his mom, "how would you like to try acting lessons?" She knew the answer before she asked and the following Saturday, she escorted him to Star Time Studios where he learned how to act and polish his singing skills.

To be accepted, an audition was required. Selecting "Rags to Riches," he made the cut and immediately began taking classes. Later on, if the studio deemed him worthy, they would put him on the live television show, but before he had the opportunity, the money ran out and his chance fizzled. Too young to understand that Elizabeth had used up every dime of her savings, he was sorely disappointed when the classes stopped, but while he was there, the lessons were enlightening; they were stored and never forgotten. For the first time, he was exposed to pop songs, crooners such as Frank Sinatra, and jazz artists. Soaking in the new music as if he were a bottomless pit, he picked up a new sense of rhythm, harmonies, and melody lines. His dancing and acting skills improved and when he returned home, he spent hours repeating the lessons. All of this would eventually pay off.

As a great mother but sometimes lacking in money, Elizabeth made up for it by affordable outings, Anthony's favorite being Coney Island, home of endless rides, a wide wooden boardwalk bursting with shops and eateries, and an aquarium packed with exotic fish. It was late spring, Thomas had gone into work on a rare Saturday, and Elizabeth grabbed her youngest son's hand for a day at the beach and the world famous Coney Island Amusement Park. The late morning clouds parted just as they emerged from the subway, and they walked directly east to the Atlantic. Anthony's eyes dilated and his heart began to pound when he spied all those colorful rides in motion. Plucking change out of her pocketbook, Elizabeth took her son first on the merry-go-round; even though it was beautiful, with its gilded horses, for a ten year old, it was boring. Running to the redbugs, he patiently stood in line and when the gates opened, he flew into the car at the farthest end of the floor. At the sound of the buzzer, he was off and having the time of his life negotiating the turns as if he were a racecar driver. Too soon the buzzer marked the end of the experience. Next they rode the Ferris wheel, which gave them a complete view of Brooklyn and the Atlantic Ocean. It was late in the afternoon, time to leave as Anthony begged his mom to allow him just one last ride: The Cyclone, an enormous roller coaster. "No," she yelled as they walked west onto the boardwalk in the direction of Nathan's. He consigned himself giving up that ride for the sake of the best hot dog in the world, and not pushing his mom any further, but he would be back and he would go on that ride. he was undaunted by his mom's fears.

Inhaling the last crumbs from the soft bun, Elizabeth grabbed his arm and they disappeared into the bowels of the subway. In the distance they heard the rattle of metal wheels echoing throughout the inky black tunnels. A loud whoosh and the doors opened as they quickly slipped inside, where they found two seats at the front of the car. Licking off the mustard from the roof of his mouth, Anthony vowed he would be returning to Coney Island, but it would be with his friends and he would show no fear as he envisioned climbing on all those rides his mom feared.

When Monday rolled around, Anthony met with two friends and they made a pact: they would go to Coney Island the following Saturday. But they needed money. Anthony begged from his aunts, borrowed from his father's pockets, and stole from his mom's coin purse, until he had enough change for the next adventure. The three boys hopped on the train for the quick trip to the Coney Island, marching with great anticipation toward the boardwalk. The sun was shining brilliantly overheard, and a cool sea breeze was blowing across their faces as they zipped up their khaki jackets. Anthony pointed to The Cyclone; there was no option than for it to be the first ride of the day. He picked up his pace, and his friends followed closely behind. After purchasing tickets, they waited twenty minutes, and jumped into the front cab while the ticket taker secured the metal bar. The sharp sound of a whistle blew as the coaster began a slow ascent to the first rung of the tracks. With each notch of the metal track, Anthony could feel his heart begin to race, and then down they plunged. His head shook and his body rattled, and then back up again for an even higher view and back down again. His stomach felt like it had been coughed up to the back of his throat, and his breathing was fast. This was exhilarating, and more exciting than anything he had ever felt. When the cab came to abrupt halt and the metal bar released, he stumbled out and completely lost his balance. What a ride! The three boys walked away, and turned to look back at The Cyclone. Wow, that was the biggest thing they had ever seen, and they had conquered it! They would all tell this story to their children.

There was one more ride they had to conquer and that was the parachute ride at Steeple Chase Park. The boys patiently waited for their turn to be strapped into the seat, but this ride was different: only one person per seat. They had to be brave since they would be alone. Carefully pulling the buckle tightly around Anthony's thin waist, the engineer nodded his head, and up, up, up so slowly and purposefully until the tip of the parachute tapped the top, and exploded open as a wave of salt air rushed into Anthony's mouth, and then he sailed to earth at a rapid speed. Jumping out of the seat, his legs felt like jelly as he again lost his balance toppling to the ground. Catching his breath, he waited for his friends and they jumped for joy as they flew out of the seats.

"That was the best, I thought I was going to sail all the way through the clouds, but I have to admit I was worried what would happen if the parachute didn't open." Anthony's friends looked at him and laughed – the parachute always opened. They spent the last of their change buying sodas and pink colored cotton candy, and grabbed the first train home. Another pact, they would never tell their parents of this adventure, nor the daring rides, nor where the money came from for this one great adventure. But decades later, this scenario still plays out in Anthony's mind as his passion for all those daredevil rides remains intact. "This is why I am always going to one or another amusement park. Now I use the excuse of my grandchildren, but I'm still a kid at heart and there isn't any ride I won't go on."

CHAPTER 5

One of the best places to hear new music was at the Apollo Theater, and as Anthony became of age to ride the subway by himself, he would spend his Saturday afternoons at the back alley, watching the acts come and go and trying his damnedest to sneak in. When the door would periodically open, he would capture an earful of whatever act was on the stage. He loved the music, he loved the smell of the stage, and the performers. He had found his home; now all he had to do was get through the front door. "I could never bust into that theater, the security was so tight and boy, did I try. I was there so often that some of the performers got to know me but they would never take a chance and allow me in. So I settled on standing in the alley waiting and hoping.

"One spring Saturday afternoon, Willie John, one of the greatest Blues singers alive, arrived in a small limousine. He was a tough dude, with bulging muscles, cropped hair, and a broad chest. Just before he went into the theater, he turned to me and said, 'Son, can you hold this for me until I'm done?' And he whipped out a snub-nose .38 handgun. I was really young and I had never seen a gun, let alone touch a gun, but I happily obliged. I would do anything to try and get into the shows and I thought holding his piece just might be the ticket. An hour later he returned and I happily handed over the pistol. He smiled and thanked me, but getting into the show still eluded me. I thought, *One day they will let me in, I just have to figure out a way.* Front door, back door, I didn't really care. I just knew this was the place I wanted to be."

Anthony's first chance at acting came in an unusual way. Aunt Ethel, his godmother, was partially blind and went to the Blind Institute on weekdays. The school would put on plays as a way of making money. At eleven, he auditioned for the role of John, a son in *Life With Father*, and he was given the part just as he finished uttering the last word of the scene. After rehearsals, the play was open to the public; the seats were filled and the neophyte actor had butterflies swarming in his stomach. Playing his part, as a bratty kid, perfectly, he was attuned to every cue, his performance seamless as he moved from scene to scene. His voice filled the auditorium with an authenticity rarely heard from any actor, let alone one so young. When it was time to take their final bows, it was Anthony who scored the loudest and longest applause. This was his first taste of live theater and for him it was inspiring and life-changing. Elizabeth had brought along a friend who had been stunned by his ability to speak several dialects, thinking perhaps he bordered on schizophrenia. After the show was over, Elizabeth nudged her friend, saying, "This was what my son has been practicing, this was what he wanted to be and now his dreams have begun." Her girlfriend just shook her head in agreement, thinking how she had misjudged his talent.

"Now, when I talk in different dialects, I get applause and nobody thinks I'm crazy. I found that my talent superseded my looks. When I entertained, people listened and they responded. No one ever called me ugly when I was on stage."

Other family members provided venues for Anthony to exhibit his talent. It was cousin Earl and his friend William who asked Anthony to join them singing Gospel. Initially they complained that he sang in the wrong key, but listening carefully, Anthony picked up his portion of the harmonies and the three decided they sounded so good they should try to cut a record. Earl contacted Poke Studios and they recorded their first song. Although Anthony loved the experience, summer had arrived, and still a child, he relinquished his career in Gospel singing to playing baseball, which became his second love.

With a perfect eye, a great sense of timing, and the natural ability to run at superfast speeds, he became an accomplished baseball player. Playing right field or short stop, he saw a successful season and finally after years of passing through Central Park, became a participant in an interleague game. Taking his position on the field, he couldn't help but notice the abundant beauty and vastness of the park, the hordes of people, the horses, the runaway dogs, the police walking their beat, and the rambling fields of green grass. It was as glorious as he had imagined, and he was finally there to take it all in. That summer, when he wasn't playing hardball, a cousin introduced him into a young adult softball league; he was the youngest member on the team, but when he batted the ball, it sailed three hundred twenty-five feet into the air: a home run! He had made his mark, and they invited him to stay for the remainder of the season.

In the fall, Elizabeth nervously took him to his first day of high school. It was rare that his parents argued, but Elizabeth believed he should go to the high school for performing arts, while Thomas was steadfast on his son learning a useful trade. On the day after Labor Day, she reluctantly walked Anthony to Boys High, and stood at the far edge of the sidewalk, spilling tears as he entered the gates of the campus. Dabbing her wet cheeks, she glanced around and discovered she wasn't the only mother who was saddened by day: their sons were growing up, the innocence of youth vanished in a split second.

When lunch period arrived, he entered the huge lunchroom with several other freshmen, taking in the novelty of the scene. Several kids owned transistor radios and without thinking, Anthony began to sing along. As usual, he was ignored until he opened up his chops, and then heads turned and listened. "Hey man, you can really sing," shouted a kid one table over. "How about joining our group, we need a strong lead singer." With a dramatic flair, he pivoted around, walked away from his classmates and joined the group of older boys who had named their group The Duponts. They sang everywhere and anywhere they could attract an audience. For two years, he remained the lead singer as they entertained audiences in subways, high schools, and underneath the ever-famous gas lamp poles. Placing a hat on the ground, coins constantly jingled as they were haphazardly tossed by passersby. At the end of the night, the boys split up the paltry change and headed back home to begin again the next day.

Singing in subway stations near the turnstiles, the sounds bounced off the tiled walls giving an added dimension and eeriness to their voices. While passengers waited for the trains to arrive, they listened to the music, tossing coins into a hat. Later, several other groups followed, creating a battle of the groups, although no one was ever declared the winner. The Duponts picked up on catchy cover tunes that would entice an impatient audience, adding their own unique style. "Gloria," originally sung by The Cadillacs, was one of their favorite tunes to perform; snapping their fingers, they glided into the melody using harmonies that were perfectly sung and when they finished, they had sounded better than the original recording.

Feeling their oats, the guys began flirting with success. They met with Paul Windley of Windley Records who took them under their wing, and helped them obtain an audition at the Apollo Theater for amateur night where sadly they failed to make the cut. Rather than send a harsh reply, Paul advised the group to practice more, saying they hadn't become seasoned. "Come back when you have it together." And that was exactly what the boys did. Returning months later, they knocked on his door, auditioned again, and this time it was a go. Paul loved them, and knew they were ready to be heard. "You" was the simple name of their first recording, becoming a local hit on the soul stations, but it wasn't the song to escalate them to the next level, so it was back to the drawing board. Saddened, but not discouraged, the group continued practicing together with the hope that something would pop up in their future, and luckily for the youngest guy in the group, it did.

Music could be heard drifting out of Anthony's window, especially when the warmer weather had arrived and his window was always ajar. Clarence Collins, who lived directly across the street, had passed by on numerous occasions, but one day he literally stopped and listened to the music: the sounds of his neighbor singing flawlessly. Hearing somebody scream up, "Who's singing?" Anthony popped his head out of the window. Clarence instantly recognized him from the Duponts. Anthony raced down the four flights of stairs and the two began a lengthy conversation about music and singing. Clarence, a bit younger, had been shown the ropes of the game, spending time in Manhattan at the two buildings warehousing the industry. With him were Nathaniel Rogers, Tracey Lord, and Earnest Wright, who would eventually become The

Imperials. But for the moment, Clarence and Anthony shook hands and went their separate ways, but fate would eventually bring these young men back together.

Maybe because Anthony was small, or because it was something his older brother had done, or from a compelling need to fit in and just be one of the guys, Anthony joined a gang, the Chaplins, and he began sporting their sign, a blue vest. The gang had their own territory which they protected and when they crossed into another territory, the vest came off; no one wanted to rumble with another guy. "We did bad things, we fought," regretted Anthony, "But I wanted to be accepted."

On a late fall Saturday evening his quartet ventured down to the subways for their weekly battle of the groups, but Anthony not thinking, had put on his gang vest, the very one that marked him as part of the Chaplins. He wasn't concerned about territories or fighting; all that was on his mind was music, and spending time with his group. Preparing to sing, they overheard whispers from the other end of the subway, "Hey those guys are part of the Chaplins." The rattle of chains and the stomping of leather boots hitting the cement floors of the subway station escalated, as the gang boys neared the turnstiles.

Anthony was terrified, as were his friends, and they began running for their lives. Anthony had made a dire mistake, had worn hostile colors on someone else's turf, and now they were coming to collect on that mistake. It wasn't rumors; it was a plain fact that gang members killed rival gang members. They were right to be terrified. The singers disbanded, running in several directions. With his adept athletic skills, Anthony jumped over the turnstiles and galloped up four flights of steps to the highest point of the train tracks. It had grown pitch dark, the moon was cloaked with thick rain clouds, and the only light was from a streetlamp. Spying a thin dark edge, he burrowed into the alley between the brick walls, concealing himself. His heart was racing and his hands were trembling as he waited, listening for sounds of the chains. In the distance the bright light of the train marked an escape. With the intensity of a condor circling overhead, he waited for the train doors to open, and just as they were about to close, he sprang out of the darkness and landed safely inside. Grabbing a metal pole, he stood silently inside the cloistered safety of the subway car, furtively looking around to see if he had been followed. He removed the vest, folded it up tightly so the colors were hidden, and made it home safe in one piece. A lesson learned, he would never share this incident with his parents. It was all too scary.

When the cops walked the beat they put the fear of God into the kids who wore gang colors, but that night, he didn't need any reminding; his fear had been very real. He had tasted the fear of death and it wasn't pleasant. That sleepless night as he tossed and turned, he vowed never to return to the gang. He had witnessed firsthand the ugliness of hate, and it wasn't a feeling he admired or needed; that wasn't the path he wanted to take. When morning arrived, he buried the vest at the bottom of the closet and never wore it again. It represented all that he didn't want to be.

The original Imperials, Nathaniel, Tracey, Ernest, Clarence, and Sammy, were all born and bred on the streets of Brooklyn, all living in one of the endless projects. Street smart, coming from similar homes, they shared similar values, but what drew them together was their shared passion for music, highly attuned ears, and complementary voices.

"I met Anthony when I was a kid, living in the Fort Greene

projects," said Nathaniel. "We attended the same high school and saw each other often as we took turns at the Friday afternoon sock hops, playing with our own groups. At the time, I was the bass singer with the Mints, but the group broke up, leaving me by myself. I wasn't happy. I'd figure I'd find another group, and luckily I did. It turned out that Tracey and Ernest, who were with the Chesters, had suddenly lost their bass singer, Ron Ross, and were in a hurry to replace him. I remember I was carrying a large load of dirty clothing to the Laundromat and they stopped me and asked if I would be interested in joining their group. Would I? I was thrilled, the timing couldn't have been better. I raced back home, tossed the dirty laundry at the front door and ran off with Tracey and Ernest. At fourteen, I began singing with the group. Initially it was just for fun; we sounded great, but it wasn't as if we were doing it for the money."

"Nathaniel was one of the gentlest guys I ever knew, but he was a weightlifter and no one messed around with him. He was incredibly naïve, and we all had a great time pranking him. He was the youngest among us and believed everything we said. He had a beautiful deep voice and when we got together, the music was amazing. Our sound was so unique and I attribute a lot of that to his deep voice," said Anthony.

"Tracey was also fourteen when we met. Both his parents and mine were close friends. When the weekends arrived, if my parents weren't in the mood to take the train up to Harlem, they took turns having each other over for dinner parties. although it was just dinner, they always said it was a party. Tracey was a super sensitive guy, who loved to sing Gospel and was kind of a loner. He was content being by himself and loved to dream. He never told me what he was dreaming, but he was always hopeful and a super positive person. I think one of the things he was constantly dreaming of was girls, and since he was extremely handsome, they would fall all over him. Tracey was the true definition of a chick magnet. In so many ways he was cool, suave, he knew who he was and wanted to become. I loved being around him, he was always fun and never complained about anything except one thing: who started the group. That would be a thorn in his side until the day he died."

"Sammy Strain came into my life when I was fifteen. We were living in different sections in the same borough of Brooklyn. There was a local talent show scheduled at PS 67, an elementary school a few blocks from my home. It was a way to make a few dollars and show off your talent, and of course, I was the first to sign up." The lunchroom had been set with three hundred metal chairs in anticipation of a packed house, and two ticket takers holding a shoebox with a carved-out slot collected the money. There was one microphone, a small stage, and intermittent lighting hanging from the rafters. All in all not a glamorous place, but a stage none the less. Meticulously dressed in a dark brown jacket, striped tie, and shiny black shoes, Anthony walked to the microphone and began singing a ballad. His smooth voice filled up the room as he captivated the audience. Suddenly, a series of gunshots rang out, sending the audience into panic mode. People ran in every direction, out emergency doors, through the entryway, while others dropped to the floor, hiding behind large posts. It was the Bishops, a rival gang that had decided to wreak havoc on the Chaplins, and in doing so, had frightened hundreds of young kids and adults. When everyone had dispersed, Anthony and a couple other singers surveyed the damage, collecting spent shells. The saving grace of that night was that no one was killed, but the terror never left his memory.

"Ernest was the least educated among us; he never graduated high school, said he didn't learn anything, that it was for buffoons.

He always had a scheme, but rarely followed through on any of them, that was just the way he was. I met him at the projects. He was fifteen and had a passion for music and singing. That was almost all he talked about and that was pretty much all he wanted to be. He stepped into the group singing lead, but when I came along –taking over the lead he begrudgingly sang as second tenor. There were so many ups and downs with Ernest, but most of them were caused by his lack of education. Because he wasn't a reader, he believed only what he heard and saw, and was blindsided too many times by not taking the time to find the truth. Years later, when money had gone missing, the rest of us joined forces, had a meeting, and released Ernest from the group. There was no proof and certainty he had cheated us, but we felt there was no alternative solution at that moment. That was when we hired Kenny Seymour. To this day if you ask me if Ernest had taken the money intentionally, I would say no, it was his lack of information that caused the disparity. Eventually Ernest would come back to us a different man: grown up, mature, and learned. He would never make those same immature mistakes again.

"Clarence was the last one to come along as one of the original Imperials. Like the rest of us, he had a passion for music and singing. I met him when I was eight and our families were living at the Fort Greene projects. He was so slick and cool; the women loved him, he was a lightning rod, and was super charming, but he had his dark side, which manifested itself as drug use. He was part of a huge bunch of kids, and when he was still in elementary school, his young mom died, leaving their father to raise a house full of kids. The love and bonding that he needed from a mother was gone and his dad, who was torn in so many directions, could never replace that love and nurturing.

"The family became dysfunctional, all going in different directions, but for Clarence the direction lead to drugs. I love Clarence, but I never felt he loved me, simply because he didn't know how to love. There was no doubt his childhood was hard. He lacked direction and guidance from the very person God had seen fit to take away. He was sullen, sad, and empty. One day, I remember, he told me that I didn't know who I was, but I realized it was his way of admitting that he had lost his own way. Then he turned around and complimented me, admitting that he didn't have the chops to sell the songs, but he could blend and harmonize. He was a selfish individual, but not when it came to the success of the group. If singing back-up made the song work, that was what he was satisfied doing. In other areas, I considered him a selfish guy, but I think it was his own form of self-preservation."

"On a wintery Saturday afternoon, Clarence, Ernest, and I were in the park flirting with a couple of girls. We were singing and dancing around, just kind of showing off, and the girls were giggling and laughing. Apparently that didn't sit too well with a group of gang boys who were watching the scene and becoming more jealous by the minute. Out of nowhere, a guy runs over, and starts punching me with brass knuckles. He screamed that I was messing with his girlfriend as he slammed his fist into my face and chest. Ernest twisted around, pulled the guy off of me while I scrambled to get up, and then the guy ran back to his gang. What I couldn't figure out was why Clarence didn't budge. He just took in the scene but did nothing to help me. That's when I realized his true colors. I would never want him in a foxhole; he didn't have my back that day, and I doubted he ever would.

"When I walked home, my mom could tell I had been hurt, my face was swollen, my eye bruised, and my lip bleeding. Alone with my mother, who loved me unconditionally, I knew it was okay to cry. Hugging me, she explained it was part of the life I had chosen, but I knew she was worried and trying to figure out how to end this brutality. I knew I was lucky to have loving parents, and that Clarence wasn't as lucky, but from my perspective it seemed as though instinct should have taken over, and he should have rushed in to help one of his own, but it didn't turn out that way. I learned a sad lesson that day, but I also realized how lucky I was to have the constant love and attention of two parents, and how that made me who I was."

It was one year later, that Anthony met up with Sammy at the Brevoort Theater. He was singing with The Chips as a tenor. Sammy had a certain class and persona that screamed success; he excelled at singing, choreography, and song writing. The two were destined to meet: both grew up on the streets of Brooklyn, with the love and passion of music playing a central part in their homes. At a very young age, both were shuttled up to the Apollo Theater to witness live music at its very best.

Sammy began his singing career at Hamilton High School, harmonizing with a group of guys, who sang everywhere, from the bathrooms to the hallways to the playgrounds. One day, a teacher, who had been listening carefully, invited the guys to sing at one of the assemblies. Excited, the guys practiced relentlessly and then made a big splash when they performed at their very first gig. Calling themselves "The Hamiltonians," they produced a couple demo records and then fizzled out. Shortly after that, Sammy's high school days were cut short when at sixteen, he was kicked out; gang life had gotten the best of him. While he was moping on the stoop of his walk-up apartment, a classmate meandered by and asked him if he could sing first tenor. Having nothing else on his plate, if he had been asked to sing anything, he would have said yes so later that afternoon, he joined the group for his first rehearsal. They met in apartment, practiced harmonies, and began walking through the streets singing, meeting other groups along the way. The street corners were filled with small clusters of teens all engrossed in a cappella music, rising above the rumblings of the city streets. People stopped, listened, sometimes tossed coins into a hat, and then moved on. No one gave these kids a second thought.

They called themselves the Chips. Using the sidewalks as their stage, they attracted enough attention to capture the ear of Harry Austin, who offered to manage the group. Their first big hit, recorded in 1956, was "Rubber Biscuit," which found a lot of play on the Black radio stations in New York City. The time had finally arrived and the Chips were invited to the Apollo Theater. The guys were so excited; it was the very first time they would perform on a big stage. They had a group slumber party, rose early, grabbed their rented tuxedos, and took the train up to Harlem. Walking into the tomb of the theater, they rehearsed while hearing bands wailing above their heads. Though nervous, as any neophytes should have been, they were in excellent company that night. The first show of the night, they were out of sync with the band, but by the second show, they had picked up the pace, getting a standing ovation from the forgiving crowd. Smiling, the Chips strutted off the stage; Sammy felt like he was the king of the world and had slain a mighty dragon.

Backstage, Anthony and Sammy began chatting before they were slated to go on and Sammy started talking about the Bishops, and how he was involved with gang life, admitting that he had been at an elementary school shooting. For Sammy, that was the end of gang life. Shocked, Anthony's eyebrows arched, and his brow furrowed as he turned to Sammy and told him he was there that night, singing and trying to raise money. "What a hell of a way to stop a show; the streets have no sense." The two later joined forces, and instead of being mortal enemies, they became the closest of friends. "One moment shooting up, and next minute, I'm singing with you," said Sammy, who was well aware of the fear he had put into the hearts of so many innocent people that dreadful night. That was the end of gang life for him. "It was senseless."

Sammy continued on with the Chips as they polished their act and became strong performers. That summer they sang at the State Theater in Hartford, one of the largest stages in the country, wowing the crowd by jumping high up in the air and landing by doing the splits. Once in a while, one of them would miss and bust their bottoms, or split their pants. In the early fall of 1957, they performed at the Empire Theater in Brooklyn, and again Sammy met up with Anthony, who was singing with the Duponts. Chatting backstage, they talked about music, mutual friends, disasters, and the fun they were having as performing artists. "This sure beats a day job," laughed Sammy.

The Duponts never gave up, even after their first record dove into the abyss of songs not played, but then, along came "Prove It Tonight," which slowly inched its way up the pop charts, and captured the attention of Alan Freed, the man who coined the phrase "rock 'n' roll." Out of nowhere, he took a chance on the group and asked them to open at the New York Paramount Theater for one of his extravaganzas. That night, Alan Freed announced a line-up which included The Platters, The Cadillacs, and Frankie Lymon & The Teenagers, but that, first, an up and coming group would open the show, the Duponts. From the side of the stage, dressed in brown checkered jackets with dark brown tuxedo pants, the group apprehensively took the spotlight. On cue, the band thrust the first drum beat, and it was smooth sailing from that moment. Gazing up at massive crowd, The Duponts gave it their all, and when they finished, they heard thunderous applause. With joyful smiles, they walked off the stage, bursting with pride. They had gotten their first big break and from the audience's reaction, it was successful.

Soon after that evening, Anthony left the group and joined the Chesters, who later changed their name to The Imperials, and that was the beginning of the fame that would adhere to Anthony for the rest of his career. After obtaining an agent, Ernie Martinelli, the group began performing at the hottest nightclubs throughout the city. "At sixteen I was playing at Town Hill in Brooklyn. It was a jumping place, with a huge crowd on the weekends. Everyone came to listen, dance, and have a great time." A mixed crowd, and so too was the music: rhythm and blues, pop charts hits and jazz. They shared the stage with stars such as Nancy Wilson, Diana Washington, and Jackie Wilson. Fame came to this young kid at age sixteen, a kid who was mixing it up with the greatest singers, agents, and producers in the industry. They all saw something in him that they hadn't seen in any other performer, but he was way too young to notice. Anthony was having the time of his life: the next day was as far down the road of life he could see.

In spite of a spike in fame, Anthony kept singing and performing at the local sock hops. During an interview he gave for Billboard writer: *the Time/Life Collection*, he said, "I sang in school, at Boys High when I was sixteen and seventeen years old. There were also school dances at PS 17 every weekend and the only reason I went was to look for girls. There were Catholic school dances at the Center and I went to those too. The dances of the day were so important, and you had to look sharp. I'd wear argyle socks, a cardigan sweater – but no jeans allowed, only dress pants. The girls would wear petal pushers and poodle skirts. We would do the 'grind' dance- that was the big one. We'd also do what they called 'slow jams' until some nun or priest would pull you away from the girl you were dancing with. My favorite artists were my buddy, Frankie Lymon, The Moonglows, The Flamingos, and Laverne Baker, who would sing 'Tweedly Dee.'" When asked if he removed his shoes, Anthony said, "Remove your shoes and socks? No way, man. That was uncool and being cool ruled. Still does. I sang at a lot of sock hops. That is how you would promote your record. I would travel to Philadelphia, Pittsburgh, and cities like that. The only thing that held true about going to sock hops was you could meet the prettiest girls. I remember that and it motivated me- if you know what I mean."

The Chesters were dressed somberly when they walked into George Goldner's record company. "Okay, young men," barked the receptionist. "The studio is free." She pointed down a brightly lit hallway and directed them into one of the small recording studios. With sheet music in hand, they began rehearsing "Cha Cha Henry," when the owner walked into the room. Listening critically, he asked if they remembered "Tears On My Pillow," and of course they said yes, even though they had never laid eyes on the music. Goldner told them to go practice the song and he would record it. Stunned, the young men acted confidently as he left them alone. "I read the words and immediately memorized the melody. Since none of the guys knew the melody I suggested they use the Penguin's 'Earth Angel' background harmony. When George reentered the room, we did three takes and the song was recorded. I never sang the third set of lyrics to the song. I just repeated the second verse." The lyrics, written by Al Lewis and Sylvester Bradford, were some of those most passionate, heartfelt words ever written and reflected the pangs of love to a new teenage generation, who needed outlets for their intense, misunderstood feelings. The flip side was 'Just Two Kinds of People In The World', and that record also sold like crazy. We were the first group to ever have a two-sided back-to-back hit; this song ran up the charts, stopping at nine in the top one hundred, and 'Tears' made in all the way to number two. Our records were literally selling like hotcakes. The irony was the Grammy Awards hadn't commenced until 1959, so we weren't in the loop and never received a Grammy. That is one of my few regrets, but also one of my goals."

Goldner rubbed his chin and bobbed his head as he stared out the window. He needed a name for this up-and-coming group. Goldner turned to Anthony and asked him who his favorite singer was and he quickly responded, "Why, Nat King Cole."

Goldner then offered up some advice. "Enunciate and sing the song like you were talking; you can talk with a high voice, try that." The young singer listened and sang it precisely that way. The words were likened to a teenage crush: as he imagined sitting in a malt shop, gazing into his girlfriend's eyes, and singing those words, he meant every single syllable. Looking down several stories from the building onto the bustling streets of Manhattan, Goldner saw a regal black Chrysler Imperial pull up to the front of the building. Lou Gally, his assistant, stood next to him, staring at the same car, "How about naming the group the Imperials? It's a name that we trust, and it represents the top of the line."

The two men walked out of the office, into the recording studio and dubbed the five teens The Imperials. At the time there was an Imperial record company, who tried to sue them for use of the same name, but it was tossed out of court: imperial was considered a generic word, one that could not be limited to one company. The cover on the first album displayed Anthony adorned in a crown with the Chrysler Imperial's insignia. Sometimes genius comes at odd times, wrapped up in many ways, and on that auspicious day at George Goldner's recording studio, history was made, and The Imperials were born.

Months later, Goldner's company recorded another set of songs by The Imperials. "The Diary," written by Neil Sedaka, with the flip side "So Much." The lyrics of "The Diary," played on the heartstrings of teenaged girls who fell in love with their unique romantic sound. *How I'd like to look/ Into that little book/ The one that has the locking key/ And you know the boy that you care for/ The boy who is in your diary….Make all my dreams come true/ You know how much you mean to me/ Say I'm the boy that your care for/ The boy is in your diary*. While George was away in Europe, the group was called into the studio to record "So Much," which did little on the pop charts and then "The Diary," and although it sold well, had it been released on the heels of "Tears on My Pillow," it would have sold much better. Timing and placement was so important in the business, and this judgment call did little to catapult the group. The lyrics and melody of "So Much" proved less than inspiring, *I'd move a mountain, if you want me to, though it's hard, so hard, It's oh so hard….I'd give you my heart, If you want me to, You know I will, Cause I Love you, I need you, I need you so much*.

When George Goldner returned from Europe and took notice of the record sales he was so angry that he fired the head of production, and then sat down with the group and reviewed a new strategy. He would personally oversee of all of their releases, hovering over their careers like an expectant father; too much at stake to screw it up. There was a lull in their careers, a loss of momentum. A couple of months later, George thought he had found the right tune, something that would make them stand out on the charts: "Shimmy Shimmy Ko-Ko Bop," written by Bob Smith, was essentially a song about nothing. In addition to producing the song, he brought in a choreographer who invented a dance to go along with the melody. *Sittin' in a native hot/ All alone and blue/ Sittin' in a native hut/ Wonderin' what to do/ Along came a native girl/ Did a native dance/ it was like in paradise/ put me in a trance.* The song was released and before George could blink an eye, the sales were soaring. Anthony figured it out: it was the preteens who were buying this nonsensical tune; they liked the silly words and the idea they could dance along. It was fun, and not a lot of music was just fun. In the neighborhoods, the music stores played the new releases, allowing the sounds to filter out to the pavement, and when young kids walked by and heard the music, they begged their parents to purchase it. That was how they jolted their career back into the limelight. "Alan Freed believed in the song, and the day it broke, it was like a chain reaction, as each radio station began playing the tune, a tune that easily crossed over to almost every genre." Fifty years later, Anthony was privileged to be in Washington D.C. singing at an event, "It was amazing to see our congressmen and -women get up and dance when we sang this song. Those were the very preteens who had bought our record when it was released a half-century ago and here they were today, still remembering the words and the dance."

Anthony went to high school, did what most teens did, and there he met fourteen-year-old Judy Fonseca, who became the first true love of his life. Living in the same projects, attending the same school, they shared similar values: a devotion to family and the ability to love. The problem back then was Anthony's parents failed miserably in explaining the birds and the bees. His older brothers were gone: Donald in the Navy, Elliot in the Air Force, and Sonny in the Army, and there was no one to impart that very important knowledge. Schools didn't teach sex education, and the topic, other than at a men's locker room, which Anthony never had the pleasure of entering, was taboo. "The only thing I ever remember my mom telling me about sex was that you could get worms. Worms, I asked her, what are those? She shot me a 'don't ask me any more questions look' and I left it at that. But I don't think she did a good job of convincing me not to have sex."

He ran into Judy occasionally and would look her way, admire her sweet smile and her cute face, but she was always surrounded by a clutch of boys and Anthony never had the nerve to intrude. One weekend there was a party at one of the kid's homes and he got up the courage to ask her to go with him. When the coast was clear, and she was standing next to her locker holding a couple of textbooks, he walked up to her and boldly asked her to the party. Smiling, she accepted, and they agreed to meet. "She was so pretty, and she was a good girl, she never did anything bad."

The party was all a young teen would hope it would be. With the parents gone, there was booze, lots of beer, and loud music blasting in the living room. As the night wore on, and the lights were extinguished and romantic ballads replaced the upbeat tempos, it became a 'grind 'em up party.' "I asked her to dance, and then we began grinding like the rest of the couples. It was so hot and so romantic. At least it felt that way to me. After that, Judy and I began seeing each other; we were always together and we thought we were in love. She had one tough sister, Bea, who hated me, and was always saying awful things about me, and then there was Judy's father, who was even tougher and meaner than Bea. A Merchant Marine, he towered over me, and didn't like the idea of me dating his daughter. For some reason, Judy's mom really cared for me; she was the one member of the household I could always count on." The teens dated throughout high school, oftentimes on the sly, to avoid confrontation with her father. In the three years they dated, their relationship remained platonic: both too young for sex, they wisely held off.

As the end of his senior year approached, Anthony got the spring bug and decided that going to school wasn't all that much fun. He was having a lot more fun singing, recording, and playing around. He didn't see the need to get a high school diploma and so for the last two months of his senior year, he played hooky: hanging out with friends, partying, messing with cheap wine, and just doing a lot of nothing. "I was drinking that cheap wine, Thunderbird, and hanging around with a group of friends in Red Hook. I was being rebellious and just wanted to be one of the guys." He had already tried the gang stuff and that was not what he wanted, but with those kids up in Brooklyn, he felt happy, safe, and content. That was until he got home one night.

Elizabeth ran to pick up the ringing phone, and was surprised to hear the voice of the high school principal on the other end. It seemed as though her son had been missing in action for almost two months and that he would not be graduating, which sent her spinning with anger. As soon as she heard her youngest slam the front door, she bounced out of the kitchen, set him down at the dining table, looked intensely into his dark brown eyes, and asked him where he was that day. Stuttering, Anthony, who was never at a loss for words, couldn't summon up the courage to answer his mother. She asked again, and with the sad eyes of a guilty person, he spoke the truth. Fuming, the next morning the two appeared at the office of the principal, who with a heavy hand, and a loud harangue, told the truant student that he had to attend summer school in order to receive his diploma. He didn't cry in front of his mom, or the intolerant principal, but he cried when he got home, and realized that the fun stuff of summer wasn't going to happen. No trips to the beach or Coney Island, no afternoon movies or horsing around with the girls; it was study, study, study. He had to pay for his mistakes, big time.

"Damn, it's hot," he complained as he entered the subway and began a tedious summer of studying. He knew his parents would be watching, and that the teacher was keeping track of the whereabouts of each kid. Looking around the crowded classroom, he realized he wasn't the only truant among the group. He bonded with other boys who had decided they, too, would skip school. There was no air-conditioning except for cracking open a window and hoping for a breeze. He endured the pain and suffering as the teacher imparted knowledge of history, math, and just enough science to see them through their summer finals. Anthony never missed one hot, brutal day of summer school. He had learned his lesson, and promised himself never to screw around again. Walking home from school each afternoon, he was reminded of all the fun he was missing as he observed his friends playing stick ball in the street, or throwing baseballs around.

Completing the last exam of summer school, the students placed their pencils on top of the wooden desks as one of the girls picked up her transistor radio and turned it onto the local pop chart station. Whispering into her girlfriend's ear, they giggled and pointed to Anthony, who was seated at the back of the room. "Tears on My Pillow" was playing. A broad smile crossed his face: his song, The Imperials and his group, were on the radio! The teacher, who was usually stricter than a nun, allowed everyone to listen, and then the class applauded their famous young student. In a hurry, he rode home on the train; he could hardly contain his sheer joy as station after station picked up the requested tune. "When I got home, the phone was ringing, and I picked it up. Goldner's company said the record was a smash and that the group should come down to the station. I never gave school another thought, and neither did my parents. It was fifty years later, when Boy's High was cleaning out old records that they discovered they had never mailed out my high school diploma. Stained, and yellow, it finally arrived in the mail."

Clarence had spent his summer working at a butcher shop. The work was as arduous and as gruesome as he could ever imagine, but he made a decent wage, and his family needed the support. The radio was on as he was pounding the life out of a row of veal chops, and that's when he heard "Tears on My Pillow." At first he wasn't sure it was his Imperials, but he turned up the volume, and yes, it was his group. It was at that very moment he knew where his heart belonged and where his future would be. Untying the bloodstained white apron, he tossed it in the air, screaming that he quit!

The next afternoon, the five teens met at the recording company, and they were treated like heroes who had returned from battle. There were contracts to sign, plans to make, new songs to sing, and tours to plan. They were officially a viable group who had made it big, and Goldner's company was going to make sure the group they had launched continued on an upward path.

Busy singing gigs, they were out in the clubs performing, going to parties, and celebrating as young rock stars. It became their new lives; singing, rehearsing and performing. Clarence hadn't graduated high school, and per state law, the record company had to provide him a private tutor. During the day, if they weren't rehearsing, he was compelled to complete his high school education. Anthony, who had the summer school experience freshly engrained in his memory, pushed Clarence to accept the tutoring, otherwise he would end up in hellish summer school, and that was definitely no place he would ever want to be.

That was truly the summer of their rising fame as the song played over and over again on the radio stations. Legend says that Alan Freed, the one person who you wanted to break your record, loved it, and asked, 'Who was the girl on the record?' He later found out that the girl was a guy, and the very next time Freed played the song on his watch, he renamed me Little Anthony. Alan said that any guy would can sing that high, has to be little. And so the group became *Little Anthony and The Imperials.* The name stuck, and has remained that ever since, but it separated Anthony from the other four guys and it caused a rift. "I became more important than the other four, we lost our shared camaraderie."

Later that year, Imperial Margarine decided that the Imperials had tread on their territory and sued to cease and desist from using the name. Being young, none of the guys much cared or paid attention to the lawsuit, but they saw it as a great opportunity to play a prank on Nathaniel. "We were singing up in Harlem at a huge ballroom and Ernest took Nathaniel aside and told him something terrible had happened. We were being sued for inflation."

"'Inflation!' he roared, 'Now what the hell is that?' All of us started laughing at him, he was genuinely scared.

"'I'll get you guys for that,' he promised."

A week later, the group was performing at the St. Nicholas Arena in the Bronx. They were in the dressing room changing into their new costumes when Ernest exploded into the room and yelled, "Our bus is dancing on the stage!" When no one else moved, Nathaniel should have taken the hint, but he raced out of the room, and ran to the stage. When it was empty, he returned to the dressing room hearing the boisterous sounds of his friends laughing their heads off.

Again he promised himself that he would get even at those guys, but with his sweet affable nature, that would probably never happen. He was duped again.

The guys were young and in need of a road manager: William Parker showed up for the job. His only credentials were that he was strong, feisty, and a pimp of ill repute, perfect for handling young men on their way to stardom. He was hired by Richard Barrett, our manager. "He taught us how to be street savvy, and took us to prostitutes where our wildest sexual fantasies were fulfilled. He allowed us the freedom to sow our wild oats, introducing us to drugs, wild parties, nightclubs, and alcohol." To ensure his charges were content, William invited the group to his apartment where he hosted parties that were beyond the boys' imaginations. Basically the parties were orgies, with the women providing the reality of their sexual dreams. "At eighteen, we were welcomed at all the nightclubs, served the best drinks, and later we joined our manager in private rooms where we smoked the best weed. Boy, did I grow up fast!"

Some years later, a tour was booked for the rising stars down the southeast corridor. Cocky, William thought he could save a lot of money by eliminating what he referred to as the middlemen, the people who marketed the shows, sold the tickets, collected the money, and made sure the house was packed. He had no qualifications for the job other than the paltry few already listed. Thus when the young men arrived on their southeast tour, there was a plethora of empty seats, and little money from the ticket sales. After a few gigs, they were disgusted and began making inquiries. On top of all the disasters, as they were driving down one of the interstates the bus driver had a meltdown and went a little crazy. "This tour is stupid," he shouted and then began to turn the bus around. William was aghast and lunged at the driver, grabbing at the wheel. The bus began weaving all over the road until one of the guys found an empty space and slammed his foot on the brakes, stopping the bus abruptly. The cops were called, and took the driver to a safer place, a room at the county jail. William then called the bus company, frantically screaming and the next day a new bus arrived. Between the lackluster audiences, and the bus fiasco, William cancelled the tour, and they headed back to New York. From Knoxville to New York was the longest two day drive Anthony ever endured. We were broke disillusioned and disgusted. They had to get rid of William and the sooner, the better. He had fast tracked their careers into a downward spiral and none of them were stupid enough to sit back and let him take away their fame.

When they returned to New York, they were set to record "Goin' To Take A Miracle," but William refused to record the track without first getting paid for it, and so a classic standard hit slipped through their fingers. William went beyond his call of duty, he didn't have the authority to make this call. Because he didn't understand the nature of the business, his obstinate ways caused the group to lose momentum, "and we never gained that momentum again."

Years before it reminded the guys of their fiasco with Neil Bogart, an attorney, who became their next manager, and booked the group wherever he could guarantee a quick buck in his pocket. Handing them a roadmap, a set of directions, and some cash to cover expenses, he instructed them to go to Butler, Pennsylvania, where the theater had already been sold out for Friday and Saturday night performances. The singers took the Mercury Station Wagon, provided by Neil. Ernest opted to do the driving as Anthony read the map, directing the caravan of two cars in a northwesterly direction. The deep burgundy Mercury was stuffed with four suitcases, a couple of guitars, and playlists. Without a care in the world, they began the four hundred mile trip, leaving the densely crowded streets of Flatbush Avenue for the Pennsylvania Expressway.

Stopping periodically for gas, food, and bathroom facilities, they made decent time until they hit Oneida Valley Road. Clarence was sleeping in the back seat but the smell of smoke penetrating a crack in the window woke him up. "Guys, I smell something burning," he said. His warning was ignored as they plodded ahead. Another mile down the road, they heard the loud horn of an eighteen wheeler blast in their ears. Pulling up beside the Mercury, the driver screamed out to Ernest to stop the car. "Do what he says," said Clarence, "I told you I smelled smoke." Bringing the car to a sudden stop, Ernest popped the trunk while the others flung open the doors and fled to the side of the road. They could see the muffler was lying underneath the car, black and smoking. The heat was rising near the side of the car. They raced to pull their suitcases and instruments out of the trunk and ran several yards to safety. Less than a minute later the entire car exploded in flames, the sparks from the dragging muffler had ignited the fuel tank.

The group stood in shock as they saw the car burn to the ground. Had they waited a moment longer, they might have all been burned to death. The truck driver pulled over and called for help. Grabbing the fire extinguisher from the cab, he ran over to the burning car and tried to put out the flames. Several other cars also pulled over, stopped, and offered the young kids assistance while they waited for the fire trucks to arrive. Hitching a ride with the Highway Patrol, the group was dropped off at a rental car agency and made it to the gig on time. "Sometimes I wondered about how our agent could have given us that broken down car, knowing the length of the trip and the amount of luggage. We were his meal ticket, why would he put us in harm's way?" This was just another lesson of life on the road. They vowed never to allow this to happen again. When they returned home, each of them had their turn at letting Neil Bogart know angry they were with him: they could have died!

The group was in big demand and was featured on Dick Clark's show, the one place all groups wanted to be seen. On being scheduled with an endless series of one night stands, Anthony recalled, "I didn't see the light of day as we were chauffeured from place to place performing. If we weren't on stage, then we were rehearsing, trying on new costumes, or learning new dance steps." The women had no qualms throwing themselves at the young men.

CHAPTER 6

Anthony had met her at one of the night clubs. Just seventeen, Mary, two years his senior, had taken a liking to this teenage heart throb, seducing him in a way no other woman had done before. He could have and maybe should have felt guilty for cheating on Judy, his childhood sweetheart, but when the opportunity arose; he was unable to turn down the beauty and intrigue of an older woman. It didn't take more than an instant and Mary became pregnant. "I was a celebrity and somehow the story leaked out to Jet, the most popular Black magazine in the city. My dad was getting his hair cut at the barber shop, and while he was waiting, he just happened to pick up the magazine, and read a story about me and my love child. Both my parents were shocked and angry. When I came home that night, there was hell to pay as my parents began ranting and raving about my unruly life. They yelled that they had taught me better than that, but I think they forgot that they hadn't taught me anything."

The second big tour began as Anthony sat on the bus with Dick Clark. This time, everything was in order, properly marketed, and highly organized. They had met Dick Clark in 1958 when he had invited the group to sing "Tears on My Pillow" on his famous television show. "I remember watching his afternoon dance shows, the pretty girls, and the famous groups, and then we got a call and the next day we were on the show. When I met Dick, he looked at me and said, 'Don't tell anyone where the fountain of youth is.' We both looked so young. He put me on pedestal and treated me like royalty, not knowing I was just as bad as all the other guys."

The Caravan of Stars was split up into two separate groups, West coast and East coast, and throughout the months, he would have the performers fly back and forth refreshing the shows. Clarence, Ernest, Sammy, and Anthony, shared the spotlight with Herman's Hermits, Bobby Vee, the Hondells, The Caddies, Freddie Cannon and the Delrons. There were two sections on the plane, one for the singers, who got up front seats, and the other for the musicians, who sat further at the back, but Herman's Hermits always felt above the others and had their own private plane.

"When our plane landed outside the rural town of Paducah, Kentucky, we decided to introduce the British to some American customs. We shared a dressing room and after the performance at the local high school, we took them out for a real soul food dinner, treated them to steins of local beer, and of course, home grown pot. But their favorite American food came in a cardboard bucket; one taste and they had fallen in love with the Colonel and his Kentucky Fried Chicken. After that first taste, that's all they wanted to eat.

"When Dick heard through the grapevine that I was corrupting the foreigners, he set aside a seat for me right at the front of the bus. I thought, here I was sitting at the front of a bus and this was a far cry from when the Blacks were regulated to the back of the buses. I got the seat of honor, right next to Dick. We all felt like free spirits, not a mean bone in our body, but I think he just wanted to keep an eye on me. This was the infamous tour where Buddy Holly ended up on the plane that killed him. Had I been on the western tour, there was no doubt I would have been on that plane. I was adventurous and unafraid; I would have been the first person to fly despite the inclement weather. I felt invincible."

Unlike the first tour, this one was mostly north of the Mason-Dixon line, where blatant segregation was long gone. Travelling through Missouri, Virginia, Ohio, we all stayed in the same hotels, ate in the same restaurants and used the same bathrooms. Dick wouldn't have had it any other way. As he saw it, we were all equal, the only difference that defined us was our talent. Here, prejudice was more of an undercurrent. There were some things I did that I knew I had to keep below the radar, especially when it came to women coming in and out of my hotel room. They would hide and come up the back entrances, or take alternate elevators so we wouldn't be seen going into the same room together.

"Fabian had joined the tour and he was most unhappy; he just didn't have the moves or the voice, but what he had was a handsome face. Some performers were simply a creation, put together by an agent who was marketing an image, but such performers, like Fabian, didn't have the talent to compete with the rest of us. One night me and Clarence took him aside and started showing him some sexy moves. Clarence demonstrated how he should dance on stage, doing this move and that move, but in the end, singing was not his talent; he gave up singing and became a very famous movie star."

One of the last stops was in Toronto, Canada, where Frankie Avalon joined the tour. The girls were all over him likes bees to honey. Anthony had gotten used to screaming teens, but it was nothing compared to the hordes of girls who stalked Frankie. "The show was over and we were looking for a place to have a drink.

Frankie told me he knew this secret tunnel underneath the Queens Auditorium where we would be safe from the crowds. I followed him into the long dimly lit channel, and as we were about to emerge onto the sidewalk, we saw a crowd that appeared to be ten thousand screaming girls, running in our direction. I was terrified we would get trampled. Frankie yelled, 'Follow me,' which I was a bit leery to do, and we started backtracking through the tunnel underneath the auditorium. Running as fast as we could, and we came out at the other end of the auditorium, right where we started. We ran and ran, until we ducked into the first hotel and stayed there until the coast was clear. I don't think I had ever been that scared!"

When they arrived home from the Caravan of Stars, there was lots of buzzing on the street about Motown records and the music Berry Gordy was recording in Detroit. The group had a gig booked in Detroit and decided to pay his place a visit. Modest, as had been portrayed, the store front was littered with young kids milling around singing, dancing, flirting, and writing songs. It almost felt like a commune for aspiring artists. The air was filled with excitement and anticipation as they waited for the producers to pronounce the next hit record.

By then, Little Anthony's group had made the big time and people wanted to emulate their success. "Motown started a charm school to teach the singers how to perform with class when they were on stage. We were cool and moved in a way that no one had done before. We were true performing artists, more than just singers. The greatest performers in the world came out of vaudeville. Sammy Davis, Jr., Redd Foxx, and we had caught the tail end of that era learning from the best. Later, when Richard Barret had discovered us and made us sing 'Bubbles, Bangles and Beads,' he was trying to instill in us a quality of enrichment that as true performers, we should be able to sing anything, because if we could sing anything it would give our careers longevity."

Sent on a series of gigs across America, the group landed in Las Vegas, home to casinos, shopping, restaurants, and great entertainment. "The first time I met Sammy Davis, Jr., one of my heroes, was in Las Vegas, where he was the headliner at Sand's Hotel and we were at the Sahara. Skip, from the Treniers, introduced us and as the years progressed, Sammy and I played in the same towns, and became friends." Skip was another contemporary, a nephew, who sang with his uncles. Anthony and the Treniers often crossed paths, and Skip, the youngest, found a fast friend in Anthony. For making the initial introduction to Sammy Davis, Jr., Anthony would be forever grateful.

"Later, we met again, when Sammy was playing at Caesar's Palace, the most prestigious venue in town. He had invited the entire group up to his suite, which was bigger than most penthouses: six thousand square feet, overlooking the Strip." Punching the private elevator, the smell of soul food and fried chicken permeated the air as the host, dressed in a tee-shirt and an apron stained with tomato sauce, opened up the suite door. Welcoming the crew into his humble quarters, he asked them if they wanted something to eat. Not waiting for a response, he returned to the fully stocked kitchen putting the finishing touches on cooked cabbage, ox tails, fried chicken, and collard greens simmered in a tomato sauce. Grabbing a beer, they dug into the soul food and later, Sammy put on a movie. There were over twenty people at the party that night, some of the most beautiful women on earth among them. He had all the ladies he wanted, and they all wanted him. "I hung around with him a lot, visiting him at his home in Los Angeles. He was kind, witty, and the most gifted entertainer I had ever met. Sammy was forever giving us tips on how to perform, or sing, or how to tell a joke. He wasn't afraid to share his talent with us, which seemed to be true for so many other stars who crossed my path.

"When we were singing at the Flamingo, Ertha Kitt caught our show. After she had finished her act she asked me to have a late supper. She was so educated, warm, a truly sophisticated woman, who spoke seven or eight languages. I was drinking an ice-cold Coke and she chastised me, saying that I should never drink anything cold when I was singing. I never forgot that piece of advice. Performing in Las Vegas made us a better group and gave us the opportunity to meet so many people in the industry who became friends for life."

Several months later Mary gave birth to Antoinette. Anthony was only eighteen, a baby himself, and in no position to be a father to that child. At first he denied the baby was his, and had it had happened when DNA testing was in its prime, he might have been proven wrong, but at the time it was Mary's word. He had to suck it up and accept that he was the father. It was his mother who always saw the glass half full, and at the birth of this precious infant girl, a granddaughter, she volunteered to help raise the child. Mary, who was still a young teen, seeking a life of her own, thrust the baby into the arms of a caretaker who became so enraptured with the infant that she stole her away. Elizabeth, the proud grandmother, had been busy shopping for her new granddaughter. Carrying a bag of winter clothing purchased from A&S, she and Mary knocked on the door of the caretaker's home, where there was no response. She knocked again and again, the door finally opened and Mary and Elizabeth said to the caretaker, we have come to take the baby home. But Antoinette, didn't want to go, she had grown to accept the caretaker.

They returned the next to pick up the Antoinette. They were gone. They searched frantically, but never found the caretaker or Antoinette until years later. "I had incredible guilt that there was a baby out there and I didn't know where she was, or how to find her. I suppose my guilt was even heavier when I hid this baby and my relationship with Mary from Judy."

In 1988 Anthony, at forty-seven, received a letter postmarked from a state prison from Antoinette: "I think you are my father," she wrote plainly. When she was released, she was finally reunited with her father and they have been close ever since.

Anthony came to believe that he was a rock-star and could have any woman he wanted, which is a dream come true when you are a teen. "Judy came to see me perform at one of the nightclubs. She waved at me and I said to myself that I could have any hot woman in the room, and I totally ignored her. I was adamant in my belief that I was living in a man's world, and could go and do as I pleased. I wasn't nice to her and we broke up for a year."

The timing was auspicious, as Irving Feld put together another tour: Little Anthony and The Imperials would be going on another road-trip, one that would last three months. By now the group had the two bestselling records in the country, "Tears on My Pillow," and the flip side, "Just Two Kinds of People in the World."

"We went from not having a pot to piss in to having the top-selling records in the nation, all before any of us had hit eighteen." It was explained that the tour would promote the group in markets around the country. It was the fate of recording stars: you made records, then you went out to the public, performed the records, and then the records sold, and that is how everyone made money in the industry. Their first album, now complete, was named simply Little Anthony and The Imperials, with ten brand new songs.

"Everybody did everything for you. All we had to do was just show up and sing. People were kissing our butts and did everything for us. They would constantly tell us how great we were, while they packed our bags, ironed our clothes, and brought us whatever we wanted to eat or drink. Our wishes were their commands. We all had money in our pockets. I was happy with the beautiful girls hanging around us all the time, doting over us. But what I didn't like was the strain and the burden of my name separated from The Imperials. It was not joyful to me."

CHAPTER 7

Anthony had lived life through rose-colored glasses. Although he had suffered heartache, experienced fear and the pains of a whopping, he was for the most part happy and content. With the enduring love of his family and the sudden climb to fame, he had more than he could ever hope for. Those glasses shattered as he climbed onto a Greyhound bus heading out for his first intense southern tour. The first time touring the southeast corridor, it was short, with just a few quick stops, as were all the initial tours. It was hard to believe, that the group had been together for over two years, recording, travelling, meeting world-class stars, and making sweet music together. In their first foray through the South, they were unknowns, and few seats were filled, but this time would be a lot different.

When the bus crossed over the George Washington Bridge, Anthony twisted his head around, took one last lingering look at the city, and began to cry. He was already homesick. It all happened so fast; it seemed like one minute they were singing at the Apollo Theater, being waited on hand and foot, and then the next moment he found himself sandwiched into an uncomfortable seat headed for places he had never seen. It was Christmas Eve when the bus pulled into Richmond, Virginia, the tip of the Deep South. Exhausted from lack of sleep and miserable after being confined for endless hours in an upholstered chair, he staggered out of the bus into the cold and damp night air. Although he was with his four friends, he had never felt so alone in his life. This was Christmas Eve; he should be home standing around the tree, exchanging gifts with his family, hugging his aunts, and singing with his mom. Instead, he was lugging a heavy suitcase into a third-rate hotel on the wrong side of the tracks. He was tossed a key to a single room and told to walk down to the end of the hallway.

Collapsing onto the springless mattress, he gazed around the dingy room. A dim lamp lit the tiny space. The door to the small closet was ajar, concealing a bathroom that hadn't been remodeled since the opening of the hotel decades ago. Grabbing a thin bath towel, he took a shower, thinking it would make him feel better, but all it did was make him cleaner. Tears continued to flow as he lived his first Christmas Eve on the road. Fixing his gaze onto the ceiling, which was filled with peeling gray paint, he grew severely homesick. Three months of this would be such a long time. He had never been away from home for so long – he wouldn't return until early spring. He was missing his favorite holiday, his family, his friends, and the comfort and security of his home. He was absolutely miserable! After a sleepless night, he borrowed a phone from the front desk clerk, and called his mom, lamenting his homesickness. But she was stalwart and told him he had to continue. By the time the conversation was over, he knew he wasn't going to quit, but he also knew that the gnawing in his stomach wasn't going to go away.

The name of the tour, Biggest Show of Stars, was appropriate, as they had the hottest line-up of pop singers in the country on those two buses: The Coasters, Chuck Berry, Frankie Lymon, Chantells,

Big Joe Turner, and Bo Diddley were some of the artists. Early the next morning, Christmas Day, the performers heard the cacophonous honk of the bus, and knew they had ten minutes to board the Greyhound. As the driver eased out of the parking lot onto the highway, Charlie Carpenter, the tour manager, stood at the helm of the bus providing instructions to the novices. Words sprung from his mouth that were so foreign that Anthony thought Charlie was speaking another language, which in some ways he was. So intermingled in his Brooklyn community, Anthony, along with Nathaniel, Tracey, Clarence and Ernest, had grown up color blind. People of every color, background and nationality shared the same neighborhood and the same apartment buildings. They got along, never singling out their differences; they all went to the same schools, churches, movie theaters, ate in the same restaurants, and shopped in the same stores.

"We are going into a hostile environment and you must learn to play by their rules," Charlie admonished. It didn't take but another moment and tears rushed down Anthony's naïve face. It was Bo Diddley who spotted his tears, took a seat next to him, and befriended the terrified, homesick teen. "He became my mom and dad, mentoring me on the road. The next day we landed in a small town south of Richmond. As we departed the bus, we saw signs that said 'Coloreds,' which was posted above water fountains, restaurants, movie theaters, and bathrooms." This was the first sign they had entered the Deep South, where Blacks were treated as second class citizens and hated with a vengeance that only the Ku Klux Klan could spawn. In spite of Charlie's warnings, nothing could have awakened their senses to discrimination and prejudice more than those unimaginable signs. The five teens walked through the center of town, and, as Anthony recalls, "I couldn't get a seat at the counter drugstore." If they were hungry or thirsty, they could order, but they would have to take the food outside the premises.

"That night we stayed in a horrible hotel on the other side of the tracks, it was worse than the night before. With bugs running around the room, no heating, and a bed that hadn't been changed, I couldn't stop crying. All I wanted to do was pack my bags and go home. Here I was a big national star, with my music played across America. Everyone knew who we were, but in the South, all they could see was the color of our skin."

Their agent also failed to mention the pecking order on the tour. As newcomers The Imperials got last dibs on anything of meaning and value. If there was a worst room, or someone needed a go-for, The Imperials were the men for the job; mostly, they were picked on and made fun of by the rest of the artists, until one day they would bond together as one person and then it would be everyone for themselves.

When the two buses pulled out of the rural town, Anthony found he had an empty seat next to the aisle and just as he was about to stretch out, Jimmy Reed, a man several years his senior, known as a blues singer, grabbed the empty seat. He was an artist of profound talent, but struggled with alcoholism, and was drunk pretty much most of the time. "I don't know how he did it. He would barely be able to stand, and a couple of the guys would dress him up, walk him onto the stage, and then Jimmy would sing as if he had never taken a drink in his life. He would walk off the stage, and then stagger back to his dressing room, or crawl up the three steps back to the bus. Jimmy always had a flask of mint gin and gave me a taste. It was powerful stuff!"

Besides Bo Diddley, Jimmy became Anthony's sidekick when they were on the bus together. In spite of his drinking, they got along; Jimmy was kind and nurturing. "We stopped to gas up the bus and went in different directions finding food. Jimmy, now completely drunk, handed me a brown paper bag and asked me to watch his precious fried chicken. I wasn't quite sure how I would watch his chicken, so I took the bag and hid it above our seats in the overhead compartments, and then I went in search of food for myself. The smell wafting from that bag must have been a little too tempting for some of the singers. When the bus pulled out, Jimmy turned to me and asked for his chicken, so I reached up, grabbed the bag, and handed it to him. When he opened it up, his eyes were wide, and his smile had turned ugly. He started screaming that someone had eaten his chicken. I swore that I hadn't eaten the chicken, as he continued ranting that he was hungry, and demanding 'Where is my chicken!?'"

Although their friendship continued, Anthony never again volunteered to take care of Jimmy's food; it was all too much pressure in such small quarters, especially with Anthony's standing at the bottom of the pecking order.

"No matter what, our two tour buses became our family, and we had to stick together, there were rough times ahead. Now, when Jimmy became incensed with the loss of his chicken, we held a trial. On the bus, we had a makeshift court where there were lawyers, prosecutors, a judge, plaintiffs, defendants, and witnesses. In order to keep things in order, the mock courtroom solved little grievances between the artists. For each cause of action, they voted for a judge, and then sang the spirited lyrics of 'Here comes the judge.' After it was decided that there was no contest for Jimmy's stolen chicken, since no one would attest to the fact they saw someone eat his precious food, the investigation continued, and the mystery was finally solved: it was David Lynch of the Platters. Jimmy was happy as a clam that the culprit had been named, but there was no restitution, he would never get back that chicken.

"The next case involved a much more severe matter. It was Ernest's birthday, and a group of us guys pooled our cash, and hired a prostitute to surprise him in his room that night. When we found out that he never used her services, but merely talked politics, and then fell soundly asleep, he was tried for being dumb. A jury of his peers found him guilty of being dumb, and awarded Ernest the nickname DA Wright, (short for Dumb Ass)."

Anthony was to have his own private trial, but it was held by Nathaniel and Tracey Lord. "You smell something bad?" asked Nathaniel as he turned to Tracey. Twitching his nose, Tracey sourly remarked that indeed he smelled something awful, and it seemed to grow more pungent each day. "Wherever I go, that smell seems to follow me and I believe I know exactly where it's coming from." Casting his eyes over to Anthony, Tracey nodded, concurring that it seemed the teen had forgotten to take a shower, lacking some coaxing from his mother. Whispering, they plotted to enlighten Anthony to the virtues of showering each day. That evening, when the bus had pulled into the motel, they noted his room, and in the middle of the night, the two snuck into Anthony's room, twisted the shower nozzle until hot water flowed abundantly, grabbed the sleeping body, and thrust him into the steaming hot water. Tossing Anthony a fresh bar of soap they warned him not to leave until every inch of his stinky body had been thoroughly scrubbed. The trial by two of his peers seemed to work, because he never smelled bad again.

In the morning Tracey and Nathaniel were smiling when Anthony met them at the breakfast table. "Do I smell nice? Here, smell my arm, does it smell nice?"

They looked at each other and burst out laughing, "Yes, you smell nice," they said, "And make sure you stay this way!" Anthony was not well-behaved in so many ways. Entangled in the arms of a young beauty, he hadn't heard the first or the last call of the bus. When the maid knocked on the door and announced there was but one other person in the entire motel, he jumped out of bed, and screamed for help. Luckily Lloyd Price, one of the performers, had taken his own car, a sleek, long, shiny, black Cadillac Fleetwood, and hadn't left the premises. He always slept in because his car could outrun the buses by miles. Hitting a hundred miles an hour was an easy task for the elegant car. Seeing the sad pout on the Anthony's face, Lloyd ordered him to grab his bag, and join him for the ride of his life. While roaring down the Interstate at ninety miles per hour, the sound of a siren filled the air Signaling, Lloyd pulled over to the side of the road, and waited for the sound of the State Trooper's boots to come to the side of his window.

"You were doing twenty over the speed limit. Did you know that?" he asked. Looking at Lloyd and then at Anthony, he asked them what they did.

"We sing. You know the song, 'Personality?' That's my song."

"Then sing me the song," the cop demanded. Not to allow Lloyd total humiliation, Anthony joined in and they did a wonderful a cappella rendition. Still not satisfied, the cop asked, "How does a nigger like you get a car like this?" Waving his hand in the air, the cop pivoted on his heels, dug his leather boots into the dirt, and let them go.

"And just another experience in the life of a Black man once you cross the Mason-Dixon line. I'm sorry you had to see this. I feel like crap and I know you do, too. Those white folks are only too happy to pay good money to see us perform, but out here, where no one is looking, they get us, they get us good. I guess we should consider ourselves lucky he didn't pull out his gun and shoot us," said Lloyd.

"The next day the bus rolled into Motel AJ Gastin, the best accommodations for Blacks in the suburbs of Birmingham, Alabama. For once, we slept in a clean, well-lit, well-decorated motel that was only a few miles from the theater." The group was herded into a small, family-owned coffee shop serving the best in homemade Southern cuisine. "I was sitting in the restaurant eating grits and heard a pop, pop, pop. Someone in the back of the restaurant yelled out that the cops had killed a young black boy, right there, right in front of my eyes. I was sick to my stomach. You could smell the hate in the air and it was brutal. That was an awakening that made me grow up. From that moment on, I stopped being a young weak kid, and was determined to get strong. Nigger this and nigger that was all that I heard. I needed a backbone to be able to endure the atrocities as I toured the southern states. People didn't realize I was in a war, and could never imagine how badly I was treated. Here we all were, famous stars, filling up huge theaters, young women throwing themselves at us, and down here, we were treated like trash, second class citizens."

A couple hours later the performers entered the back entrance at the Birmingham Theater, and began their sound checks and rehearsals. They noticed something very odd about the theater: it had two separate sides. Later, when the audience arrived, the Blacks and whites each took their respective sides. After Anthony's jump to manhood that afternoon, he decided, along with his four singers, they would not comply. They would not turn their backs on the Black audience, and just sing to the white people, the very people who loathed them, murdered them, and segregated them. Instead, when their group was called, they took the stage, turned their microphones to the center, and sang to the back wall. Instead of a grand round of applause when they had finished, they heard the KKK yelling threats. Walking off the stage, they scampered out of the rear of the theater, and into the back of the bus.

That night Anthony had played his trump card as a grown-up, had acted courageously in the name of justice, but in doing so, he put his fellow artists in harm's way. When everyone was assembled on the bus, and everyone was accounted for, they received a strong reprimand from Charles who again reminded the young teens, that you play by the rules or else you put everyone's lives in jeopardy. He got a promise from the boys that they would never again pull a stunt like that. "That young Black kid who was murdered this afternoon could be one of you if you don't listen to me." After that, they listened and followed the rules as they walked on eggshells through the heart of Dixie.

The next day the tour rolled into Prichard. The bus stopped in front of a large, inhospitable, dilapidated boarding house in the Black section of town. The pale yellow paint was chipping off the front door, the wooden floors were warped, and the brocade wallpaper was peeling off the walls. Setting the suitcase in the corner of the room, Anthony pulled back the covers of the twin bed, and saw tiny black bugs scurrying over the stained sheets. How was he supposed to sleep when he knew these tiny creatures would be crawling over him in the middle of the night? Walking down the flight of steps, he caught the attention of the owner and complained bitterly. "Honey, I'll get those bugs out of your bed before tonight," she promised. He didn't believe her. After the show had ended, and it was time to face the gloom of the boarding house, Anthony shook out one blanket making sure it was free of bugs, wrapped it around his body tightly, and fell asleep on the floor. Closing his eyes, his last thought was, "The life of a famous star, so glamorous!"

The next day, with the entire afternoon to kill, and the sky filled with dense rainclouds, several of the performers grabbed the bus driver and coaxed him into taking them to the movie theater. "We bought tickets, and walked into the empty theater. The man took our tickets, and pointed to the stairs. There was a sign posted 'Coloreds' at the base of the steps, so we reluctantly walked up the two flights and took our seats. Peering over the edge, there were four people sitting on the first floor. I was disgusted, humiliated, and angry. What difference did it make where we sat? Later I got up to use the bathrooms, and again that ugly sign was posted above the door. I can't even remember the name of the movie, all I can remember is how awful I felt. Those same fellows who sold us our tickets, and directed us upstairs came to the show that night. They were clapping and cheering as if they had amnesia and forgot how terribly they had treated us that very afternoon. Nothing made any sense."

There would be two long, boring days on the road travelling on the bus to Texas, and so Clarence and Anthony made the best of those two days and hopped on the first jet flying into Idlewild Airport. The young singer was so homesick even a two day respite would help mend his chronic queasy feeling. Grabbing a cab, they fought the late-night traffic, arriving home after midnight. When Elizabeth heard the door open, she jumped out of bed and bear-hugged her son. After an hour of kisses, snacks, and testing out his bed, he called several friends and left to party, and run around the city.

It was a girl he ran to see first, Bea, who was older by ten years. "She was more woman than I had ever known. At the time, the fact that she was ten years older than me was crazy; guys didn't run around with older girls, but I was infatuated and nothing deterred me. My friends told me she was too old for me, and that she was just looking for security, but I couldn't help myself. I was drawn to her; you might say I became obsessed. I spent most of those two days at home with her. This was the beginning of an affair, though I can't say that I knew or understood what real love was."

Bea was dauntingly beautiful, with her deep brown eyes, caramel colored skin, and an oval face that flushed rose in the sunlight. Her body was curvaceous with large breasts and long legs; she was two inches taller than Anthony. They spent most of the next day in her bed where she initiated him into the art of love making. The ethereal delights went beyond anything he had ever imagined; she had taken him to a place beyond his imagination.

Later, they went out for a late lunch, and between the sodas and the hamburgers, she proposed marriage. Taken aback, he was all too happy to acquiesce, but he wasn't of legal age to get married and he would have to obtain his mother's permission. "I was so happy, I had never been so happy. Home just one day, my girlfriend asked me to marry her; it was usually the other way around, but I said yes." They finished their lunch, and arm in arm, they took a taxi to city hall, and obtained a marriage license. After the clerk reviewed their IDs, she handed the document back to Anthony, explaining he would need a parent's signature to legally approve the marriage certificate; he wasn't yet eighteen. He could read the disappointment on Bea's face, but he knew he couldn't fight city hall, so he slipped the certificate into his pocket, and vowed he would return to her later that day with his mom's signature. Grabbing another cab, he dropped her back at home, and then sat pensively by himself for the next half hour until he arrived at his apartment. Brazenly entering the apartment, he waved the certificate in the air, and announced he was getting married.

"You're doing what?" Elizabeth screeched, "No, you're not!" He began crying, and begging his mom to sign, but she was steadfast and refused. She was his mother, and no one knew him better. This was a train wreck about to happen and when she found out that Bea was ten years older, she was even more adamant. From the passion in his eyes, she sensed that reasoning with her underage son wasn't the route to take, so she simply stood her ground, refusing to allow this marriage to take place. The more he pleaded, the stronger she became, until he finally gave up.

"I was mad, really mad, at my mom. If she would have signed the certificate I would have found myself married by the end of that day." Since marriage was out of the picture, and he still had another entire day at home, he called another girlfriend, Yvonne, and arranged to meet her. "She was the most beautiful girl I'd ever seen. The first time I met her was at the Brooklyn Paramount Theater, she was wearing a sash that read Miss Harlem, and she was gorgeous. I was drawn to her too."

It was as if Anthony had amnesia, as he became steeped in one sexual relationship after the other. Or perhaps it was the fact that the teenage years had passed him by, as he travelled from childhood to adulthood. "I think I was in love with love."

After a brief dinner at a local Italian bistro with Yvonne, his mind returned to Bea. He had to see her again. Excusing himself to the bathroom, he deposited some change in a payphone, and arranged to see Bea in a couple of hours. Dropping off his current date, he rode up to Harlem, but instead of going directly to the restaurant, he got off at the front of Bea's brownstone. There was a black car parked in front of the residence, one that was familiar. It belonged to Jay, a singer, a member of The Crests. Curious, Anthony speculated why the car was there, and rather than barge into her home, he waited on the sidewalk.

After a few moments he witnessed Jay leaving Bea's apartment. They were laughing. He grabbed her waist tightly, kissed her good-bye, and then sprightly jumped into his car and sped away. "I knew she was cheating and I became so angry." A rage set into him unlike any he had ever experienced. So consumed with passion, he wanted revenge. It was earlier that day she had proposed, and she was already cheating, but he never took a good look at himself to admit he had done the same.

"I went home, stormed into the kitchen, and found a meat cleaver. I hid it underneath my sock, and prepared to meet Bea at the Palms Café. As the cab approached the café, I began to cry. I was so hurt, I wanted to get back at her, I wanted to punish her for cheating on me. Instead, I went to the nearest phone, and called my oldest brother Sonny, and cried hysterically."

"Hey, little brother, if you want to kill someone, then come to my home and I will give you a gun," he offered. "Come on up, I'm home, and I will pull it out, and get it ready for you, I have plenty of ammunition and there are plenty of bullets to do the job." As Anthony pondered the situation, he realized how fanatical he had become. Sonny had used a psychological approach, and had tamed his mind, roping it back into reality. Hoisting the knife out of his sock, he tossed it back into the kitchen drawer, and then planted himself in his bedroom, and cried himself to sleep. Too much passion, too much sex, too much high-strung emotion for a young teen who was home for forty-eight hours. One day left at home, and he felt the need to resolve the relationship.

Early the next morning, he borrowed a station wagon and drove to Bea's home. She had been on the lookout for Anthony. She had found out that he had found out about Jay, and that he was filled with jealousy and rage. When she heard the motor die, she armed herself with the largest knife in her kitchen, and nervously opened the door. Displaying the large weapon she screamed, "Get away and don't come back, we're done!" With the shoe on the other foot, and a weapon starring him the face, he turned around and left.

On the drive home all he could think of was the fact that his mother had been so right in not signing the marriage certificate. What a complete disaster that would have been! Tears ran down his face as he eased through the city streets making his way back to the security, warmth, and simplicity of his home. He never saw Bea again. Devastated from the fact she had cheated on him, he would never recover. A whirlwind of passion, love, sex, and turbulent battling had left him emotionally spent.

It was Sonny's advice that got Anthony through that rotten ordeal, and he knew he owed his oldest and wisest brother a debt of gratitude, perhaps even his life. Had Sonny not calmed Anthony down, his passion may have ended him up in jail. Decades later as Sonny walked down the aisle to receive his master's degree, Anthony remembered his brilliant mind, and how he knew how to solve every family problem. It was always Sonny the siblings turned to when they needed advice, and his advice was always well taken. Six weeks after receiving his degree, at the young age of 56, Sonny died. The trauma of his death overcame the Gourdine household. He was beloved by his family, and by his wife, Billie, who never remarried. "I could never find another love as great as the love I had for Sonny."

Twenty years later Anthony was performing at show and was asked to join a special table of women for a drink. Walking over he shook hands with the women, smiled, and then departed backstage. The person inviting him to the table was Bea, but she had turned old, and her once shapely body was heavy, her once radiant face hung with thick layers of skin; he had no idea who she was. Later that evening someone told him who that woman was, and he smiled to himself. He had gotten his revenge – he had humiliated her by not recognizing who she was. It was worth the wait.

CHAPTER 8

Before leaving New York, Anthony had just enough time left to meet up with Taffy, another beautiful teen, who had fallen prey to his charms. He arranged to meet her at her apartment, and after a couple of quick beers, they had a jubilant and carefree roll in the hay. She was fun, young, playful, and wasn't after a long-term anything. Smiling, he held her tightly; this was the kind of relationship he needed.

Kissing her good-bye, he went home, gathered a few clean clothes, kissed his mom, and took the first cab to the airport. Elizabeth had tears in her eyes when she saw Anthony walking down the steps, but then he stopped, and turned. "Mom, I'm sorry for what I put you through, I know that you were right not signing the marriage certificate. I'm sorry for being so stupid and fighting with you." He wrapped his arms around her and promised he would try to do better. That was all a mom could hope for, and that was all she would ever ask.

Clarence met him at the airport, impatiently clinging to the two tickets back to Texas. Racing through the long corridors, they ran to the gate as the staff announced the final boarding. After finding their seats, Clarence turned to his friend and asked him how his vacation was. "Relaxing," smiled Anthony as he closed his eyes, getting the first trouble-free moments of sleep in over two days. Next time he would stay with the bus; things would be a lot smoother.

Travelling west to Houston, the artists had plenty of time to think about the idea of arming themselves with guns. Several singers walked into a gun store, purchasing pistols, hand guns, and an assorted array of ammunition. Both men and women were easily swayed into carrying a small but formidable form of protection; they were only halfway through the tour, and there were plenty of stops left, south of the Mason-Dixon line. If nothing else, they could whittle away idle hours with target practice, and even hold a contest. So yes, the tour bus was now armed to the teeth as the driver reversed his course heading toward Valdosta, Georgia. Unlike Atlanta, which is nicknamed Oasis of the South due to the fact that Blacks were well treated in the city, Valdosta was just as unwelcoming as all the other hick and uneducated towns in the South.

Although it was early February, the humid air was already warm and sticky. Bored, a group of guys bought some softballs, a couple of bats, and some mitts, and started playing a game in front of a huge barn that they would be performing in later that night. Marking out the field, they picked sides, and began tossing the ball, when a huge farm truck pulled up to the side of road, with three rednecks inside. "You Niggers are going to sing tonight, you better sing to us," they yelled as they brandished their guns, and sped out in a red cloud of dust.

The artists and musicians nodded to each other, set down their equipment, went to the bus, and extricated their weapons hidden in their suitcases. They were prepared, and if need be, they would meet those low sons of bitches head-on. Picking up their bats and balls, they continued playing until they spotted that same truck returning from the opposite direction. Running for their weapons, they waited until the truck stopped, and then wielded their weapons, pointing them right at the truck, shooting several rounds directly above their heads. This time when the truck peeled out, in the same cloud of dust, it was to save their own skins.

Quietly walking together, the men were all secretly shaking in their running shoes but inside, they were bursting with pride: they had defended themselves. After the truck departed, they set up a bunch of empty beer cans underneath a magnolia tree and spent the rest of the afternoon target shooting.

Handling a gun requires some skill and training, and not everyone who had made their purchases in Houston had thought much about how to use their gun. Richard Barrett, their manager, was one such person. After squeezing off several practice shots, he became distracted and forgot to put the hammer back down. Inserting the gun down the front of his pants, he was unaware that it was still cocked, and ready to go. As he jogged in the direction of the barn, there was a pop sound, the sound of his own gun, shooting himself in his own leg. Several heads turned in unison as they heard their friend screaming, and saw him writhing on the ground in agony. "I could see the bullet hole in the back of his leg, and Richard passed out from shock." Their manager spent a few days in the Valdosta hospital before he was shipped home for the remainder of the tour. Again, it was Charlie at the front of the bus, lecturing everyone on the safety and use of guns, a lecture well served had it had been made as they departed Houston.

The tour performed that night inside the big red barn, one that seated the Black audience upstairs and the whites on the main floor. There was a huge white cop, a state trooper, standing at the edge of the stage, sporting a gun twice the size any of them had purchased.

The trooper was tapping his foot to the music, as Bo Diddley did his thing so well. Anthony was standing back stage, tapping his foot as well. In his mind the cop was enjoying the music as much as the next guy, but with a magnum .45 holstered at his waist, he was not quite like every other guy.

"I walked over to the cop and asked him what kind of a gun he had, I had never seen one so large. He turned to me and said, 'This gun is to kill little Niggers like you.'" Disgusted, Anthony slinked further backstage; he was sick to his stomach and didn't feel like performing. Hatred was so abundant that it sapped the life out of his body, taking away all that he had grown to believe. Maybe he was a man now armed, but his insides hadn't changed; his morals, and values were still intact. Hatred, bigotry, and prejudice were not part of his vocabulary. Perhaps his parents had sheltered him a bit too much, but then he reflected on their lives and how from the earliest he could remember, everyone got along. Was America really that different? Was the South another country where the rules of civility didn't apply? He had a lot to think about as he buttoned his jacket and prepared to strut onto the stage with his fellow singers.

They got through the show, and the next day, Anthony was rewarded with an unexpected gift: Frankie Lymon was going to teach him how to drive a car. "Tennessee was where Frankie Lymon taught me how to drive. With the afternoons free, and rehearsals completed, we had several empty hours to kill. Frankie rented a station wagon and said, 'Let's go for a drive down to Chattanooga for a little sightseeing.'

"When he asked me if I could drive, of course I said yes. I was the can-do man. I could do anything I set my mind to. Frankie hopped into the driver's seat, and we began driving down a deserted country road. Frankie said, 'Take the wheel.' I hesitated, but then grabbed the wheel. Frankie almost threw up as I swerved the car all over the road, but at least I got my very first taste of driving a car."

The next day Johnny Maestro asked a few of the guys if they would like to go horseback riding. "Do you know how to ride?" he asked. The can-do teen answered in the affirmative and off they went to a top notch dude ranch. The horses were not the typical rentals, they were thoroughbred quarter horses. Never having ridden a horse, nor seen up one close, other than the police riding them in Manhattan, Anthony thought it would be simple, just like driving the car. He had seen Western movies, and remembered how the Lone Ranger looked so happy when he was on top of Silver, his trusty steed. Yes, he certainly could do this.

Setting his left foot into the stirrup, he flung himself over the top of the horse while a handler adjusted the height of the stirrups. Holding onto the reins, he was ready and excited. This was going to be fun. Last in the parade, Anthony was told his horse would follow the others. The virgin rider nodded in agreement. With a subtle slap on the lead horse, the group began a slow, lazy trot, which quickly escalated into a full gallop. Anthony was breathless as his horse kept up with the rest of the pack. This was fun, although he was clinging onto the saddle horn for dear life.

In the distance, he spotted a wall, one that appeared close to six feet tall. All the horses were still at a heady gallop when Anthony noticed the men took the reins and twisted to the left of the wall. Anthony neither knew how to steer his horse, nor did he have the experience to see what was coming. The horse kneeled down, and he went flying over the wall, landing on the other side directly on his butt. It was hard to enjoy the screams of laughter from Johnny and the other guys on the other side of the wall when he could barely stand up. "How I did the show that night, I don't know. I was in so much pain, I could barely walk." After that, the can-do man stuck to things he was good at, one being romancing women.

"After a while, the tour became a drag, and I would hang out with women. I found sex was the one thing I looked forward to; they made it fun. Back then, they called the girls backstage Annies, who were very willing to have sex, they just wanted a piece of the entertainer. I spent many an afternoon in the arms of these willing women and they all made it worth my while."

The tour began to wind back north, stopping in Madison, Wisconsin. Anthony was in a stall in the men's room, when he overheard several white men saying, "Niggers are this and that way." I walked out of the stall. They knew who I was, but it never stopped their tirade. "I said to myself, as I was washing my hands, that here I am a world-class performer, and this is how people treat me? I really didn't expect this as far north as we were."

Johnny Maestro was the only white person on the tour and was as disgusted by racism, as the Blacks were treated differently. He found himself isolated, forced to sleep in a "white motel" away from his peers, his friends, his colleagues, his equals. One day, he had had enough, and rebelled. Locating black face paint, he covered his face, put on a fedora, walked in with a group of the guys, and slept soundly and peacefully with the rest of the performers.

The calendar read March when Anthony finally returned from the tour. The air smelled so sweet, the trees were budding, and the morning air less harsh. "I didn't realize how long I was gone, I was too busy counting the moments until I returned. I found out that show business was not that glamorous." When Anthony walked through the front door, Elizabeth saw a different person. Her teenager had grown up, and had become a man. The road had toughened him, made him physically and mentally stronger, and although she missed the soft, sweet child, she knew if he were to succeed in the entertainment business, he had to grow up. Hugging him, and planting several kisses on his cheeks, she told him how much she loved him. There was no doubt it felt great to be home, and when he opened the door to his room, stacks of gifts were piled on his bed: Christmas gifts along with birthday gifts. He had turned eighteen on the road and for the first time in his life, there was no birthday cake or family celebration.

No sooner had the group unpacked their suitcases than they were summoned into their manager's office with the promise of more work. The young guys strutted into the large conference rooms excited about their future prospects. "I'm going to present a new look for you guys and a new sound. We are going to cut an album called *Shades of the Forties*. Now before you disagree with the idea, I want you to listen to me. The sophisticated sound will capture the adult audience, and lend credence to your true singing talents. I promise you, it won't destroy your bubble gum images."

Handing out the list of songs with the lyrics, he told them they had a couple weeks to practice before recording, and that they would have a very special reward upon completion of the album. "When the music from the new album began to play on the adult pop stations, I was told that I was like a young Sinatra. We cut some of his biggest hits. No one had previously thought to do such an album. Our manager had made the right choice for us. The music was way ahead of the times and sold over a half million copies, which was unheard of. Critics didn't know where to place our music, all they knew was that it sounded real good."

Cub Koda, a music critic, stated, "There's music on here so finely wrought and so heartfelt, certain passages of it will give you the cold chills by its sheer, unaffected beauty. There is so much more than dry history, The Imperials made some mighty music that truly deserves a much wider hearing and here's exactly where to start absorbing their genius."

Again seated in the same spacious conference room of their manager, Richard Barrett, the guys appeared edgy and anxious as they waited for the promised surprise. They did as requested and cut the album. They worried over the loss of their teen idol status, and now here they sat, impatiently waiting for his announcement. "Young men," he announced, "I'm sending you on a dream tour, an entire month performing in the islands of Hawaii. I promise, none of you will feel the pangs of discrimination; hell, your skin is lighter than most of the natives. You will be treated well, like kings, I promise. Now go home and pack your bags." Handing Anthony, Tracey, Ernest, and Nathaniel their plane tickets, he admonished them to make sure they were at the airport on time and to behave well in the newest state to join the union. "I have rented a limousine to pick you up in the morning, and there will be one waiting for you at the end of your journey." Hugging his favorite clients, he showed them to the elevator, yelling, "Knock 'em dead!"

"I was just eighteen and one minute I was in Brooklyn, and the next on a huge plane flying across America. We barely made it to the airport. Our limo driver had taken us to the airport. He dropped us off, and we walked into the terminal and got comfortable, but when we walked up to the ticket agent to check in our bags, she informed us we were at the wrong airport. Grabbing our bags, we ran for a taxi, since our driver was long gone. Hailing an empty limo, we flashed some cash, and explained our dilemma. Used to us New Yorkers in a hurry, the driver slammed the trunk closed, gunned the limo, and raced through side streets, dropping us at the edge of the luggage check-in at the right airport. Running down the long corridors, we reached our seats just as the stewardesses slammed the door shut."

William Parker, the appointed chaperone, was standing nervously and pacing, waiting for the guys to appear. It's not that their agent didn't trust the lads, but it was that he didn't trust the young lads, so William happily volunteered to supervise the boys while sipping on tropical island drinks, not a bad gig for a month. Now William was beside himself with worry. When he saw the guys running into the gate area, he was both relieved and worried. At least they arrived, but if they were going to behave like this, he would have a lot of babysitting to do.

"Can you believe this?" said Tracey, sweating from head to toe, "Going to the wrong airport. Our agent would have killed us had we missed our flights." Turning to Ernest who was also sweating, he could sense something was wrong.

"Oh, Tracey, you know what? I think I left my costume at the other airport!" Once airborne, Ernest began rummaging through the bags; nope, he had left it back at the other airport hanging on a pipe. What to do? "I'll call our agent when we land in Dallas, he will figure this out. This isn't the first time I've done this, but what a distance."

The flight crew paid special attention to the young celebrities, plying them with beers despite knowing full well they were underage, propping up their pillows, bringing extra nuts and snacks, which made up for the anxiety of almost missing the flight. Eight hours later, they landed in Dallas, the first leg of the very long journey. There was just enough time for Ernest to place a frantic call to their agent: "Yes, everything is just fine, but please, can you find my costume and have it delivered to the hotel?" he requested in a guilty tone. "Thanks, gotta go, the flight has just been called." Yet again leaving another mess for their agent to clean up, but he would come through (he always did) he would find the renegade costume and have it on the next plane in no time.

From Dallas to Los Angeles was another six hours of flying, and after that, they boarded Pan American for the overnight flight into the Hawaiian Islands. On this flight was the famous Sam Cook, who was also part of the show in Hawaii. The moment they entered the plane, it was a completely different experience; they each had a sleeping berth with pillows, blankets, and a small reading light. Two full meals would be served, along with drinks, and snacks, and when the drone of the engines was too pronounced, they covered up their ears with the pillows. After twelve hours, the captain announced they were descending into Honolulu and it was time to fasten their safety belts. The trip took this long because the planes were four engine constellations, jet engines had not placed in commercial service. On their trip home, they landed in Los Angeles to switch planes and they were offered the first commercial jet flight, a 707 on American Airlines to New York. We were told the flight would be no longer than four hours. On that plane was Ed Sullivan.

Tropical air, carrying the sweet scents of flowers, rushed into the cabin, as they lumbered down the steps onto the tarmac and received leis from the darkly tanned island girls. Walking through the small airport, they noticed the islanders had darkly tanned skin, just as their manager had promised, and after a day of travelling, it was reassuring that they would fit in and feel at home. William declared two days of vacation before performances began, but each guy had to check in with him at least three times a day; he wanted to know where they were at all times. "No crazy stunts, no swimming out into the wild ocean. Stay around the pool if you want to swim, the ocean is treacherous. And no getting crazy drunk, no smoking, or wild parties…" by then William had lost them as they hurried to their rooms and dressed for the beach.

"It was the most beautiful place I had ever seen, and it was a place I knew I would want to come back to. At night I looked out from my balcony and saw Diamond Head. It appeared like an over-sized Christmas Tree, with small lights blinking on and off. The smell of the air was so sweet, the beaches were so white and clean, and the ocean was so warm. Going from island to island, the more I saw, the more I fell in love with Hawaii, especially the gentleness and kindness of the people. I have to admit, I was a little homesick, I felt like I was in a foreign country even though we were all there to welcome Hawaii as the newest state."

The first and last leg of the trip would be spent performing at the same hotel, and the next three weeks were spent hopping from island to island in tiny prop planes holding no more than a dozen passengers. The guys had the time of their lives and made William's job easy as they dutifully checked in three times a day. On their last performance of the tour, they were back at the original resort. A young girl and her father introduced themselves to Anthony. They had seen the show the very first night and returned for the last show. "My daughter is in love with you and your music," he said.

"May I have your autograph?" she asked timidly. Scribbling his name into her book, she asked for his phone number and address, which, for some odd reason, he provided.

If that is what would make this preteen happy, why not accommodate her; besides, she would be the first one in line to purchase all their new releases, he thought. Giving her a hug, he thanked them for coming to the show. The next day, the group and William boarded the plane, and another day later, the limousine was at the ready to cart their weary bodies back to Brooklyn.

Unbeknownst to Anthony, that preteen in Hawaii had become obsessed with him, so much so that she began to cry the moment his flight left Hawaii. Being an only child, having parents who were apparently well-heeled, they were willing, and apparently able, to do anything that would soothe her distraught heart. They booked passage on a cruise ship, loaded on their car, drove across the entire country, and rang Anthony's doorbell.

"Anthony, you have visitors," yelled Elizabeth, as he dragged himself out of bed from an afternoon siesta. Standing in the foyer of the apartment was that young girl with her parents. He was so shocked, he couldn't speak. "Well, you remember how much our little sweetie loved your music and we couldn't make her happy, so here we are in New York," boasted her father. Stunned, Anthony didn't know what to do. Luckily Elizabeth had received a call earlier that day that they would be visiting and she invited them in, set three extra plates at the dinner table, and they all sat around chatting as if they were next door neighbors. The obsessed teen kept in contact with Anthony for years, sending photos of her budding career as a fashion model. When her face appeared on the cover of Vogue, he rethought his first image of the little preteen, but by then, she had fallen in love a half dozen times. Having learned his lesson, he never again gave out his address to fans.

CHAPTER 9

The gang made a date to meet at The 1650 Building. Things were brewing: new songs, new rhythms, and it was time for them to record again. Anthony, dressed in an updated Italian navy pea coat and tan leather boots, looked like a photo out of *Gentlemen's Quarterly*. He and The Imperials were on top of the world and the world was responding in kind, purchasing their albums, going to their performances, and calling the radio stations clamoring to hear their songs. Coming off an earlier Southern tour where he was introduced to hatred, he was elated to be back home among people who loved him, regardless of his color.

The walk light had turned white and the troop of young men stepped into the street, crossing over to the west side of Broadway when they spotted a man strumming a guitar, sitting outside The Turf, the restaurant adjacent to the Brill building. There was no hat to catch coins, nor was this scraggly man begging for money, all he was asking for was to be heard. "It's only twenty bucks, man, for this song," he yelled. His beard was rough, his face reddened from years of drinking, but his fingers were adept as they flew over the guitar strings. "Hey guys, listen to this cat, he ain't half bad. In fact, he is really good." At once they formed a circle around the vagrant and paid him the respect they thought he deserved.

"My name is Run Joe Taylor, most guys just call me Run, since I have no home, but they love my music. Just listen to this tune, I promise you it will be a hit, a big smash and I will make you guys richer than you already are," he lamented. Although Anthony's group never did hand over twenty dollars for his hit song, the Platters did, and they got "The Great Pretender," one of the most played songs in the world. Anthony would pass Run Joe Taylor throughout the years, and wonder why they never took him up on his offer, but they never forgot him. You can never tell a book by its cover. It was 1960 and a lot would happen this year, but first, the group found their way back into the recording studio to cut "My Empty Room," which titled their next album. The melody was public domain, although Welch was given credit for the lyrics. Another passionate love song that teens and the ubiquitous romantics could relate to, it sold well, crossing over R&B into the pop charts. *Why must I sit here in my empty room/ why did you leave me darling oh so soon/ was it a game dear/ am I to blame dear/ your memory lingers on like sweet perfume/ I sit here in my empty room and cry/ my heart is aching since you said goodbye.* Heart wrenching, it spoke to the passion of young love, offering a form of understanding and empathy. The music gave a voice to the emotions of a new dynamic generation, the teen generation. Not only did they have money, but they began carving out what was to be defined as a fresh segment of American society, they were a power to be reckoned with, respected, and deserving of a valued position in society. They had an insatiable thirst for music, especially that which captured their emotions. No longer did the young teen feel alone. When they flipped on the music, their personal heartaches, passions, secret loves, and bottled up emotions became mainstream. The adage that children should be seen and not heard was incinerated, replaced with new ideas, new passions enlightening the old guard that the new generation impacted the economy. Timing is everything, and the music Little Anthony's group cut was at the right place and right time.

The next tour would begin in New York City at the Apollo Theater. It was called the Chitlin Circuit, which was a series of theaters scattered throughout the country that showcased Black performers in Black neighborhoods. The best performers would show up on those stages, especially at the Apollo. Although known for singers and musicians, The Apollo was also the place for the hottest comedians to be heard. When Redd Foxx, Moms Mabley, Slappy White, Stump and Stumpy, or Bill Cosby were slated on the marquee, one could spot a cluster of white comedians sitting in the audience taking notes. Breaking into national television was particularly hard for Black entertainers, which made it easy for the white comedians to steal jokes from their Black counterparts. It took time, but the Black comedians got their reward, appearing on national television, especially the late night shows, where they breathed life into a new era of comedy.

The Chitlin Circuit was comprised of theaters dotting the Eastern Seaboard, with a pocket in Chicago. It was a safe place where Black entertainers could perform before Black audiences in a free and unencumbered way. When segregation was still an epidemic in America, those theaters provided a perfect platform for Black artists to show off their talents. At this juncture, most of their music had not crossed the sacred but invisible line into mainstream rock and roll. The Circuit thrust these brilliant artists into the spotlight, allowing the population to fall in love with their sounds. Even though the radio stations segmented them into R & B, a euphemism for Black music, anyone could scroll their transistor radios freely to a station of their liking. When the soulful sounds were being listened to by a cross-section of America, and fans were inundating the rock and roll stations with requests, the deejays listened and soon the Chitlin Circuit songs were flying across the airwaves faster than the deejays could spin them. Music became one of the most effective elements to blast through the racial barrier. Here is a shout out to all those gutsy deejays who gave the American public what they wanted, and helped obliterate segregation. In so many ways, deejays, like Murray the K, and Alan Freed, had more gumption than combat soldiers; they helped guide the culture into an understanding and acceptance of every human being as equal.

After climbing out of the car, the guys dropped their costumes in the dressing rooms, and then walked up the metal steps to the third floor of the Apollo; food was always being at the top of the theater. A cook from the neighborhood found a need, and prepared all of their favorite comfort foods for a reasonable amount of money, they could purchase a home cooked meal. Anthony's Aunt Sarah lived but a half mile away, and when she found out her favorite nephew was at the Apollo, she began preparing fresh meals, bringing them to the theater for the remainder of their gig. "She made me fried chicken, collard greens, coleslaw, and biscuits. The guys were so jealous that Aunt Sarah began bringing enough for all of us to share. Boy, could that woman cook!"

"Are you guys ready? It's curtain time in a half hour," announced Mr. Spain, who headed security, and took great pains to make sure the entertainers were ready to go on. That evening a movie was shown to keep the audience busy until the headliners appeared. Anthony was always curious about the audience, and he stood behind the movie screen scanning the crowd. "I could see through the movie screen, but they couldn't see me. It was fun to see who was sitting in the seats, and it made me feel good to know all of the seats were filled.

"There were an awful lot of young girls in the first couple rows; they were all so pretty and dressed up. I wondered if I would get to meet any of them after the show." The line-up that night was stellar, Frankie Lymon, The Dells, and The Flamingos, guaranteeing another sell-out crowd. In the back dressing room, Clarence, Ernest, Tracey, Nathaniel, and Anthony were putting the finishing touches on their hair and make-up, as they waited for their cue to take the stage.

It was an odd night as Frankie Lymon opened up the star-studded show; there was even a premonition that things would not go as planned. "I was standing in the wings watching him go on, but he was stoned out of his mind. He actually walked into a pillar in the corner of the stage as he stumbled to reach the microphone. I was feeling scared for him, and frankly I couldn't figure out how he would be able to perform. In spite of himself, when the keyboard player cued his opening note, Frankie sang like a trooper and none of the audience detected he was as high as a kite. I really felt sad for him, so on top of the world, and ruining his life with drugs. Right then and there I should've sworn off drugs, but I was young and had many lessons yet to learn."

Dressed in black suits, red ties, and white shirts, the group sparkled as they stepped up to the microphones. Young teens were screaming and clapping wildly, as The Imperials performed their latest top-charting songs. Anthony leaned over to shake hands with the girls lining the edge of the stage when one girl grabbed his hand, and then another grabbed his arm, pulling him off the stage, and down into the seats. "They began tearing at my clothing, leaving me almost stark naked before Mr. Spain rescued me from their clutches. The band kept playing as if nothing was the matter. I wasn't about to hop back on stage without clothes, so I rushed back to the dressing room, and threw on the jeans and jacket I wore to the theater, rushed back to the stage, and finished the song. After that, I never got that close to the audience again. I was truly scared." They took their bows, and the group left the stage with Anthony still shaken from the incident.

As with all live shows, things sometimes go awry, and somebody else needed to be saved that night. The Flamingos, who were slated last, discovered the tenor's voice was knocked out from a nasty cold virus, and he was unable to sing the high falsetto notes in "Golden Teardrops."

"I knew the part and was happy to help them out, so we set up an open mic backstage, and when the tenor's part came, he lip-synced on the stage, while I sang live from back stage. Nobody knew, and they were able to get through their entire set. The audience gave them a standing ovation, and none was the wiser that I had sung all of the high notes. I think we must have invented the art of lip-syncing that night."

What a night! And yet, it wasn't over. That was the evening Anthony would meet his next squeeze, Melba Sanchez. "She was a hot Puerto Rican chick, and had come to the show with a group of her friends. When the performance was over, she was waiting at the backdoor. When she introduced herself, I was taken by her beauty, and I suggested we go to the Palm's, the best restaurant in Harlem, and hang out for a while. Everyone was really dressed up: men in suits and the women in sexy cocktail dresses with stiletto heels. You had to look sharp if you wanted to hang out at that restaurant. It didn't matter what color you were, it was the in place to go if you wanted to see the singers and performers. The waiters served us drinks – back then nobody cared if you were under twenty-one." Melba's olive complexion, long lustrous black hair, and dark brown eyes captured Anthony's attention. She was strikingly beautiful, and when she spoke with her hint of a Puerto Rican accent, he was entirely captivated. The two dated for a while, and soon enough, another shocker: Melba found herself pregnant. Nine months later she gave birth to Liza, a perfect baby in every way, but with no father in sight. There were many other women who had set their sights on Anthony, one in particular: "Big Gert," whose weight hovered around two-hundred fifty pounds. Over six feet tall, she was a scary lady for a young teen. Her advances were met with disdain, as she tried relentlessly to bed him. "I did everything to remain out of her clutches, but one night she got lucky. Enticing me with the promise of the best weed in the city, we climbed into a taxi after the show, and went to her apartment. It was dark and late, but I could see that we were in a bad neighborhood. Stores were boarded up, and thugs were walking the streets carrying tire irons and guns for protection from gang members. We walked up two flights and she unlatched the door, flipped on a light, and then relocked the front door. With every different sound of another lock secured in place, my heart began racing. What the hell was I thinking when I said yes to this mammoth woman, and how the hell was I going to get out of this place?" Walking to the window, he looked for an escape route, perhaps a set of steps that would lead him back to the street, but no luck. He would have to fight his way out if it came down to it.

True to her word, Big Gert went into the kitchen, opened up the cookie jar, and pulled out two joints of substantial proportions. Scraping a match on the countertop, she put both joints in her mouth, lit each one, and then offered one to her new beau. "It was sheer heaven, she was right, it was the best weed I had ever had. As I kept smoking, Big Gert kept talking, and after a while she didn't look that bad to me."

"Are you going to make love to me?" She smiled. "Now, my Johnson has a mind of its own, and although she wasn't pretty (but pretty big), she got me! We had sex. She took my hand, put her hands around my neck, and began kissing me. She kissed my ears, and mumbled something, and then slowly took off my shirt. She pulled me in toward her mammoth breasts and they parted like the Red Sea as my head nuzzled in between.

"She had quite a technique. When she was naked on the bed, her obese body no longer seemed to matter. She knew all the right moves to get me going, and go I did. I was so stoned I guess I didn't care, and when it was over, she unlocked the front door and let me out. I remember running as fast as I could until I found the first subway station, and dove down the stairs. The next day before the show, I was the laughingstock of the theater. Big Gert had let everyone know she and I had done the deed. She had conquered me. Oddly, after that she never raised an eyebrow; all she wanted was the conquest, not a repeat performance, and boy, was that a relief." The week run at the Apollo was over and Sunday morning all of the acts piled into their cars heading down to Baltimore, the second leg of the Chitlin Circuit at the Regal Theater. "The town was tough. The Circuit was in a Black neighborhood that was dangerous and unwelcoming because of the local street gangs. They were hardened dudes, and didn't think twice about showing their strength in bar brawls or street rumbles. These were guys you didn't want to get near. They thought all of us artists were pansies, and intimidated us whenever they had the chance. When we arrived, the theater director told us to be conscious of the audience, and keep our eyes on the crowd, that sometimes things got out of hand. Yes, they had security, but by the time the security officers interceded, it was often too late. The guys and I had a meeting, and discussed how we could get through the weeklong gig. I felt like I had a target on my back, and I needed Clarence, Nathaniel, Ernest, and Tracey to back me up. I was the front man, and if something was tossed on the stage, it would be me who took the fall.

"On the first night, the line-up began with Laverne Baker, a soulful blues singer with a dynamite body to match, followed by Slappy White, an outrageously funny comedian. All was well until we took the stage. I can't say why, but some of the audience didn't appreciate our music, and began tossing stuff onto the stage.

"A bottle was thrown right at Joe Richardson's guitar, and the glass exploded right in his arms. He was terrified and then mad as hell. We were there to close the show, but as far as I was concerned the show was already closed. With my short build, short enough to be known as 'Little Anthony,' I wasn't about to tough it out with the big guys. The lights in the theater brightened and the emcee announced the show was over. The five of us ran back behind the curtains, making sure the crowd was leaving, and then we went to our dressing rooms in sheer relief. It boggled my mind to think what would have happened to us had we played our full set that night. That was a scary time, and a very scary town. The incident took away from the glamour of being a world-class act!" Things were looking up after that gig, as they travelled to the Howard Theater in the heart of Washington, D.C. "The ratio of women to men was three to one and the women were stop-traffic beautiful and smart; they were running our government. I was so weak, I fell in love with so many of the women.

"There was a boarding house directly across the street from the playhouse where we all stayed. It was one week of partying and having a wild time after each performance. The crowds loved the show, and we were all back to being rock stars. There were more than enough women to go around: at the end of the evening we had our arms filled with at least two gorgeous girls. After the second show two women came to my dressing room, Peaches and Candy, both beyond beautiful. They had fair skin, great bodies, and long, flowing, dark brown hair. I had one on each arm as I lead the way to the café around the corner. When I walked in, all of the guys were jealous, because those two women lit up the room.

"I didn't know which one to pick, and I couldn't have them both. I ended up with Peaches since she made my heart pitter-pat. Sharing is part of brotherly love, and Tracey gladly brought over his chair, sitting next to Candy. They seemed to hit it off, although I was too busy to notice. Peaches took me everywhere, and really showed me the town. We went to museums, listened to jazz in small bars, toured the national landmarks, and walked through the parks. I ended up seeing Peaches until the last night of the gig, when she announced that she had fallen madly in love with me – that is, until I came clean and told her I was already committed. That put a damper on our sex life, and for her, it was the end of the relationship. She wasn't about to share me with anyone, especially someone I had given my heart to, namely Judy. I just couldn't handle another serious relationship. Oh yes, and I never bothered telling her about my kids."

Clarence had begun a whirlwind affair with a stunning beauty, only to find out that she was the police lieutenant's daughter. One fine evening, shortly after the partying had begun, her dad knocked on the front door asking to see Clarence. Pulling out his sidearm, he pressed the cold metal to Clarence's temple and strongly suggested Clarence not bother his daughter again. Clarence was clear on the promise, and watched his step the rest of the week. After that, we all inquired as to the position of the parents; one threat was more than enough and we didn't want to cause any waves in the community.

Philadelphia was an important stop on the Chitlin Circuit, as the town had a huge teenage population thirsting for new music. The week the tour was booked, it had already been sold out. It was going to be easy performing in the City of Brotherly Love. The theater was well-appointed with deep plush seats, red velvet curtains, opera lighting, it was called the Uptown Theater. Georgy Woods was a famous deejay who sponsored those shows. The stage was wide, with endless outlets to plug in the microphones, and the stage hands were accommodating to every need. On the show were Jackie Wilson, James Brown, The Dells, Little Stevie Wonder, The Flamingos, and many more. What was most convenient was the boardinghouse, located directly across the street and run by Ms. Pearl. Ms. Pearl loved the artists, and showed that love by preparing meals from morning until night. At sixty, she was still spry, with thick, dark brown hair laced with slivers of gray, large oval coffee eyes, and an ample midriff, which had grown over the years of sampling her soul food. She never asked for a dime, instead happy to attend the shows in lieu of accepting money for the food. Her house had a small dining room, but a large living room, filled with sofas and overstuffed chairs. She would hand plates of food to the artists, insisting they tell her how they got to be. Ms. Pearl loved the stories and the lives of the entertainers. It was as if she were living vicariously through their lives.

In the middle of the week, the peaceful evening was interrupted. Nathaniel was at the back of the theater, milling around with the Isley Brothers, when a group of thugs walked into the alley and began beating up on the guys. Even though Nathaniel was a weightlifter, he was no match for the chains and clubs carried by the hoodlums. Rudolph, (one of the Isley Brothers), was a strong street fighter, and knocked out one of the guys just as he was about to clobber Nathaniel. Later that night, when they were sitting in front of the fireplace, and Ms. Pearl had attended to his cuts, Nathaniel looked up at Rudolph, and thanked him for saving his life. "I owe you one."

Shaking her head in disgust, Ms. Pearl was filled with anger. "You boys come to town and give us your talent, and just look what happened. I'm telling you those jerks who attacked you today, they were just jealous. They have no lives and are envious of anyone who is successful. None of you will ever want to return here," she cried. "I'm so ashamed of the way you were treated. Please promise me you will return." Everyone got up one by one, hugged her, and solemnly promised they would return. They all kept their promises, returning to the city, but the next time it was quite different. The next time Dick Clark would be host, ensuring their comfort and safety. But no one ever forgot Ms. Pearls' boarding house, nor the meals she so lovingly prepared. Clarence retrieved the car and honked the horn, signaling it was time to go. Ms. Pearl stood at the door, and handed each performer a care package, so they wouldn't forget her or go hungry. Standing in the cool morning air, she waved until she could no longer see the taillights, and then strolled back into her kitchen to prepare for the next coterie of arriving entertainers. She had three days to wait until the next artists arrived. Extracting the cake pans from the cupboard, she began again.

At times, the car rides were monotonous as the caravan forged through Interstate highways, twisting and turning southward onto a two-lane country road. The sterile view from the highway drastically morphed into lush farmlands with intermittent family-owned businesses dotting the fringes of the road. After checking the fuel gauge, Clarence announced the next rest stop and said they should take advantage of the facilities, because it would be hours before they arrived at the motel. Even though it was only four in the afternoon, they knew this would be the only meal they would eat until the following morning. Crossing the imaginary border into redneck territory, deep in the heart of Virginia, they worried about the bathrooms; would they be allowed to enter or would a sign marked "coloreds" be posted on a separate door.

Bringing the car to a halt, Ernest opened up the door, lumbered out, flipped open the gas flap, and fed the empty tank. Anthony jumped out and dashed into the bathroom. The first in line, young, and naive, he was in and out in just a few moments. He was unaware of the other guys playing lookout, guarding the door for possible troublemakers. Although there was no sign above the bathrooms, they were in the Deep South and they didn't want any trouble. Rubbing his wet hands together as he slammed the bathroom door, Anthony looked at the concerned faces on his fellow performers, shrugged his shoulders, and walked into the adjacent store. Several others were standing around, picking up bags of chips, sodas, candy bars, cookies, and pre-wrapped sandwiches. Nothing was fresh or appealing; these slim pickings would be it for the next fourteen hours. In the corner, at the very bottom shelf were cans of anchovies. Grabbing three small tins, a couple of sodas, and a bag of chocolate chip cookies, dinner was done. Nathaniel stood in line next to Anthony as they overpaid for the snacks. The cashier, who was also the owner, asked them where they were from. "Don't see too many people like you in these parts," he said, while collecting the money, and stashing it quickly into the register. "Would you guys like to see something real special, something that no one else has?" he asked in a sinister tone.

Anthony's intuition told him to avoid this suggestion, but Ernest, the least educated and the most gullible among the group piped up, "Sure, why not? What could you possibly have that no one else has?"

"Come with me," said the shop owner, as he waved his hand and enticed the young singer behind the back of the store. There was a muffled bark, and the sound of scratching at the rotted wooden door. Unlatching the door, Ernest peered inside and screamed. Anthony heard the screams and ran to the back of the building, and saw his friend shaking and completely stunned. Pointing to the door, Ernest stuttered, until he released the words, "That is the biggest darn dog I've ever seen. In fact, it looks just like a horse!"

"He won't bite," said the store owner, "But this doggie is the largest St. Bernard in the entire world; hell, he is listed in the *Guinness Book of World Records.*"

Ernest turned to Anthony asking him if he wanted a look-see and before he got his answer, Anthony was already running to the car. He had heard and seen quite enough. When Ernest came running into the car and yelling out he had just seen the biggest dog on the planet, everyone laughed. Turning to Anthony he said, "Now tell this them this true. I just saw this St. Barnard as big as any pony." Anthony decided he would have a little fun with Ernest, and admitted that he hadn't seen any dog, which in actuality he hadn't. "There is no such thing, you must have imagined this," he joked. The rest of the guys had assembled in the car and were quiet as they listened to Ernest describing this big dog. With smirks on their faces, they looked at Ernest and laughed, and went back to eating their dinner of chips and assorted junk food. Disgusted, Ernest folded his arms across his chest, looked over at Anthony, and swore he would get his revenge. This time Nathaniel honked the horn and three minutes later they were back on the two lane road travelling toward Richmond. The sun had set, and the road was pitch black, save for a few houselights sprinkled in the distance. The road narrowed as the car began to climb the hills leading into the heart of the city. Anthony saw it first: a brilliant, piercing, white light illuminating the top of the hill. Shaking Clarence awake, Anthony pointed to the light, "What do you think that could be?" Still angry from the trick about the world's largest dog Anthony had played on him earlier, Ernest replied, "I don't see any light. You must be crazy!"

"Okay, then I will get someone else to see it." Tapping Tracey on the shoulder, Anthony told him to look at the bright light, and just as he twisted his head around, the brilliant light extinguished without a trace. Tracey closed his eyes, and went back to sleep; he never saw a thing.

"So now you know how it feels," niggled Ernest. "But what do you think that is? I saw it blink out without a trace. Do you think it could be an alien ship? Or how about a secret explosion from the military? But whatever it was, it's gone." When the car came to the top of the hill, the very place where they had seen the light, there was nothing there: not a house, a barn, or even a tree. There was no explanation, but they both knew what they had seen and it was eerie. They were quite happy when the car had crossed two more hills and pulled into the motel for the evening. Civilization at last!

Some years later, they picked up the bus tour beginning at the State Theater in Richmond, which wasn't memorable – still too much prejudice for their liking. The buses contained stars that everyone wanted to see; The Orlons, Billy Steward, Solomon Burke, Dion Warwick and the Imperials. With that line-up, the crowds came out to support the shows, packing the theater every night. The schedule was tight; they had finished up the last night in Charlotte and had to be in Raleigh the next day so instead of sleeping at the hotel, they hopped back into their respective bus and spent the night driving through the countryside.

The road was filled with curves as they traversed the mountain passes, which lulled most of the guys to sleep, but not Solomon, who was becoming car sick. Previously seated at the back of the bus, he lumbered up to the front, taking a seat behind the driver. The sway wasn't as bad closer to the front, but he was still unable to sleep.

Sometimes things happen for a reason, and Solomon's weak stomach was more than made up for in the strength of his hands. The driver had also been lulled to sleep, and the bus began to move erratically, rotating back and forth across the highway. Solomon grabbed the wheel, woke up the driver, and tried to straighten out the bus. Boxes, food, bottles, and garbage went flying everywhere as the bus took a dive down the side of a ditch. What saved the lives of those musicians was the fact it had just rained, and when they plunged into the ditch, the nose of the bus got stuck in dirt and the wheels were securely planted into a foot of mud. Because Solomon had been there to wake up the driver, no one had suffered any severe injuries; they were just shell-shocked. Another glamorous day in show business, and thank God everyone lived to talk about it.

The tour finally arrived in the northern states, in the heart of Chicago, but by now because of the distance between gigs, they were travelling on planes. The venue was known as part of the Chitlin Circuit; the Regal Theater in the center of the hood in downtown Chicago, another tough neighborhood, but like the Apollo, it drew a diversified audience, Black and whites came to the shows. Even though the city was desegregated, there were plenty of hotels where the artists weren't welcome, so they stayed at a hotel bordering the

Black ghetto. In late evening, after the shows had finished, the group toured the city with strikingly beautiful women, who took them into the cozy jazz clubs, where legendary artists made their livings. "Ironically Dizzy Gillespie was also staying at the same hotel. We were talking, imagine that, the Great Dizzy Gillespie!"

Chapter 10

What Anthony shortly discovered was even though he could have all the women he wanted, life wasn't the same without Judy. Despite all those love songs that poured from his heart, his was still an empty, loveless life. He loved her more than he realized, and a year later, they picked up where they left off, madly in love with each other. The pain in his heart prompted him to write his first song, "Fires Burn No More," a ballad about the heartache of love and breaking up. "When I saw Judy running around with another guy I was heartbroken; it hurt me so much. Even though I was the one who made her angry, the pain I felt when I saw her giving attention to someone else was devastating.

"It was a Saturday morning and I was taking the train up to the Harlem for my weekly visit to see my aunts. As usual, I walked to the very front of the train and looked out onto the tracks. I loved to pretend that I was driving the train, and that I was the one in charge. The forty lonely minutes got my mind thinking about Judy, and how miserable I was. I wrote the lyrics and when I got to my aunts' house, I asked for a pencil and paper, scribbling down the words so I wouldn't forget; the name of the song was Travelling Stranger." Nothing had changed in Judy's home. Bea was still carrying her torch of disapproval, as was their father, but the mother welcomed Anthony back with open arms. Anthony had had a taste of sex and was ready to take their relationship to the next level. The two became inseparable, spending all their free time together. It was at a friend's house when they were grinding away to the music and playfully fooling around that he took her into the only private room in the house: the guest bathroom. They had sex, which wasn't that romantic, nor so wonderful for Judy who was a virgin, but like an opiate, they were hooked. With each meeting it became more pleasurable and more exciting, until the inevitable happened, and she became pregnant. He was only nineteen, and cried out that he was much too young to get married. He was at his wits' end with no solution in sight. "By then, I had numerous girlfriends. I guess you could have called me a womanizer, but I enjoyed being around women, and having sex with them. They made me feel so important and loved."

Andre, a healthy, happy baby boy, was born in 1961 to a teenage couple who loved each other a little too much. "There I was at twenty, and now I had three kids! My mother went bonkers! The women found out about each other and they were mad, really mad. I just couldn't keep my pants zipped, and the women just couldn't say no. Judy's parents were as livid as mine. They arranged a meeting, and in no uncertain terms, told Judy and me they were planning a wedding, and the two of us were going to get married, and that was the end of the discussion. I loved her, but the thought of marriage, and being tied down to one woman, didn't sit well with me.

"Opening up the front door, I tossed my jacket down, kissed my mom, all the while smelling a delicious aroma coming from the kitchen. I could tell she was upset: it was the middle of the week, and fried chicken was usually reserved for Sundays. 'Sweetheart,' she said to me as she gently handed me an official looking envelope, 'this arrived for you today.' I tore open the letter, and it was a draft notice.

"I didn't want to go into the army, I had my career. It was all over the news about the pending war with Vietnam, and I didn't want to be sent there." President Kennedy had set an edict that if a man was married or supported a child, then he didn't have to serve. Andre was born, and I was supporting him. In a way, Andre saved my life." When Anthony reported to the army recruiting office, and told them he was supporting a young child, he was released from the service. Had he been inducted, he would have found himself on the other side of the world, involved in the most horrific war of the decade. "To this day, Andre has been a blessing to me."

Walking down the aisle in a white satin gown, Judy was a beautiful young bride. Smiling, she held her bouquet of cream-colored roses, as her dad clung tightly to her arm. He didn't need a magic globe or Ouija board to predict this marriage wasn't going to last forever, but what he did want was a proper marriage for his daughter.

"The Imperials stood by my side as groomsmen. My best man was Ronnie Sherman, our road manager. At the time, all my older brothers were tangled up in their lives, or away on military duty, so my singing group became my family at my marriage." As the couple said their wedding vows, and exchanged rings, Anthony was nervous and anxious. At twenty he was in a pickle, one that he felt unable to solve, but his parents had placed a strong moral fiber into his soul, and he wanted to do the right thing, not only for himself, but for his family. It was as if his Aunt Bessie was perched on his shoulder, pushing him into the right direction, and making him believe, and live the life that wedding vows dictated.

Later that night, as he lay in his wedding bed, he cried himself silently to sleep. He was a kid himself, but he had three young babies. How would he ever handle all this? Three women, three babies. He felt stretched in so many directions he didn't know which way to turn. With a ring on his finger, his life belonged to Judy, but there was still two other tiny children who needed his support and love. Antoinette had disappeared but she was still out there somewhere, and she weighed heavily on his mind. "I felt like Don Ameche in 'Girl Trouble,' with so many women. It was like Pandora's Box, each woman was something new for me to experience and I had to have them all. I was living the life of an entertainer. Everything was in excess, from women to drugs to rock and roll; I was living a crazy life, but it sure was a lot of fun although it got me into trouble a lot.

"My mother met Melba, and offered to help care for baby Liza. The moment my mom looked into that baby's face, she was smitten. Melba was demanding, and said that Liza was my child, and I should help take care of the baby. I was married, but I gave Melba money to care for Liza, and I also spent time with her. When Judy found out, she was pissed. I had kept the baby a secret from her. Judy had known I had Melba as a lover, but I never told her about Liza."

One afternoon, Melba and Judy took their babies and met at Central Park. The sun was shining and the crisp spring air was warm, but their relationship was cool as a January morning. They were angry, as they talked about their shared lover, but they came to the realization that their lives would be forever intertwined. What Anthony had done was beyond the bounds of civility, but he was a teen, already famous, and the world of the common life had escaped him. He had reached a point that few would ever hope to achieve, but it was fraught with the pitfalls of celebrity. As Judy's father had emotionally predicted while walking her down the aisle, within a year, the marriage had ended. "Judy caught me cheating with a model. She was so angry, and so hurt, she couldn't take it anymore." At twenty-one he signed another contract, the one ending his first marriage and leaving behind one beautiful son: Andre.

CHAPTER 11

"I met friends along the way, people who are so imbedded in my memory, that I see them as clearly as if they were standing in front of me. One of them was Teddy Randazzo." A singer with Chuckles, the two shared adjoining dressing rooms, and quickly became friends. He was Italian, and had made movies, but his passion was singing. Alan Freed loved and believed in Teddy and his group, promoting them on the live shows and his radio broadcasts. "Let me show you something special," said Teddy as he made Anthony follow him up an endless hill of metal stairs backstage at a Brooklyn theater. When they reached the top rung, Anthony saw it had been worth the climb. They were at the dome of the theater overlooking the stage; it appeared to be a hundred foot drop. They stood there, with a couple other young guys, and watched the rest of the show. That was the beginning of their friendship.

"Someday, kid," said Teddy, "we are going to work together."

"He disappeared from my life, and I didn't run into him for another nine years." As things go in the industry, and people talk and network, someone knew someone else and through a chain of networking, the two men found themselves sitting outside a recording studio chatting away. Ernie Martinelli was walking down

Broadway and he ran into Teddy Randazzo. Teddy found out that Ernie was managing Anthony. Teddy asked if they were recording and Ernie said "no." Teddy said, "I have this song that I would like Anthony to record, I think his voice would be great on this song; "I'm On The Outside Looking In." Teddy was the most prolific song writer of the time. Those notes, handwritten on sheet music, became "Going Out of My Head," "Outside Looking In," "I Miss You So," and "Better Use Your Head," songs recorded by Anthony and The Imperials, selling over sixty million copies. Teddy was the most prolific song writer for the group. It seemed as though all he knew was how to write chart-topping hits.

"These are some great lyrics," said Anthony. It was getting late, and he didn't want to walk away from Teddy again, so he invited him back to his home, where his mom cooked them dinner. The entire night Anthony couldn't shake that music. He kept humming the melody lines in his head. After nine years, Teddy had matured into a super handsome guy; a true "Italian Stallion," with thick dark wavy hair, dark, deep-set eyes, and a muscular body. He was truly a chick magnet. "I had a man crush on Teddy he was really great looking and he had the women coming after him." Not only was Teddy a writer, but also a producer, and one of the greatest arrangers in the business. Working with the best performers, his name was cemented in musical history by producing albums for Anthony's group.

The group was ensconced in the recording studio, as Teddy walked in carrying his lyrical bag of tricks. Handing the guys the song, "I'm On The Outside Looking In," his eyes drifted toward the corner of the room. He was sullen and deep in thought. "This song, these words, are an outpouring of my soul. As you know, I got divorced, and I was in so much pain that the heartache fell onto these pages. Now when you sing this song, you are my mouthpiece, and I want you to feel the suffering. There I was, young, alone, and I went to see my ex-wife, but there she was inside the home with another guy, living another life. The hurt I felt when I saw her with someone else, enjoying her life; and me, on the outside watching someone else love my lover, was so painful. Sing the pain, sing it from the depths of your heart," said Teddy.

For a moment the room was deadly silent as Anthony took in all that the song writer had to say. Anthony was an actor at heart, he knew how to transform the words into meaning, but when Teddy was so forthcoming, it gave a depth that none of them could have ever imagined. When the song was released, it became one of their top hits: that melody line combined with The Imperials' harmonies elevated the song to a heavenly experience. Of course it made sense that the next song Teddy would compose was " Goin' Out Of Head." The group had four back-to-back million record hits, making Little Anthony and The Imperials one of the most famous and sought-after groups for an entire generation. Despite rotten management, but having the knack for selecting the right songs and genuine talent, they set the standard all other groups hoped to meet. Teddy's ear for music was insatiably seeking new sounds. He travelled to Europe, where he recorded several tracks using a massive symphony orchestra. After recording over two dozen tracks, he brought them back to America, and the singers combined their voices with the prerecorded tracks; this was the first time such a thing had ever been done. The full sound was unparalleled, providing elegance to the music. When the deejays played the new music on the radio, it had that wow factor that appealed to an entirely new group of listeners.

The following Thursday morning, Don Costa, President of

D.C.P., had reserved the recording studio. This was the day they were going to produce Teddy's "Take Me Back" and Don could smell the success in the air. Sammy, Ernest, and Anthony stumbled into the studio after a hard night of fun, but Clarence was nowhere to be found. They had called, and even stopped by his home, but no one knew where he was. They would not disappoint their manager or the producer, so they conceded that the record would be produced without him. "I feel like crap with this awful head cold, and my voice sounds like a frog, but I'm here. Where the hell is Clarence?" Anthony lamented. The receptionist brought in three cups of tea, as she was used to the craggy morning voices, especially with guys, and the constant whining of sinus infections and head colds. Setting the steaming cups on the sideboard, she shook her head in disgust as the boys moaned about all their illnesses. Teddy walked in with a big smile, handed out the music, and told them the orchestra was the best in the world. "Orchestra? What orchestra?" said Sammy. "No one is here." Maintaining his Cheshire cat's smile, Teddy instructed them to put on their headphones, nodded to the technician, and let the explosion of a hundred strings ring in their ears.

"The tea didn't help; I still had that awful, raspy, frog sound in my voice. So I did something different: I sang as though I was whispering the song, a technique known as hiss singing. For all I know this was a made-up word, but it worked for me. The trick I had to remember was once the song had been recorded, I would have to duplicate the same sound live. Later, I found out that many artists had used the same technique." Anthony recorded the song alone, and with the technician's genius, blended his voice with the prerecorded track. This was a first for music, laying the groundwork for all future recordings. The sound was full and vibrant, bringing out the best in their voices with the best musicians. It would have been difficult to put them altogether, but Teddy made the unthinkable happen. What a sound this music made when it hit the airwaves; it made people purchase music. It also served to create the value and importance of well-produced music, into our culture, spurning the success of the transistor radio and an entire industry devoted to listening to music.

It was 1961. Little Anthony had turned twenty-one, and Little Anthony and The Imperials had lasted for three years and split up. the Imperials went their separate ways, performing and recording some lackluster tunes. It just wasn't the same. Perhaps it was youth, or the headache of supporting three children, but Anthony was taken in by Gloria, an agent who promised him the world. She told him she would make him a movie star, that he should go out on his own, that he didn't need the support of three back-up singers. He took her up on her offer and left the group. After a few months had passed, and there were no acting jobs on the horizon, he came to realize she was a fraud who had handed him an empty bill of goods.

He only sang sporadically at nightclubs around the tri-state area, his career was capricious as his name bounced up on a marquee, only to be taken down the next night. He had made a big mistake, and would extricate himself from her clutches. As he was plotting his getaway, he received an odd phone call: "We got your contract, we bought you from Gloria, and from now on you will be working for us. You don't want to mess with us, we are connected and you'll do what we tell you to do." Terrified, Anthony hung up the phone and called the police. Gloria had literally gambled away his contract, illegally selling him as if he were a commodity that could be traded and it quite obvious that it was to unsavory men. Slavery was outlawed, but apparently his agent hadn't read up on labor laws passed in the last century. Luckily, he never heard from guys again.

Another lesson well learned.

1963 was a year well-remembered by Anthony: President Kennedy was assassinated and later, he had a reconciliation with The Imperials, Ernest, Sammy and Clarence. Perhaps one precipitated the other, but the fates chose these two incidents to come together.

"Of all the leaders in our country, it was Kennedy who inspired me the most, the leader who was unafraid to slam the doors on segregation and to open up America's eyes to see his vision of a country free of prejudice. He was a man's man. When I read about him jumping out of the PT boat, and saving the lives of the guys, I thought he was a real honest-to-goodness hero. But yet when he messed up, he admitted it. The Bay of Pigs was a mistake, and he owned up to the responsibility; he didn't sugar coat the truth. He truly helped the Black culture in our society become equal. It was Lincoln who began the fight, and later it was Kennedy who picked up the ball and ran for the touchdown. He wasn't afraid to fight for what he believed in, and he wasn't afraid to share his feelings with the public. He truly was one of the most transparent presidents we ever had. I remember so clearly, as if it were yesterday, when America's guns were pointed to the tiny Cuban nation, and Kennedy refused to back down until all those boats, loaded with nuclear missiles, had turned around and sailed away. Even though I was really young, I was scared there would be a nuclear war."

That fall day, Anthony had a lot on his mind, a meeting at Rockefeller Center to discuss a new record, finances, and the possibility of getting back to the men he loved. Early, he was strolling around the building when he noticed a group of people huddled around a television set behind the plate glass window. He saw a man fall to his knees, and he heard wailing from young teens and mothers.

Picking up his step, he joined the group, and was shocked at what he saw: the beloved President had been shot in Dallas, in an open motorcade. Stunned Anthony stared at Walter Cronkite's teary eyes, Cronkite trying so damn hard to be the professional newscaster America had all come to know, but this scene was so overwhelming, even the strongest fell into a state of shock and many into a state of depression. "My heart went boom, and I went into a numb state of sadness. This was the President who stood up to segregation, and now he was gone." Anthony forgot the meeting, hopped into a train, and headed home where he spent the next couple of days glued to the television and embracing his family. The meeting with The Imperials never came to fruition.

Anthony, at the urging of Ernie Martinelli, met with The Imperials at the Town Hill in Brooklyn. Ernest, Sammy, and Clarence hadn't lost sight of their lead singer; they loved him, missed him, but figured he needed a little time to get his head back on straight. When Ernest made the call to Anthony and suggested they get back together, Anthony jumped at the chance. There was guilt tugging at the back of his head. He had left his favorite men, and it had all blown up in his face. He wouldn't ever let them down or disappoint them in the future. He had to let them know he was ready to commit, and he hoped they felt the same. He took pains to find the right worsted navy suit, plied his hair with the special goop of the month selling at the barber shop, and took the subway to meet the guys. He was as nervous as the day he got married Walking into the room, he tentatively glanced over at the three men, not knowing how they would react. They jumped up, clasped his hand, exchanged bear hugs. They jointly decided to reunify.

That was cause for celebration and they ordered a bottle of champagne. Ernie Martinelli, taking over the role as their manager, explored the back-together-again theme, booking them tons of gigs. They were working the clubs a steady six nights a week, and every show was sold out. Money was flowing to the guys' bank accounts and they were back in the saddle for the joy ride of their lives.

Town Hill, keeping with a wide range of genres, was the reigning number one nightclub, attracting a wide range of customers. "Lots of women, the elite of the city, pimps, and rich people came to hear us sing. We packed them in and ended up staying there for months. Everyone was happy: the customers, the nightclub owners, The Imperials, and our families. We were making lots of money, and we didn't have to travel the road." With two young infants living in the same borough, Anthony had to use his money responsibly. Never having learned the whereabouts of his first child, Antoinette, there was always that pang of guilt and wondering. Years had passed since he had laid eyes on her.

The summer was approaching, and the circle of elite, top-charting artists was a very small world. Talent attracted talent, and one fine day, Kenny Seymour met with Ernest, Sammy, Clarence, and Anthony and reinvented their music. Kenny's dad, who was an operatic singer, handed down the genetic pipeline his creative DNA to his son. As a young kid, Kenny picked up the piano and guitar, playing by ear, later expanding into singing, arranging, and choreography. From a skinny pimple-faced preteen, he grew into a tall, thin, handsome kid who overflowed with musical talent. After creating an explosively innovative sound, they agreed to launch their new show in the Catskills, a place where half the Eastern Seaboard vacationed from Memorial Day to Labor Day. With lots of money and time on the vacationers' hands, big shows were in demand. But first, Sammy insisted on a new haircut, dragging Anthony along for a modern new look. Johnny's House of Styles, sandwiched in between a pizza parlor and an Italian bakery, was where the cool kids went to preen for the babes. As it turned out, the barbershop sold more than just haircuts, but asked if you wanted some of the "girl," a slang for cocaine, while waiting for the next barber. "Nah," the singers responded, "we came for haircuts." Sammy had done a good job convincing Anthony to try the relaxed look, and so he sat in the red leather chair, while his hair was processed with lye. Ten minutes and voila, he had a new, easier look. "What a smell! Does this stuff ever go away?'

"Sure," laughed Sammy, "but then it's time to have it done again." Such irony: the Black kids were straightening their hair, while the white kids were giving themselves permanents to add kink. When the sun came out, the Blacks would run for cover under a beach umbrella, and the whites would lie prone on the beach, slathered with baby oil and surrounded with sun reflectors to get a deeper dark tan. By the end of the summer, everyone looked just about the same. This infusion of cultures was aided by the cross-over music of Little Anthony and The Imperials, and many other performance artists. America was finally synthesizing into one holistic culture, and music played an important part in making this happen.

Later that afternoon, Anthony met Clarence so he could show off his new hairdo. "What did you do?" laughed Clarence as he inspected the sleeked down transformation. "Turn around, well, it ain't half bad, but boy do you smell awful."

"It's just the stuff they throw on your hair, but I really like the way it looks," Anthony admitted. Still laughing, Clarence picked up the ringing phone. Covering it with his hand, he yelled out it was their Ernie Martinelli. "I just got off the phone with the agency and there was a request that we open for the Beatles, and he has requested you guys open their show."

"Yes, the who? The Beatles? I hear you and I will run this by Anthony. Yep we will call you later today," said Clarence as he turned to his friend with a perplexed look on his face. "Our agent just offered us a gig opening up for the Beatles at Shea Stadium. We are already booked for the summer, but he seemed to think this would be a big deal. What do you think?"

"I've heard of the group, but, I'm not sure we should open for them. I don't open for bugs. Other people are opening up for us. I say, na, let's pass. Now that we are the headliners, I don't think we should have second billing," said Anthony. Years later, Anthony admits that this was the dumbest mistake that the group ever made.

Sporting his new hairdo, early one Saturday morning, Anthony paid a visit his tailor, F&F Clothing. The bell attached to the heavy metal door rang as he clicked open the brass lock. The narrow store was stuffed with bolts of fabric tucked neatly in rows of shelving, stacked from the floor to the ceiling; it smelled of wool and canvas, and he heard the faint sound of a sewing machine coming from one of the back rooms. Sol shuffled out carrying a cup of steaming coffee in one hand and a box of labels in the other. "To what do I owe this visit?" he asked his youngest customer. "Sol, can you fix me up with a few new suits? I really like those light weight mohair and the dark linens; very chic, very in."

While gulping down most of the coffee, he pondered just the right piece goods to make that happen. Setting down the cup, Sol drew the step ladder closer, and began yanking out bolts of fabric from the top tiers. "These you are going to like," he promised. Dropping the goods on the large, flat table, he gently unwrapped each one as if encased in gold. A cashmere blend, several navy, black, and dark brown linens, and three finely worsted wools with the tiniest of patterns represented the best he had to offer. Anthony had been to the shop before, but he had never noticed the numbers tattooed on Sol's forearm. Sol looked into his customer's eyes. He knew Anthony was seeking an explanation.

"I was in the prisoner camps in Poland during Hitler's reign, and unlike so many millions of Jews, I was one of the lucky ones; I survived. You can see from my gait, and my limited use of my left arm, I didn't survive untarnished. I can tell you my story, but another time. It's Saturday, and you are young, and don't need the burdens of an old man such as myself. Suffice it to say that as much as the Blacks have been tortured, murdered, and abused, so have the Jews, that much we have in common. At least we both have the good luck to be alive, and enjoy whatever God sees fit to provide."

"I lost so many: my family and friends. I was sent to Poland, to the work camps, while the rest were marched into the ovens, stripped bare of all of their belongings, and burned alive, stark naked." Tears trickled down Sol's face. Anthony felt his pain, joining him in sorrow. Coming to see Sol that day, he got a lot more than he had planned. It was those tears that struck a delicate chord in Anthony's heart. He had to learn about the Holocaust; what was it about the human race that could spurn such intense evil? He had asked himself that question before on his second bus tour through the southeastern states, but he had never even considered that another culture, whites loathing whites, could be just as devastating. He learned a lot that day, impressions that would never slip out of his memory.

"I was sick to my stomach. I could see the pain in his eyes. He didn't give me any details; it was too painful." So l needed to abruptly alter the mood, otherwise his only customer of the morning would walk out empty handed. He walked back to the workroom, and dragged out his wife to meet Anthony. "What do you think of the selections?" Smiling, she scrutinized their customer up and down. "You need some nice new clothes to get those girls screaming? Well, I think these will do," she advised, as she pulled out several additional bolts from the far end of the counter. The three decided on a dozen fabrics that would take care of the upcoming summer season. After Sol's wife returned to the sewing machine, he wagged his finger, offering up his best advice: "If you have to make friends, make sure they are rich, smart, and successful. If you surround yourself with those kinds of people, then you will become one of them. Just look at me," he laughed as he turned around in circles, raising his hands to the ceiling.

Anthony's interest never waned concerning the Jews, and the Holocaust. He learned to sing songs in Yiddish, studied Jewish culture and religion, and made a solemn promise he would one day visit Israel.

CHAPTER 12

Kenny Seymour loved the ocean, and suggested to Anthony and Clarence they go fishing. "Have you ever fished before?" Anthony, the can-do man, answered that of course he had fished. Early the next morning the three guys met and took the train to Sheepshead Bay. It was one of the rarest places on the southern shore. A wide bay with a panoramic view of the Atlantic Ocean, one hardly noticed the sounds of the waves slapping the shoreline. In late spring, the sun warmed up the ocean breezes just enough to make wearing a jacket nonessential. The three rented a small, metal, outboard motorboat with plastic seat cushions and headed out to the ocean. There wasn't cloud in the sky when Kenny pulled the cord to fire up the small gas engine, and off the three of them sailed into the wild blue yonder. Finding the perfect spot a mile off-shore, they took out their rods and began probing the area for fish. Each had brought a basket to cart home all the fish they were planning on catching. Whatever bait Kenny had thought to purchase was obviously the right choice, as they caught fish after fish. Within a couple of hours, their baskets were brimming with flapping tails of various sized fish. A sudden cool breeze caught them off guard, as the small boat jerked upward. Clarence looked up, and saw that a huge cluster of black clouds was coming their way, creating a squall in the once calm waters. Within minutes the sky was teaming with thick, ice-cold raindrops. Between the three teens, the three baskets of fish, and water spilling in, the boat began to sink. Anthony pointed to a buoy in the distance, and suggested they make a quick swim for it, but Clarence had failed to tell them he didn't know how to swim. Dumping the fish out of one of the baskets, they began heaving the water over the sides of the boat, but the rain was relentless.

"Kenny grabbed a couple of the seat cushions, gallantly stood up in the wavering boat, and flashed the SOS sign. Luckily in the distance, a Coast Guard boat was cruising the area and caught sight of the tiny boat, rescuing the three kids. Being without life preservers, they could have easily drowned, but it wasn't their time. The thankful boys left the fish in the rented boat for the Coast Guard, while they towed them safely back to shore. Another can-do story for Anthony, and another one he would never tell to his mother. Kenny, who had spurred on the idea of the fishing trip, needed everyone to remain alive. They each had a big summer ahead of them, after all. Kenny had done his job and trained the group, and when the summer commenced, they would part company. He would be touring Europe after their Canadian gig, while Anthony's group would travel down to the Catskills for the remainder of the summer season.

Kenny taught Anthony and The Imperials the fine art of four part harmony, he created a special sound that had never been heard before. Next, they hired Mat Mattox, a Broadway choreographer, whose claim to fame was taking the classical training of ballet and revamping it into jazz movements. He created dance steps exclusively for the group, blending dance movements with the score, adding polish and a professional presentation never seen before. He was one of the principals in *Seven Brides for Seven Brothers*. After a solid month of rehearsals, fresh choreography, new clothing, and a new song list, they drove up to the "borscht belt." Even on the rainiest of evenings, when thick thunder storms flooded the muddy fields, Little Anthony and The Imperials were sold out.

Ernie Martinelli, their doting agent, traipsed up every weekend or so to check up on the boys and make sure things were going well, and everyone was behaving. He had made a heavy investment in the group, staked his reputation on the fact that the four men would stay together, and he would use these solid performances as the stepping stone to further their careers. They never disappointed. They arrived at every gig and rehearsal on time, and after they had taken the last bows of the night, happily acquiesced to the crowd's relentless cheering by singing several encores. What Kenny Seymour knew, besides music, was that if enough of the right people heard your music, it would catapult the group to the next level, and that was exactly what happened.

That June, the group took a car ride up to Montreal, where they played at El Mocambo, one of the hottest nightclubs north of the border. They were staying at a three-star hotel and taking advantage of the perfect weather. The guys punched the elevator to the top floor and began partying on the rooftop. Anthony ran back to his room, picked up his fencing gear, and began an ardent game with Kenny. Using chalk, he drew the boundary lines, slipped on his mask and bam, the two were at it for hours. Other singers, hearing about the rooftop gathering, joined the group, ordering drinks, flirting with girls, and placing bets on the two athletes. Mary, a singer with Tiffany, became enamored with the man behind the mask, although she was being pursued by Clarence.

With the last point of the saber, they lifted off their masks, bowed to the crowd, and grabbed an ice-cold beer. Mary noticed Kenny was talking to another girl, so she took her time, slowly working her way over. She smiled and introduced herself. Looking into his deep brown eyes, she was immediately smitten. "Just where did you learn to fence like that? I've never seen anyone fence, especially not two black men," she giggled.

"A hobby," he shyly answered, "But it keeps me light on my feet, agile, and keeps my mind alert, all the things I need to help me perform on the stage. Now, pretty lady, tell me about yourself. I know you can sing, but what other talents do you have?" he asked sardonically. At sixteen, she hardly had any of the talents he was alluding to, but he was immediately drawn to her.

After the show, Mary and Kenny parted ways, meeting again on a most unusual summer tour, The King Cole Review. Boarding a plane at Kennedy Airport, Mary's group, the Tiffany's, joined up with several groups touring Sweden. "It was the first time I had ever been on a plane and the first time I had ever been to Europe. At eighteen, this was very exciting time for me," remembered Mary. "When we landed and met up with the other groups, I was pleasantly surprised when Kenny Seymour was among the performers. We picked up our conversation exactly where we had left off, and soon we were spending a lot of time together. He was twelve years my senior, had just come from a short marriage with an ugly divorce, and was probably the worst choice I could have made, but we fell madly in love. Throughout the summer, on the road, we spent all of our free time together. I was mesmerized by his charms and talents as we explored Europe. Every day was a new and exciting experience."

When it was time to board the plane back to New York, Kenny decided he couldn't live without Mary, who was preparing to begin college at the end of the summer. He begged her to move in with him, and she acquiesced, even though she had a multitude of misgivings. Guiltily, she told her mom that she was living with a girlfriend, practicing and rehearsing for future gigs. After a year of travelling the road with Kenny, the couple finally tied the knot in Las Vegas.

The group finished up the Catskills tour by early July, and returned home only to then begin again. This time they packed their lightest linen suits and headed for Puerto Rico. The summer of 1969 was highlighted by an event they would never forget. They were performing in Puerto Rico at the famed El Flamboyan hotel on Collins Avenue, in the heart of Old San Juan. "We were booked for a week, the very week of the first moon landing. The hotel had set up a huge screen in the center of the gaming floor of the casino so everyone could watch the unprecedented event. On the massive screen, in a fuzzy black and white video, we saw the astronauts land and say those famous words, 'That's one small step for a man; one giant leap for mankind.' Words that I will never forget, word that have stayed with me forever. I remember everyone cheering and being so excited about the landing."

Back in Las Vegas, the group had a gig at the same hotel as Barbara Streisand. Barbara was starring in the main room, and Anthony, with Redd Foxx and Bobby Vinton, were performing in the lounge. Each night, every seat was filled, and there was a hush over the crowd the moment Barbara walked on the stage. It was as if the audience was paying reverence to the star of the show. Christmas was approaching and Kenny, who had just rejoined the group, decided that they should give the world famous star a gift to remember. "I had never met her, but we all agreed that this gift would spark up her holidays. We wrapped a spliff of Jamaican ganga in a small box and inserted a card, Merry Christmas from Little Anthony and the Imperials. Years later when Barbara's book was published she acknowledged this gift, it was one of her favorites."

It was after that auspicious performance in the lounge that Kenny took Mary's hand, got down on one knee, and proposed. They made a hasty visit to Cupid's Chapel on the northern end of the Strip, and she became his second wife. He never even bothered with a wedding ring, and later that night, after they had shared a bottle of champagne, he found his way down to the casino floor, grabbed his buddies, and celebrated until dawn.

The sun slipped through a small opening of the heavy curtains, rousing Mary out of a hangover. Despite lying immobile, Kenny had a smile on his face when Mary kissed him good morning. With the smell of liquor and cigarettes on his breath, she could only guess what time he had rolled into bed. She asked no questions; this was the very first day of wedded bliss, and he was her first boyfriend, lover, and husband. She just figured that was how they all acted.

The group stayed in Sin City, headlining endless shows in the bustling casinos, rubbing elbows with the greatest entertainers in the world. They were an elite group, living a surreal life, often commiserating with each other. Their lives became the definition of "fast": drugs, money, women, music, clubbing, and excessive indulging. "It was the excess that drove so many of these great entertainers to an early demise. With all that money, they didn't know how to spend it fast enough and for many, it destroyed their lives," remarked Mary, who had a front row seat as she travelled with the group.

"At the time I didn't know that Kenny had a lover at every gig. After the show we would come back to the hotel room, he would make up some excuse that he had to meet up with the guys, like rehearse or have a meeting, even though it was midnight. Off he would go, and I wouldn't see him until late the following morning. I was naïve, boy was I naïve, but I believed what he said, and went along for the ride. I wasn't doing anything but travelling with the group, and had totally lost focus of my own life," Mary said.

Las Vegas was followed by a short southern tour, but this time (promised their manager) things would be a lot different. This time, the performers would be staying in decent hotels, thanks to the passage of the Civil Rights Laws. Boarding the buses, Ernest, Sammy, Clarence, and Anthony were looking forward to singing and selling lots of records to hoards of screaming teens. They were tired of cold blustery winds, snow falls, and dark gloomy days; travelling the southeastern Seaboard in mid-winter seemed like a promising idea: sunnier and a lot warmer.

The performers gathered together in one large troop as they tentatively walked into the Richmond Holiday Inn. Although the desk clerk arched his eyebrows, he handed each of them a room key and watched them punch the elevator button to their respective floors. Thanks to President's Kennedy and Johnson, the hotels were forced to open their doors. When Anthony gazed around, smelling the fresh scent of a clean room, he was overjoyed. Walking over to the window, he spread apart the curtains and opened the window. Free! Although never in bondage like his ancestors, he felt like the heavy chains wrapped around his neck had been split apart. He stood in this room, like any man. During a long shower, he said a prayer thanking those Black activists who had braved the Southern drugstores and refused to budge until they were dragged away. He had to admit, he was nervous walking into the hotel, and that night, when he was able to sleep in a clean, well-appointed room, he had to pay homage to those who had paved the way.

The short tour was successful; the seats were filled and there were no incidents of blatant racism. Judging by the roaring crowds, the ticket sales, and the spike in album sales, it had been a profitable tour. That was all they could ask for, and that was all their manager had hoped for.

Less than a week later, the group reassembled at the airport. They were flying to Jamaica to perform at a four star resort. Anthony looked over at Kenny, and said, "What the hell are you carting?"

"It's a cane. It was given to me by Na Binge to take to Jamaica to the Prince of the Rastafarians, Daddy Bill," he answered. He showed Anthony a small map of Kingston on a wrinkled piece of paper, and pointing to a tiny dot, said, "He lives right there. I made a promise to Na Binge I would one day return this cane, and this trip seems like the perfect opportunity."

Judy, Anthony, Kenny, and Mary sat together as the plane ascended into the bright morning sky over the Atlantic Ocean. After a couple of hours, Judy turned to Anthony and commented on the smooth ride. Jokingly, he suggested it was Kenny's magic cane. The uneventful trip ended as the plane landed gracefully off the coastline of the aquamarine waters of the Caribbean. The group gathered their luggage, grabbed a couple of cabs and headed to the white sandy beaches. The two wives sat side by side underneath a thatched roof hut watching the four guys racing around the beach and plunging into the water like porpoises. It was heavenly, the clear skies, the cool, salty breezes, the palm trees waving, and an occasional bird dipping into the water.

Clarence and Kenny planned on making the trip to Kingston the next day. They were fascinated by the wooden knobbed cane, and wanted to see who was the rightful owner and what powers the cane possessed. A guy named Na Binge, who owned a Jamaican Voodoo store in the heart of Brooklyn on Nostrand Avenue, had entrusted Kenny to take this sacred cane back to its rightful owner. Na Binge had called ahead and alerted the Prince that Kenny would be returning the cane and to allow him safely in and out of his home.

That night there was a crack of thunder as thick black clouds opened up drenching the streets with over an inch of rain. The next morning the streets were filled with mud from the heavy overnight downpour. They rented a small jeep in hopes they could traverse the roads the safely. Clarence drove while Kenny read the directions.

"It's just up the hill," said Kenny, "about a quarter of a mile."

Clarence looked at Kenny, down at the muddy road, and over to the temperature gauge on the rented car. "I think we better walk up, this car isn't going to make it. I don't want to take a chance of getting stuck in the mud and having no way back to the city. Can you see the two of us trying to hitch a ride?" Kenny grabbed the cane and they trudged up the side of the mountain. With each step, the foliage became denser, the trees higher, the leaves greener and wider. There were pungent-smelling flowers huddled underneath the palm fronds, with an occasional brightly-colored butterfly, or green spotted tree frog interspersed. As they continued hiking, it was silent except for the sound of a squawking bird, or Clarence's complaints about the endless piles of mud.

"Did you hear that?"

"No, what?" They froze in midstride, as they heard it again, there was the sound of a small herd of goats. Without uttering another word, they turned their slow march into a running marathon until they reached the top of the hill. By then they were all pretty much covered in mud. "Are you happy," Clarence screamed to Kenny, "Now we all look like natives!" Gathering their breath, they followed the dirt path until it lead to the home of Daddy Bill. Along the way several natives joined them, chanting, "Burn it, burn it." The tribesmen surrounded them and directed Kenny and Clarence to a metal-roofed hut. Bowing, Kenny introduced Clarence, held up the cane, laid it ceremoniously across his wrists, bowed again, and offered it to the leader of the tribe. Ritual has it that the ganga pipe was smoked before any conversation took place. Kenny and Clarence took a seat on the floor of the hut, and became instantly stoned. Smiling, the darkly tanned Daddy Bill pulled a pipe out of his mouth, greedily accepted the gift, and opened up the door to the hut only to disappear from view. He practiced obeah and he had felt incomplete; now the cane handed down through generations would add to his bag of tricks, giving him the symbol of his position. He needed time and privacy. He said a few words to the natives, causing them to encircle the two visitors, and safely escort them back to their car.

When the wheels of the rented car landed on the asphalt, they sighed with relief. "That was quite something," said Clarence as he fished for something to say. Could it be that he was the only one who was frightened? Nah, he didn't think so. Looking down at his mud-drenched shoes, he felt lucky to be alive. He could always buy another pair the next day.

While Kenny and Clarence were on their field trip, Anthony went on another. Their manager also managed Bob Marley, who on that very same day was cutting a record in one of the few recording studios on the island. Chris Blackwell, who owned Island Records, invited Anthony to the studio. That was the day that Bob Marley and The Wailers' legendary song, "No Woman No Cry," was recorded. Anthony sat intently, tapping his foot and listening to the beat of the reggae song, fascinated with the poignant lyrics. Great song, he thought, but so political, I wonder who will buy the record? Emerging from the confines of the recording studio, Bob shook Anthony's hand and the two stood around and chatted. Anthony commented on the nice tune and wished Bob the best when the record was released. None of them could have predicted in that recording studio, on that special day, that "No Woman No Cry" would later become a worldwide anthem.

Chapter 13

It was a rare late summer morning that Anthony arose at dawn and decided to take a walk. There was so much to think about: the lyrics, the new dance steps, and the opportunity to perform for the entire fall without being far from home. He had been blessed with preeminent talent to orchestrate his show, and perfection was on his mind. In the distance, he saw a young woman pushing a carriage, and as she approached, her face was all too recognizable. It was Judy, his first and now ex-wife. In her mini dress, her hair in the new bouffant style, her face gleaming, and her willowy shape still intact, she was beautiful.

"I looked at her and stared. I thought she was really hot looking. And then I looked down at Andre, the cutest kid, and suddenly realized how much I was missing. I was his dad and never spent time with him." A sudden flood of emotions coursed through his body, cloaking his heart. As he looked at the two of them standing unassumingly, he was inspired. In spite of him leaving, they had made it on their own; they didn't need him, his money, or his attention. What he saw when he looked at them was his home, his family; they were where he truly belonged. He joined them, and began talking about old times, how they met and fell in love, and then he found the courage to invite her out.

Preparing for their first date together in over two years, he selected a hip sweater with the latest designer label jeans, splashed on the most expensive cologne, picked up a small bouquet of yellow daisies, and pressed her doorbell. When he heard the sound of Andre in the background, Anthony opened the front door and stood in the living room. His son ran around, picked up a stuffed animal, hugged it, and then offered it to his dad. Sitting on the floor, he hugged the toy, and then offered a hug to his son. Crawling on his hands and knees, the father raced around the floor playing cat and mice with his son, when he stopped dead in his tracks, seeing the thumping stiletto heel of Judy, who was angry that her calm son had become so rambunctious. "Honestly," she said, "Now I feel like there are two kids in this place."

She was anxious to leave. Dressed in a short skirt with a printed sweater set, she was cuter and prettier than he had remembered. The two years had changed her persona from an immature teen to a young woman filled with confidence and style. She had found herself. He opened up the passenger door and waited for her to sit before shutting the door and turning on the engine. He had taken great strides in learning how to be a gentleman, a man that Judy might want back into her life. There was but one drive-in movie still left in the Bronx, and that was where they were headed. After buying a bag of popcorn and two sodas, they watched the first ten minutes of the film, and then began to talk. One kiss led to another, and before the plot on the screen had thickened, they had consummated their love. "I fell back in love with her, I couldn't resist her."

Soon after that first date he moved in, and two years later, he popped the question; they remarried without fanfare. At the time, he had split from The Imperials, and they lived on a shoestring while he performed as Little Anthony. The agent he had put so much faith in had all but destroyed his finances, but with love for his beautiful child and wife, he knew he would make it, he just didn't know when or how.

Their dingy apartment was rat infested, and in the depths of night, when Andre screamed for his bottle, Anthony would bring a bb gun into the room and shoot at the rodents trying to get into his son's crib. Sometimes he would pour hot water down the holes in the floor to deter the rats, but nothing worked. He knew they had to leave that hellhole. After suffering the indignities of the apartment for over a year, Anthony rejoined The Imperials and his bank account quickly swelled. It was a joyous day for the three when the moving van pulled up to transport their belongings to a lavish new apartment building off Bedford Avenue in the heart of Brooklyn. He took the elevator to the twentieth story, and when he walked across the floor, opened the wide sliding glass door to the patio, and glanced out, he knew they had finally arrived. It was clean, freshly painted, with parquet stained floors, three large bedrooms, a large living room, eat-in kitchen, and two full bathrooms; it was heaven on earth. The complex was home to many other singers who shared the same lifestyle. This was going to be perfect!

Each morning Judy would bundle Andre up, walk him to preschool, and then she would take the train into Manhattan, walk a few blocks to Random House (one of the largest publishers in the country) where she would park herself at a large walnut desk and work an eight hour shift She continued working until she found herself pregnant, and after a few months, she quit to become a stay-at-home mom. Her sanity was intact as was her ability to properly run the household. Oftentimes she felt as if she were the only adult living in the apartment; she had two young children, and one grown-up child. Anthony recalls, "I was truly happy. I had all the material things I wanted: cars, nice clothing, furniture, and two great young children. But I also loved to party, and my habit of cheating got the best of me. When I saw a beautiful woman I just had to have her, and I never thought twice about how it would affect my marriage. The girls were all too willing to have a piece of me, and I was all too willing to take them up on their offer. I was living the life of a superstar, running from one gig to another, one town to another, one country to another. I was smoking, toking, and trying an endless array of beautifully colored pills. A lot of the time I was as high as a kite. I never took a breather, I was on the road all the time, singing, performing, rehearsing, interviewing, and meeting people. I was setting myself up for a fall."

"Drugs, the evil downfall of so many people entered my world. I had drunk beers, been toasted on rum and coke, popped a lot of pills, and smoked a few joints, but had bailed out when propositioned with hard drugs. Constantly on the road, with little rest, I began emulating a lot of my peers and experimented with cocaine, and snorting heroin. I felt euphoric, high and strong, like I could do anything, but then the drugs wore off. I was so high from cocaine that I couldn't sleep at night so I had to learn how to balance the drugs, and I began taking downers to allow me to sleep. It became a vicious cycle of using drugs to get me high during the day, and after the evening performances, taking downers to allow me some rest. I had my drug dealers, and I always had my connections. It became a big part of my life as I continued my performing career."

Anyone and everyone, was all too happy to provide the stars with whatever their hearts desired, even their road manager, who had scored some Panama Red, a high grade of marijuana. "It was really potent, and I got really high, the highest I had ever been using that drug." Unlike the usual brown weed, it was laced with red leaves, and the sensation was overpowering. For a few extra dollars, Anthony was slipped cocaine so pure that it had been cut just once. The strength from the drug created insomnia; in spite of the downers, he was unable to close down his mind and body to rest peacefully. He began hallucinating.

"I was at home lying next to Judy. It was in the middle of the night, and a voice inside my head said, 'Jump.' I got up, walked into the living room, unlatched the sliding glass door, and stood at the edge of the balcony staring down twenty floors. 'Jump,' echoed the voice, 'if you jump, then you will finally be able to sleep.' I kept listening to the voice as it pounded louder and louder inside my head. I grabbed the railing and began to answer the call, but then I just stopped. I heard the sound of a passing ambulance, and it startled me back into reality. What was I doing? What was happening to me? Shaken, I stepped away from the rail and snapped shut the door, double checking the lock."

Padding back to the bedroom, lying in the darkness, his reneged mind had become its own conspirator, destroying the body it encompassed. He closed his eyes, but it was futile trying to sleep. Perhaps the next day would bring a reprieve. When the morning sun splayed its light into the bedroom, he dressed and took a short train ride to the Botanical Gardens, the most beautiful spot in all of Brooklyn. It housed thousands of plants and flowers and was a place to think and unwind.

"I was at the curb of the street preparing to cross, when that voice returned, telling me to jump in front of an oncoming car. It rang out louder and louder, 'Jump, jump! If you jump then you will find sleep.' As the noise was filling my head, I heard a young voice yell out, 'Hey that's Little Anthony. Hi, Little Anthony.' At once, I pulled back from the curb, stunned back to reality. No, I wasn't going to jump in front of that car and no, I didn't want to die, but yes, I really needed to sleep.

"Shaken, I walked across the street into the beauty of the gardens, and realized I had been awake for seven days straight. I thought back to that last long pull on the cocaine, how my mind had expanded as if it were an endless helium balloon, and now seven days later, I felt as if I were about to explode. I sat down on a bench in the middle of massive flowerbed and decided I needed help. I knew enough to know that I couldn't go on living like this, but that I didn't want to die. I was shaking life a leaf and could hardly walk. I walked a couple of blocks and found a phone booth. I called my dad, begging for help, and within twenty minutes, he arrived at the phone booth. I was stammering, not making any sense, my heart racing, my hands trembling. From the look in my dad's eyes, I could tell he had some sympathy for me. We drove to his doctor's office and sat in silence until my name was called." The astute physician, Eugene Quasch, was aware of his new patient, and knew the side effects of hard drugs. He didn't want to overly frighten Anthony, but he didn't want to see him suffer. "You are having a fear of failure, and you have to deal with this problem." He gave Anthony a prescription for valium, and it worked. Thomas took his son back to his apartment, gave him a glass of water, had him take one tiny pill, checked the lock on the sliding glass window, and made sure Anthony was resting in his bed before he left.

It was fourteen hours later when he finally awoke, rested and relaxed. He felt like a new person; the words inside his mind were gone, as was the trembling and rapid heartbeat. Sleep became his salvation. The next afternoon, Anthony continued his path to recovery by meeting with a psychiatrist, who he thought was crazier than himself. A chain smoker, the doctor never stopped puffing as his new patient poured out his heart and soul. "I was experiencing super highs and super lows, and when I took the hard drugs, they made it that much worse." The doctor listened intently and reaffirmed the prescription of valium, and then strongly suggested a vacation, that his mind needed some time to unwind, and decompress. It had been too long since he allowed his body to sit still, to relax, to clear all his thoughts and become peaceful.

Three days later, the couple packed for a vacation. Judy thanked her mother-in-law for watching her rambunctious boys, kissed her sons, took Anthony's hand, and left for a week in Nassau. The flight was smooth, and as they descended toward the small airport, they saw fish jumping out of the crystal clear ocean. Judy clutched his hand, wanting him to believe she loved him, and supported him, and she would be there for him. They had known each other far too long for her not to instinctively sense what he needed; she was gratified and thankful he had accepted his fate and was willing to change. The taxi rounded the curve of the downtown harbor, winding up a half mile to the apex of the hill. Hidden among a forest of palm trees was a large pink mansion, surrounded by huge flowering plants and a small army of service staff. Greeting their famous guests, the valet pulled the luggage from the trunk and escorted them to the front desk. Five minutes later they were standing barefoot on the sand overlooking the water. The suite was filled with colorful, scented flowers, in contrast to the white floors, bedspread, furniture, and walls. It was immaculate, as if they were the first guests to ever stay in the room. The oversized shower and claw footed bathtub, with thick terrycloth towels draping the bamboo racks, gave the room the feel of a true five-star resort. After rummaging through the luggage, they put on bathing suits and walked down to the edge of the water. Holding hands they walked for a long distance in silence, spotting wildlife and enjoying the smell of the ocean breezes. Behind a mossy rock, they spied a family of turtles as they began a parade to the water seeking food; in the distance they watched sailing ships, and by the harbor, they saw cruise ships gliding in and out of the port. The simple, unfettered day of Caribbean life was calming, just the tempo Anthony needed to begin the process of cleansing his mind.

"I was emotionally drained, and I knew I was close to a nervous breakdown. I continued using the valium, but sparingly. What I did enjoy was all those rum drinks. I would order one of those fancy cocktails and sit on the sand, just staring out into the endless ocean. It did calm my mind, and my nerves. My hands stopped trembling, and my mind began to slow down. I was afraid of abusing any drug, so I kept drinking the rum, and not taking the pills. Besides, the rum tasted a whole lot better." Anthony had friends who were also vacationing on the island, but he refused to see them. He was there for complete relaxation, and was terrified he would be tempted by drugs.

At the end of the week, the couple reluctantly packed up and flew home. He now knew that his mind could rest, and that he could change direction, and become in control, but he was scared, because he didn't know how long this confident feeling could last.

A month back home, in the routine of singing, and gig hopping, and he lapsed back into cocaine, and smoking laced weed. "You got to learn how to balance the drugs, it was the beginning of my recovery. I kept my mind in check, or so I thought. I started using LSD, but I wasn't alone; I did this with other members of my group. Maybe it was the overwhelming anticipation of performing with

Dionne Warwick at Avery Fisher Hall, for a special fund raiser, that got to me, but maybe I really didn't need any excuse to take the drug. Mayor Lindsey and a lot of other political leaders were also there that night. I was nervous, thinking, do I measure up to this kind of prestigious event?

"We all went on to perform, giving one of the best shows we had ever done. The drug seemed to unleash the heart and soul of my voice, disintegrating any insecurities about the high class event. I went on an LSD trip with my fellow Imperials and I thought I was walking on air. I knew we must have sung great when the entire audience gave us a standing ovation. I was so proud that I could perform so well, and that no one could tell I was stoned. The drug allowed us to focus, and put forth one of the best shows we had ever done.

"When the performance ended, one of the guys was coming down, and having a bad trip. We drove our cars back to his apartment and spent the entire night walking him through the downfall. Just as the sun was rising and we were due at the airport, his mind landed on planet earth. We were able to board the plane as one solidified group, but none of us had slept a wink. That day, we would be on stage with George Carlin at the University of Virginia, and again, we had to be on the mark and put on a stellar show. Meeting the comedian was a wonderful experience and all of us became friends with him ever since.

"Although we ceased using LSD, since none of us wanted to spend another night nursing a bad trip, the drugs still continued. It was at one of those spectacular shows produced by Murray the K, that things went awry. In all, there were fourteen acts slated to perform at the Brooklyn Fox Theater. The best of the best in rock and roll were on the roster that evening." Marvin Gaye, whispered into Anthony's ear that he had heard about Panama Red, and that he would sure like to try a hit or two. There was plenty of time before either of them was scheduled to go on, as they were in the last two groups in the line-up. Nodding his head, Marvin, accompanied Anthony, Clarence with a few other Motown stars down a series of steps at the bottom of a well, underneath the base of the stage. It was serenely quiet, dank, and quite dark. Anthony extracted the joint concealed in a pocket in his tuxedo pants and Marvin lit a match. The joint entered his mouth and then he drew in a deep breath and handed it to Anthony. They were thoroughly enjoying the imported weed, not realizing that the smoke was curling upwards, through the air ducts, and onto the stage. Because of its unusual quality, the smell was instantly detected by the various groups as they walked on and off the stage. Marvin heard Johnny Mathis sing and nudged Anthony: they had better return to their dressing rooms as it was almost time for their acts. This was the first time Marvin was high as he took in the essence of the drug, and then stumbled up several steps, until he reached stage level. He was smiling from ear to ear as he heard Murray the K announce his name. Marvin's performance was brilliant, raising the teen audience to their feet, as they exploded with applause. Lastly, Little Anthony, who was quite stoned from the Panama Red, and The Imperials took the stage and received the same rousing standing ovation. As emcee, Murray became incensed that someone, although he did not know who, was smoking weed fifteen feet underneath his own feet, and so he gathered all the artists together, and read them the riot act. "Now who did this?" he shouted. Although both Anthony and Marvin felt the strings of guilt play upon their hearts, there was no way in hell they were going to admit to such a dastardly deed. So Jay Black of the Americans, who was as clean as the first snow of the winter season, raised his hand and took the blow. The other thirteen acts were chuckling underneath their breaths; they knew it wasn't him, and they knew the real culprits would never confess to such a mortal sin- getting all of the singers high on the best weed they had ever smelled! The acts retired to their dressing rooms, smiling and later laughing.

Reaching for his overcoat, Anthony heard a crash on the wall next to him. Worried, he knocked on the door and the radiant face of Dusty Springfield flashed in front of him. "You okay? I heard a loud sound and I was concerned." Turning her eyes toward the floor she admitted that when things went bad she took to throwing dishes against walls, and tonight was one of those nights. Their eyes met and for a brief moment, he felt as if he had crawled inside her mind and could feel her pain. She thanked him for his concern, closed the door, and then repeated the process until the last plate had been broken. Maybe the Panama Red had gotten to her too, Anthony guessed, as he got behind the wheel of his car for the short trip home.

It was by the grace of God that he and Marvin, and the other performers had escaped the wrath of Murray the K, and he made a solemn vow never to repeat that incident. When Anthony unlocked the front door to the spacious apartment, all was quiet. He quickly showered, and crawled into bed next to his wife. Holding her, he felt her warmth and the love in his heart surge. Tonight he didn't need valium to put his mind and nerves at ease, as he drifted into a secure and restful sleep.

"Hey Frankie, I heard you're home on furlough. Listen, tonight is our last night at the Regal Theater and we will be home tomorrow. See you at the usual beer stop, around 6:00?"

"Sure, I've missed you too, have a safe flight," answered Frankie

Lymon, one of Anthony's best friends. Despite Anthony being a year older, they shared the same limelight as teenage heartthrobs, travelling the world, making it with beautiful girls, and singing gig after gig. Their swift trip to stardom led them both to the same treacherous path, but for one, it didn't end well.

"I considered Frankie the greatest singer ever, and I once told him so. He told me he thought I was the greatest singer he had ever heard, so at least we had that in common, the mutual admiration. We shared so many things, including two girls who lived in the same apartment building, Taffy and Cathy. I first ran into him at the Apollo Theater when we were just sixteen, and then our paths didn't cross until I found him sitting on the sofa in an apartment at the base of Harlem. There were these two beautiful girls, cousins, Taffy and Cathy, who lived together, and it turned out that Frankie was seeing one, and I was seeing the other. Many times the four of us would be singing and dancing around the place."

For years the two were friends, often meeting at a small, locally-owned restaurant that served Southern soul food with hefty glasses of beer. "Japs" was the name of the unusual place, situated in the heart of Harlem. The family had set up shop, and when Asian cuisine wasn't selling that well, they revamped the menu, adding soul food dishes. The two young singers loved the food, but mostly they loved to hear the elderly Asian mother reciting the soul food menu with a Japanese accent.

Frankie and Anthony's relationship was based upon the fact that they understood each other's lives; not too many of their own friends could possibly relate to the tumultuous careers of superstardom. They commiserated, developing a deep understanding of and respect for each other, but the one thing neither of them could do was solve the other's problems; all they could do was listen and be an open, accepting, nonjudgmental ear. Frankie's mom had drug problems which wasn't the role model a young teenager needed. In spite of his sketchy home life, he was one of the most, if not the most, talented young man to ever appear on the music scene. He wrote some of his songs, danced like Sammy Davis, Jr., sung, and was an all-around genius of a performer. When he entered the stage his presence captivated the audience. Although he was a brilliant singer, he was also the epitome of a performance artist: singing, dancing, and directing the band.

He fell heavily into drugs, and without the support of a strong family, Frankie joined the army firmly believing the regimented life would set him straight and take care of his chronic drug problem. He was willing to forgo three years of celebrity to rid himself of the nagging drugs. He kissed his wife good-bye and went through the arduous military training. While away, he fell in love, and then again, and ended up marrying three times, but there was one tiny little problem: Frankie never divorced any of his wives.

Upon returning home to his Queen's apartment, clean from drugs for months, he did the unthinkable. Friends came to see him, hugging him, and showing him love. One thing led to another and a party assembled with a prolific assortment of drugs. Just a taste, he told himself, as he assembled the syringe and tied his arm. He had forgotten that he hadn't used drugs in months, and that his sensitivity was back to a beginner status. The dose he injected proved to be fatal. He was found collapsed over a toilet with the needle clinging to his vein. The ambulance was summoned and his death hit the newspapers by the morning.

When Anthony walked into his apartment, the usual warm smile on Judy's face had been replaced with a deep frown as she related the tale of Frankie's death. "But I just talked to him last night, we were going to meet at Japs. I can't believe he is gone," Anthony sobbed uncontrollably. Taking his arm, she walked him to the sofa, took off his jacket, and brought him a cool drink. He absolutely could not come to terms with Frankie's death. He would never lay eyes on him again, share a drink, laugh, tell stories of the road; in an instant, his short life was snuffed out by an incendiary device of his own choosing.

"I didn't go to the funeral, I was too numb. I got into a shell, and I lapsed into a nervous breakdown. If that could happen to my good friend, it could happen to me. All I could picture was that syringe hanging from his arm, and his body listless. It scared me. I had lost my best friend to drugs, and he was barely twenty-five. Frankie had been bragging that since he had joined the service, he had been clean, free of drugs, and then he comes home, uses it once, and dies.

"I was unable to go to the funeral. I just couldn't handle the scene. I started remembering my Aunt Bessie's funeral, and how emotionally distraught I was, and I knew it would be impossible for me to handle this situation. There would be hundreds of people, the press, the endless sad tributes, and I'm sure people would expect me to speak, and I just couldn't face it. It was all too much grief for me, but it didn't deter me from using drugs to get rid of the emotional pain." Judy never uttered a word about drugs, she just showered her husband with unabashed, unconditional love, and constant emotional support, "You know who you are," she said.

"I believe that God puts people in your life as 'gate keepers' to guide you through the path and set you straight. I began embracing those people and I began finding my way back to reality." He seemed to have forgotten all the strong Christian values he had been taught; it was as if it had been erased from his conscience and it was the drugs that did the erasing. "I was beginning to find out who I was, and not accept the reflection of how the world defined me. I felt that God was steering my course and that if I listened and paid attention, then I wouldn't end up like my best friend. I guess you could call this soul searching, but Frankie's death was the straw that broke the camel's back. It made me take a good, hard, long look at myself, and it scared me."

Redd Foxx was one of those people put into Anthony's life to illuminate the road, and keep him on a steady, streetwise pathway. He met him at a high school auditorium; Betty Carter, a well-known jazz singer and The Imperials were sharing the stage. They met backstage and talked for a while, and observed each other's performances. Nicknamed Red because his hair was strawberry blonde, it stuck and became Redd Foxx's celebrity persona. "He was so funny, the funniest person I had ever met. I began playing his underground party records, and they were hilarious and filthy. He was tough, an ex-marine, and he knew how to take care of himself, and he grew to like me."

"You gotta learn how to survive," Redd preached, "otherwise you will never make it in this business."

"It was years later when our paths crossed at the Hilton in Las Vegas. Redd was appearing with Bobby Vinton, and told me he was offered a sit-com as the father in *Sanford and Son,* and thought I should do the show with him. As it turned out, I didn't get the part, and the show became one of the most successful comedies on network television. I often went to watch the filming, sitting backstage and laughing for hours.

"I was happy for Redd, and his great success, but as seasons passed he grew angry with the production crew; he wanted a window in his dressing room because he was extremely claustrophobic. One year he got so angry he quit the show, but when the studio called, and said they had found a dressing room with a window, he returned the next season.

"His influence in Hollywood was felt everywhere. Our group wanted to get on the *Midnight Special Show*. Redd made the call, and they gave us the gig, but only if Redd would show up and add a few jokes. We saw each other all the time; between his home in Los Angeles and his home in Las Vegas, we met up often. He once told me never to grind my teeth because it looks like you are doing cocaine. I never questioned him how he had learned that fact, so I just used the advice and let sleeping dogs lie. I think what Redd gave me was the ability to laugh, to let my mind just go and enjoy the moment. It was a high, just listening to his jokes. He was a whole lot funnier offstage than on, when the microphones were turned off, and he was uncensored. That saying that laughter is the best medicine must have been attributed to this man. I loved him and I loved the happiness he brought to my life."

The west coast proved a convenient and lucrative location for Anthony as he yo-yoed back and forth between Los Angeles and Las Vegas. Between the two locations, there was always a gig to play and money to be made. A call from his booking agent, and he and the group assembled at the Hilton Hotel and Casino, one block east of The Strip. Elvis was headlining in the main room and Anthony and the Imperials were entertaining in the lounge. When Elvis' performance was over, he sometimes took a seat at the back of the lounge and watched Redd Foxx, Bobby Vinton, and Little Anthony and The Imperials perform. One evening at the lounge, a gentleman approached Anthony and Redd and explained that Mr. Presley was in the audience and wanted to meet them. Later, after the show, Anthony, Clarence, and Redd chatted and began a friendship. It was Clarence who became closer with the famed singer. Elvis would call

Clarence and in the middle of the night, they would gather their shot guns, go out into the desert and scare the hell out of the jack rabbits. "One evening, I got a call from Elvis to join him at a movie theatre to watch the George Forman and Jimmy Ellis Fight. Clarence, Kenny, and I walked into the movie theatre and it was completely empty except for us, Elvis and his Memphis Mafia. I found out that he loved to go to the movies, but because of his fame he was never comfortable. That night he rented out the entire theater. We had free run of the place, we could order whatever we wanted; free popcorn at the movies. It was an awful lot of fun. I kept thinking about how much power this guy had to enable him to rent out an entire theater."

"I will never forget the get together Elvis invited me and the guys to at the hotel. It was after our performances and we met in the Gazebo at the Hilton. Again, he had rented out the entire venue and invited some of the top performers in the world: Jack Carter, Leslie Uggams, Dion Warwick, Redd Foxx, and Teddy Randazzo. We were standing around joking, drinking and having a great time. Teddy looked over to Elvis and commented on his extraordinary watch. Elvis said, 'You like my watch, then it's yours,' and then he took it off his wrist and handed it to Teddy. Just like that! I couldn't believe it, but that was Elvis. Teddy was floored." Elvis and Anthony remained friendly throughout the years until 1977, when Elvis was no more. In deference to the great star, the Hilton enshrined Elvis' dressing room, until 2010, when Little Anthony was asked to perform in the main showroom. In deference to Anthony's legendary persona, he was allowed to use Elvis' dressing room. "This was a quiet honor and I wanted to share this with Elvis. I sat in the dressing room and I sensed that he had been there."

CHAPTER 14

Dressed in leotards, the four young singers were scurrying around the dance floor, learning the art of flamenco dancing from Matt Maddox, the best choreographer in the business. He was screaming out directives and they stringently followed his orders as they checked and rechecked themselves in the floor to ceiling mirrors. There was nowhere to hide from the instructor's focused eyes. "I'm reminding you, gentlemen, that you are preparing for a big show at Town Hill, and you have to look good while singing, and that, gentlemen, is even harder than it looks. So again, and bend, and bend, and now place your hands back and forward to split."

The music was playing loudly so no one could hear Anthony's right knee pop out of joint as he dropped to the floor in excruciating pain. Being well-versed with dancers' injuries, Matt made an instant assessment and packed him up into a cab sending him to a doctor's office, who made a quick diagnosis, and then placed Anthony at Lennox Hill Hospital. Later that day, the three Imperials visited Anthony, whose leg was cocked up in the air with a wide sling.

"Oh, does this suck. They tell me I will be stuck like this for five days until the swelling goes down. I'm in so much pain, and I'm sorry I let you guys down, I sure wasn't expecting this to happen."

"Hey man, there is nothing to be sorry about, it was bad luck. I think I'm just happy it wasn't me, the way we were being pushed in the studio. Tell me, what can we do to make you better?" asked Clarence as he leaned over, and listened to Anthony's request. "No problem, we will see you tomorrow. Now, don't go chasing those pretty girls around the hospital with that gown on, your butt ain't that sexy looking." Anthony closed his eyes, but it was impossible to sleep with his leg elevated The worst of it all was, when he had to relieve himself, it was in a bedpan. Oh, for sure, it was going to be a very long five days. He eventually went to sleep when an evening nurse injected him with enough drugs to camouflage the constant ache. Later the next day, things were looking up, since Clarence returned with some excellent marijuana. Closing the door to Anthony's private room, Clarence carefully helped his ailing friend out of the taut sling. They slowly shuffled into the bathroom, closed the door, and lit up on a fine joint of Panama Red.

"I can feel it now, the pain is floating away. This stuff is magic, a lot better than anything else they have at this hospital." With very little private time, they hurriedly smoked it down to a tiny butt, and then flushed the remnants down the toilet. Clarence assisted Anthony in returning his leg to the sling, and then held up the second gift: a bag of Chinese food, which would kill two birds with one stone: help hide the odor from the joint and satisfy his friend's hunger. In the austere hospital room, the two were laughing, eating, and commiserating about the trick knee when a stout nurse flung open the door. Twitching her nose, she observed her patient with a sparerib in his mouth, laughing with his friend; she wasn't that naïve. Putting her hands on her ample hips, she shook her finger at her patient, and told him that smoking in the hospital rooms was prohibited, adding that smoking anything at all was prohibited. "Otherwise, none of your cute friends can come and visit you. Now, will you promise to behave?" she demanded. With a boyish smile, Anthony nodded his head and reached for an eggroll, offering it to the nurse.

"Would you like to join us?" asked Clarence, who needed to cajole the angry nurse. Giving him a grimace, she left the room, again reminding them, "No funny stuff around here." They broke into laughter as Anthony thanked his friend for saving the day. There was enough in that one joint to get him through the worst, until the night nurse returned with her trusty bag of tricks. "I can't wait to get out of here!"

He left the hospital with his knee still on the mend, and although he could sing, the flamenco steps were saved for The Imperials, who danced circles around Anthony as he stood in the center of the stage. Resting more than usual, he had extra time on his hands, and he became depressed about his future. It was so fragile; any little thing could go wrong and his entire world could vanish. "I was concerned that I wasn't accomplishing what I wanted to accomplish. None of the latest records had spiraled to the top of the charts. Our music kind of got lost in the shuffle between the English invasion, and the dawn of heavy metal. We survived this, singing endless gigs, touring the country, but our new records weren't commercial, and the public wasn't buying what we were selling. Initially, when we joined the music world, we were light years ahead of everyone with our new sounds, and our records were hot. But lately, the fans just stopped buying our new tunes." To offset this depression, he took a wide range of drugs, TCP, cocaine, and marijuana; his mind was going through turmoil and brain becoming fried.

While he recuperated, the group stayed in the New York area

with a gig at the Copa Cabana, truly living Barry Manilow's song in "the hottest spot north of Havana." That was the capstone when it came to prestigious venues, and the group had a two-week gig, a tribute to their dutiful and persistent agent. The group was booked here by the William Morris agency, the Vice-President was Lee Solomon. Costumes were restyled and choreography redone in a subdued manner to accommodate Anthony's mending knee. Rehearsing in the afternoons, they had the run of the place as the lighting and sound crew constantly tweaked the arrangements, guided by the different songs. "Jules Podell, the king of the club, accommodated our wishes, making sure we had everything we needed to bring off the best show; but he could be mean when he was drunk. He would sit at the back of the kitchen and watch everyone come and go. He didn't want any stealing underneath his nose. The front door was locked, and they only way for us to enter the club was through the kitchen door to get into the dressing rooms, and the stage. Sitting on a high bar stool, Jules ruled the roost. He was as tough as nails, and word was that he was very connected – or at least that was what he led us all to believe. Halfway through the first week, I got a case of laryngitis. There was so much smoke it really got to me. I went to the Copa Cabana's doctor who told me not to sing for one day, and then he gave me a bunch of liquids to soothe my throat. I phoned the manager of the club and told him I would be out that night, that their doctor was serious about a one day rest. After drinking tons of honey and lemon tea and other concoctions my doctor prescribed, my voice returned and so did I. When I walked into the kitchen, Jules gave me an angry stare and then he began to yell.

"'Hey, you, come over here. You don't ever walk out on my shows; remember you have to go through me. If you're not making it, you tell me, not the manager. Do you have that? Because next time I'm not going to be so nice,' Jules threatened.

"I was trembling and scared to death. I looked at him, and told him I was truly sorry, that my voice was bad from the smoke, and I couldn't sing. I really wanted to be there, but I wasn't going to do a bad show and make him look bad. I could see that he was thinking over my apology, and from that day on, he treated me well, and we became friends and, of course, I never missed another performance."

Anthony's voice had completely returned just in time for another headlining show in New Jersey. Their agent had suggested Bruce Springsteen and the E Street Band open up the show; the venue was huge, and the band could make plenty of noise to fill up the auditorium and rouse the crowd for Anthony's prodigious appearance. Although at the time, Anthony hadn't met Bruce, he and the E Street Band had opened up for him at one of the smaller clubs in New Jersey. Anthony knew their music and he loved the way they performed. So it was a go. The following Saturday night, Bruce and the E Street Band brought down the house, warming up the crowd for Little Anthony and The Imperials. The show was a huge success and early the next morning, deejays praised the two groups.

With the group in high gear and finely tuned, they packed their costumes and headed to Chicago, performing in another prestigious nightclub. With everyone on the same page, they were rocking the crowds, bringing in the fans, and making money for the venues, as well as plenty for themselves. Creating a party was what they did best, which didn't go unnoticed by Hugh Hefner, when he sat in the packed club, focused on the young singers. Seated at a table surrounded by statuesque beauties, Hugh watched the show, and then came backstage, and invited the performers to his house for a party. He handed Anthony the address, and they promised they would be there. "The next evening, we changed our costumes in record time and took a cab to the address. Our mouths dropped open when the cab entered the gate, and we saw this huge mansion at the outskirts of the downtown area. It was the Gothic architecture that made the place appear outlandish. It was ice-cold outside, with small crystals of ice dropping out of the sky, but the moment the front door opened, the temperature was as warm as the tropics. The living room seemed as big as Madison Square Garden, with a full band in the corner playing dance music, girls walking around handing out glasses of champagne and fancy hors d'oeuvres. There was a fireman's pole in the one of the other corners of the living room, a real pole! Behind the oak bar, a glass wall revealed naked girls in the swimming pool, right behind, and on top of the bar.

"I felt like a kid in an adult candy store. There must have been between three to four hundred people at the house, partying, eating, drinking, and having plenty of sex. Just as we had seen him pictured, Hugh was dressed in a silk smoking jacket when he came over to us. He asked us if we were having a good time. After we thanked him for inviting us to the party, he held his glass high, toasted us, and disappeared into the crowd. I had to try the fireman's pole, at least while I was sober enough to make it down in one piece. Since I was a kid, I have always wanted to do that.

"I walked up the steps to the second floor, and I couldn't believe all those women walking around topless. I saw couples coming in and going out of bedrooms, and I became so entranced with the women, I forgot the pole; I was more intrigued with what was inside the bedrooms. A beautiful brunette walked my way, and she wasn't shy about suggesting we share of piece of heaven; she didn't disappoint. Later, I walked down the steps and rejoined the guys. Hugh had given us all keys to the Playboy Clubs, which would get us into any club around the world. A few days later, our manager gave us a call, he had scored a week gig at the Playboy Resort in New Jersey."

"You guys must have really impressed Mr. Hefner, he is looking forward to your stellar show in his world famous club, and it comes with all the perks of a guest – complete use of the facilities. Gee, I wonder if that means the women, too."

A month later, they returned to Chicago for a one night engagement at a popular night club. They didn't worry about being arriving promptly; between the time difference and the short flight they had more than enough time. But it was February, and it was Chicago. "Ladies and gentlemen," announced the captain, "we will be a little late; we have hit bad weather, and the control tower has asked us to circle the airport until the winds die down."

"Damn," said Sammy, "I hope this doesn't make us late for the show. I hate rushing through airports, and I hate rushing to get onto the stage." But for all his hating, the plane continued to circle and circle, until it finally landed at eight in the evening. The show started at eight. Yep, they were late. The cabin crew was very kind, and allowed the group to depart the plane first. They ran through the long hallways, jumped into a waiting cab, and raced over to the club.

They were met with an angry scowl and the manager cursing at them, when they flung open the glass door and made their way backstage. Anthony didn't trust the tall bouncer, and demanded their fee before they sang their first note. After slipping the cash into his pocket, they hurried to the dressing room and put on their jackets. Clarence was looking into the mirror, primping his hair, when he saw three huge thugs staring back at him. Grabbing

Sammy's hand for security, the singers slowly turned around. Those were the scariest guys they had ever laid eyes on. "You'd better sing," they yelled, "Or we are going to make sure you never sing again." By that point, Anthony was rattling in his patent leather shoes. "So we circled the wagons and looked for anything that could be used a weapon. Those three thugs surrounded us, raising their fists in the air in a threatening show of force. A moment later the owner of the club walked in."

"Do you know who we are?" screamed Sammy. "You can't threaten us with your bouncers. We are singers, and we are sorry we are late, but we will put on a damn good show. Now please stop threatening us and let us do our job." The three huge men parted, and the singers paraded to the stage. The band, truly warmed up, got the show on the road as soon as they saw the whites in Anthony's eyes. That night the group felt like they were singing for their lives. As soon as they took their last bows, they rushed into the dressing room, collected their few possessions, and took the next cab back to the airport. "I think Chicago is not our kind of town," laughed Anthony as they plane ascended into the dark, foggy skies.

Despite the downturn in record sales, when the group was slated to perform, it was always a packed house, and the fan base continued to swell throughout the years. They all wanted a piece of the performers, and some of the more devoted fans happily supplied the singers with drugs and sex. The Imperials supplied the rock and roll. "I lost it. It was some performance in the Carolinas at The Beach Club, and we were playing beach music, which was a combination of rock and roll with a little shuffle thrown in. Everyone in the place seemed stoned. After the show had ended, a guy in the front row asked me 'How is your head?' and I answered it could be better, which was the universal accepted statement for 'Yeah, I could use a little taste." Ten minutes later, a couple of guys came into the dressing room, pulled out a small bag, and we shared quality cocaine."

Buzzed, Anthony thanked the guys and spent the rest of the evening feeling the euphoric effects of the purified drug. He was soaring above the clouds when a beautiful young woman knocked on his door. The look on her youthful face immediately grabbed the attention of Anthony's loins. After a quick introduction, he began to kiss her. She returned his advances by slowly undressing, and moments later, they were locked on the small sofa in the corner of the room. Now his day was perfect: drugs that were destroying his brain, and meaningless recreational sex that left him empty. That's when he began to lose it, and introspective thinking crept into his psyche.

The next morning the group flew into Myrtle Beach, South Carolina, in the heart of the southeastern Seaboard, where segregation was still stringently practiced. Ted Hall was the big promoter in the area, who brought in talent to perform at the numerous nightclubs lining the beach resorts. Working with the elite of rock and roll, and rhythm and blues groups, he had tentacles in every classy venue south of the Mason-Dixon line. He promised the groups high pay and excellent care while still providing the best entertainment to the club owners, and he rarely failed at keeping his promises. Upon walking into the luggage area of the small airport, Anthony spotted a beautiful young woman holding up a sign that read "The Imperials." Waving, they introduced themselves, threw their gear in the back of the huge limousine, and proceeded on their way. A few moments later, the sound of a police siren filled the air, quickly approaching the car. Easing to the side of the road, a tall, white officer sauntered to the side of the limo, conspicuously placing his hand on a menacingly large pistol. He glanced into the backseat and then into the front. "Excuse me, ma'am, where are you going with these people?" She nervously explained the name of the group, as he again asked, "Are you sure that is them?" Again he looked into the car, never releasing his hand from the gun. "Now ma'am, can you please tell me who these fellows are?" Answering with more assurance, as it was the officer's third request, he finally nodded his head, and walked back to his vehicle. "I looked back, and saw that cop follow us all the way to the hotel. He didn't leave until we had removed our stuff from the trunk. But that was just the beginning. It was unusual that we arrived on the day of the gig, and there was little time to prepare for the show. We had a sound check, and a couple hours later, the performance.

"Everyone treated us terribly. The staff ignored us, the stagehands gave us a hard time about any small request, and the managers snubbed us. We had to do everything ourselves, and that was not how we should have been treated. I was angry and humiliated. Here we were, big stars, flying into a small town, and being treated like dirt. I turned to the guys and said I was leaving. None of us had to take this abuse! With that, we walked out of the theater, grabbed our bags, and took the first taxi back to the airport. We were big stars who were singing at the Kraft Music Hall, the *Ed Sullivan Show*, travelling around the world, and in this small town, we were nothing. All they saw was the color of our skin. When I arrived home the phone was ringing off the hook. 'Yes,' said Judy, 'He just walked in.' She handed the phone to me, and I heard Ted Hall, beside himself. 'What the hell happened?' Without hesitation, I relayed the details of the trip, fully explaining the humiliation we felt and the horrible way we were treated. He apologized profusely and begged for us to return. It was a sold-out crowd, and his own reputation was on the line. The next morning, we arrived back at the same airport. Ted had purchased us the plane tickets, and we flew first class back to Myrtle Beach. The same stunning blonde was there to pick us up; she wasn't holding a sign, but we knew each other. This time she chauffeured us to a condo owned by Ted, and we stayed comfortably for a week, enjoying the beauty of the ocean, and the sounds of golf balls hitting the green grasses of the links." Feeling responsible for the inferior treatment, the promoter went out of his way to make the group feel welcome and respected. The kitchen was stocked with food and beer, the rooms freshly cleaned, and maid service arrived every evening. Later that afternoon, the limo returned for the sound check, and this time Ted's assistant stayed with the guys to make sure the staff took proper care of the performers.

Before they went on stage, Ted tapped on their dressing rooms, and invited the group to go fishing the next day. He had taken great pains to find out their hobbies, and had charted a private fishing boat. "The limo will pick you up at eleven in the morning. I figured you guys would want your beauty sleep after the performance," he laughed. When the sold-out show ended, the limo was filled with several additional people, as young women had joined the singers. Supplied with booze, several joints, and beautiful young girls, they partied until the wee hours of the morning. They were the first Blacks to ever spend the night at the condo, and certainly showed the haughty redneck-thinking people how famous entertainers lived.

The limo arrived right on schedule, as the young men lethargically piled in for a day of fishing. "This is going to be great!" The chartered boat was prepared. They jumped onto the wharf and onto the fifty-foot vessel for a day of wonderful fishing. Shaking their hands as he helped them aboard, the captain promised he would find the best places, and that night they could count on freshly filleted fish for dinner. Pulling up the anchor and unwrapping the thick twine ropes, he took a course directly into the deeper ocean waters. Without a cloud in the sky, and with a slow, warm, southerly wind, the captain knew just where the fish were biting. As they passed by numerous smaller vessels, Anthony noticed that the other fisherman noticed them, and why? It was because they were the only Blacks sailing on the ocean. Bringing the boat to a dead stop, they baited their lines, and waited patiently for the fish to bite. It didn't take long before they were pulling up fish after fish. Screaming with delight, they filled up the ice chests with fish of all sizes and shapes. In the distance, a medium-sized boat began chugging their way. Named *Billy Bob,* it was filled with rednecks, who, upon reviewing the success of the Black fisherman, were intrigued, angry, and intimidated. This was another first for The Imperials: the first Blacks to charter an expensive boat, and then have the audacity to show up all the white people by plucking the biggest fish from underneath their noses!

"What the hell you guys doing," yelled *Billy Bob'*s crew. "You Black people are stealing all of our fish. Get the hell out of our waters!"

The captain wasn't about to listen to their abuse, and returned their tirade with a few obscenities, sending them on their sorry way. "When we dropped in our lines, the fish just came. I knew how to watch the currents and to feel the breezes, as did the captain, and we had a very successful afternoon. Years ago, my friend Smitty taught me the art. and I never forgot it. Growing up in the projects, we became friends, and one day he asked me to go fishing. We left at four o'clock in the morning and traveled to Long Island where there was a group of jetties that went a hundred feet into the ocean. Smitty pointed out the currents and tested the air for wind direction, and then we walked until he found the perfect spot. We cast our lines into the water, and I remember my first fish. It was big, a big old black fish, and from that moment on I was just as hooked as the fish. I loved it." When the chartered boat finally docked, the captain doled out the fish. The guys left some for the captain, took many back to the condo, and handed out the rest to people congregated around the docks. That night, Anthony cleaned, de-headed, and fried up the catch; it was the best meal of the week. No one complained about sea sickness; the fish were well worth it.

After showering off the smell of the fried fish, the limo was at attention, to deliver the group to the last show. After "Going Out of My Head," "Tears on My Pillow," "Take Me Back," "Out of Sight, Out of Mind," they ended the run to a standing ovation. Déjà-vu. A new set of girls climbed into the luxurious limo, and it was back to the condo for a final night of partying. After singing those heartfelt lyrics, Anthony felt no pangs of guilt as he leaned in to kiss a striking gorgeous blonde haired, blue eyed girl of legal age. The song spinning in his head, "If You Can't Be With the One You Love, Love the One You're With," was his theme and rationale for cheating on his wife, Judy. "She knew I was cheating, and she suffered. In spite of it, she loved me, loved me more than I deserved, but I just couldn't help myself. On the road, sex filled the emptiness, and it was fun. The night after our wedding, I was having sex with a model. Judy found out and forgave me. With my religious background, I knew it wasn't right, but I was rationalizing that I was just having fun, and all those girls, night after night, meant nothing to me spiritually. I didn't love them, I didn't even know most of their names, it was just the sport of it, the fun of having sex. I loved women, and I had this insatiable sexual drive.

Remarkably, I even went through a stage that I questioned my own manhood. It was on my first tour; I was barely seventeen, young and naïve. We were staying in a dump that had no air-conditioning, and we all opened our bedroom doors to get whatever breeze was coming in from the hallway. There was a big, tall, Black guy standing in the hallway, and he walked into my room, 'Be cool,' he said as he sat down on the bed next to me, and began stroking my back. I literally jumped off the bed, and yelled 'I'm going to kick your balls.' Luckily, several other people heard me and ran into the room, rescuing me from the jerk. The guy thought I was gay because of my high falsetto voice, but that was as far from the truth as one could get. The gypsies got wind of my predicament, and came to my hotel room. 'You having bad luck?' they questioned. 'If so we can help you.' One of them took a boiled egg out of a large brown satchel and placed it underneath my bed, spoke some gibberish, and announced they had put a spell on me. I was going to be fine, and no one would ever bother me on the tour again. With their wide, brightly colored skirts whirling about, they clasped hands, tossed some purple powder in the air, and skipped out of the room."

It was a long trip across the country, with gusty crosswinds making the huge jetliner dip from side to side, as the nose pointed down to the tarmac. From the sky, he could see the sprawling city completely surrounded by neighboring mountains. There wasn't any snow, just rocks in varying shades of gray and rose, rising above desert foliage. The singers hired a town car, and headed toward the Flamingo Casino and Hotel. Driving north on Las Vegas Boulevard, they couldn't help but be impressed by the oversized casinos and hotels, bigger and more lavish than any they had ever seen. The city had grown since their last gigs; the Strip abounded with new facades and huge, lavish marquees. "Guys," said the driver, "I'll wait here

Anthony's parents, Thomas
and Elizabeth, 1938

Anthony with Christmas bike

Anthony at 7

Anthony and the
group, 1958

Aunt Bessie with Thomas and Elizabeth Gourdine

Rehearsing for the opening at the Flamingo, 1965, left to right - Sammy, Ernest, Clarence, and Anthony (lying on the floor)

Dick Clark's Caravan of Stars, 1965

On the Ed Sullivan Show, 1968

Anthony with the new edition

The Imperials, 1968

Album cover in California

Sonny, Elliott, Anthony, Donald, Thomas, and Elizabeth

In uniform on the set of Comtac

Married 10th anniversary

Casey

Knicks playoffs,
1994

At the Rock and
Roll Hall of Fame,
2009

June 8, 2012

with the luggage until you are situated." Surprised, the four bounced out of the back seat, and walked up to the registration desk. They proudly announced their names, and were greeted with humiliation and segregation. They were turned away; yes, they were scheduled to perform, but no, they weren't allowed to stay at the hotel. Mortification swallowed the four as they reversed their steps and headed back to the town car.

"He must have known," said Sammy. "Why else was the driver so willing to wait for us?" Being Black himself, the driver knew just the spot, a safe hotel where the world-famous group wouldn't be shunned.

"I've just the place for you. I know you will be happy and trust me, you won't be alone." He eased the long car back onto the boulevard, and ten minutes later, they arrived at the Mrs. Brooks' Motel, a homey, low-key inn a block off the Strip. Mrs. Brooks handed out four room keys and shrilled with delight when she found out it was Little Anthony and the Imperials. "We thought that Las Vegas was wide open and free of segregation, but it wasn't, at least in 1965. But we made the best of it. The hotel was an oasis, and we were treated with respect and kindness. No one bothered us; we had the run of the place. It was true debauchery, with girls running in and out of our rooms day and night, weed smoked in the halls and on the patios, and late night parties after performances. No one called the cops for all of our noise; instead, we just asked them to join the party. We met a ton of women, showgirls, dancers, airline stewardesses, and even prostitutes. The line coming in and out of the rooms never ended. Sex was plentiful in Sin City, especially when it meant sleeping with world famous performers. No one fell in love: it was recreational sex: hot, plentiful, and exhausting." Mrs. Brooks provided a large table, a barbeque, and allowed the guys to have their own private party at the back of the hotel. "Can I join the crowd?" asked Skip, a friend Anthony had met a year before. After they hugged each other, Skip took a seat, grabbed a beer, and they began a lengthy conversation about cooking. "I didn't know you were a cook," said Skip. After that, whenever the two had the day off, they could be found hovered over the tiny stoves in their kitchenettes, cooking up the best soul food in town and ruminating over the unexpected segregation in the city. Skip Trenier, born in Mobile, migrated to Los Angeles, and in the early 1960's, drove across the desert and became part of the legendary icons who performed on and off the Strip for three decades. His uncles were the backbone of the group, and he, the spry nephew, added spunk and innovation, helping keep the Trenier's prominent places on the giant marquees. Their music was original, although, unlike Anthony's, never saw the light of day in the top 100 hits. Booked almost every week for decades, they were satisfied with performing to a sold-out lounge every night. Travelling the globe, the Treniers toured in Australia, Japan, England, Manila, Venezuela, and across the contiguous states. Skip and Anthony had crossed paths on many occasions, and now were both briefly planted in Las Vegas, where they saw each other often.

"You know, Anthony," said Skip, "I think if I had to do it all again, I would have never let that Teddy Randazzo out of my sight. If we would have sung all those great tunes he gave to you, I think we would be sitting in opposite chairs." Anthony nodded in accord, and they talked about the first time they had met, in the Sahara Hotel at Lake Tahoe. The two groups shared one venue, alternating sets, and the lounge was so packed that no one could dance. In the audience, in any given night, you would see Liberace, or the Smothers Brothers, or Jerry Lewis, or Jack Benny or Liza Minnelli. "I thought we were the smoking hot group, and then you guys would take the stage and steal our thunder," Skip laughed. "But those were fun times. We all were busy, made a good living, and the crowds were at our mercy. Remember how we would introduce the stars who were sitting in the audience? Some nights it would take twenty minutes just to acknowledge them all, but it sure added validity to the quality of our music." Anthony twitched his nose as Skip carried out a heavy pot for the three in the morning meal. "That smells delicious, but I know it isn't soul food. Since I invited everyone seated in the lounge, I'm pretty sure that pot of yours will be gone before the sun comes up, so now give me your recipe." Laughing, Skip remembered when he had tried to coax a recipe out of Anthony for his shrimp patties and he wouldn't budge. "Okay, you know, I don't guard my secrets like you do, but then this sauce is my own invention, nothing like my mama cooked. First I gather up my pot, say a prayer, and tell the sauce that I love it so much, and that all of my friends are going to love it to. Sometimes, I even sing to the tomatoes so as to tease out the best flavor. It's Sicilian at heart: fresh chopped garlic, then a handful of fresh basil, pressed olive oil from Italy, several cans of tomato paste, and canned tomatoes, three pounds of chicken wings and then it simmers for hours."

"Wine?" asked Anthony. "No, the wine is for drinking!" They poured themselves two hefty glasses of red wine, and Skip began reminiscing. "Anthony, our group was a lot like yours, yet in some ways we weren't like yours. We did a lot of dancing in our acts, like you, but we did it well before your group began. My uncles and I were the headlining act, opening up Resorts International, the very first casino in Atlantic City, and boy, was the place packed. We were smoking hot. Every celebrity on the East Coast drove in for the opening, and stayed to watch our show.

"One night, Frank and Barbara Sinatra were in the audience, and I wanted to let him know I knew they were in the audience, so I cued the band to play "New York, New York." Just a few bars into the song, Frank comes up onto the stage, grabs the microphone out of my hand, and finishes the song. Out of the corner of my eye, I noticed the players in the casino heard him singing and stampeded to the lounge. It was so funny. The security guard caught my eye and told me to get Frank off the stage; the tables had emptied and the casino was losing money. I asked the guard, 'Are you nuts?' But I knew the casino did well, that lounge broke the record for the most amount of drinks served in any lounge. They were making plenty of money."

One afternoon Anthony and Skip decided to have a big bash. They could throw a party and have a great time, in spite of the fact they weren't welcome into the bedrooms of the Strip hotels. At the last set of the evening, when many of the local entertainers had gathered to hear Anthony's group play, he offered an open invitation, and asked everyone to come eat and party at the Brooks Hotel. They prepared a Southern repast of oxtails, shrimp gumbo, collard greens, fried chicken, potato salad, beer, as well as all the weed you could smoke, strung lights across the patio, brought out a stereo radio, and caroused until the emergences of the morning sun peeked through the ravines of the eastern mountains. Singers, musicians, politicians, and visitors arrived in a parade of limousines, and were escorted around the back for the best party of the week. The owner of the hotel joined in; she knew word would get out that her place was the place to be. To hell with the cops, she would handle them if the need arose, but that night, as in all other nights, nobody came to spoil the raucous party.

After sleeping in later than usual, Mrs. Brooks' daughter woke up to the sounds of her boyfriend screaming. "Get out of bed and clean up that mess in the back. All that noise last night, they could have called the cops." He slapped her on the face, and she began to cry while she hurriedly dressed and walked out the back screen door. He followed her, hitting her again, this time on the back, and then another jab to her head. The blood-curdling sounds made their way into the rooms of the guests. Anthony, Sammy, and Ernest opened their doors simultaneously, looked at each other, and yelled "Let's get that bastard." The three of them ran to the back, pushed him aside, and told him if he ever put another hand on Mrs. Brooks' daughter they would tear him to pieces. They encircled him. "What's it going to be? Get the hell out of here." Retreating, he went back to the registration desk, packed up his stuff, and left the hotel. Sammy sat the daughter down, and examined her blood-drenched head, strongly urging her to see a doctor.

"I'll be fine, guys. Thanks for saving me. You have no idea what hell my boyfriend has put me through for so many years. You guys are the first people who have ever come to my rescue. I thank you; you saved my life," she cried. The boyfriend never returned, and Mrs. Brooks, along with her daughter, led a much happier and safer life.

The hotel continued to flourish, even after the color barrier had been broken in the other hotels, and stayed flourishing until Mrs. Brooks finally retired. Her daughter moved on to a better life, met a wonderful man, and moved to Hawaii. Years later, when Anthony was headlining a show, she caught up with him and took Anthony and his wife out for an authentic Hawaiian restaurant. Turning to her husband, she pointed to Anthony and said, "If it wasn't for this wonderful man, I doubt I would be sitting here. He saved my life, threw my boyfriend out of the motel and out of my mom's and my life. We were finally safe from my boyfriend's abuses. I truly believe he would have killed me and probably my mom had Anthony not interceded." Raising a glass she toasted Anthony and Linda. "Cheers; thanks for saving my life."

"We returned a year later to Las Vegas, and it was a different town. Frank Sinatra had made a blatant pronouncement: that if Sammy Davis, Jr. couldn't sleep in the Sands Hotel, then he wouldn't perform. He and the Rat Pack were the biggest-drawing shows in the city, if not the world, and if the hotel wouldn't bow to their wishes, their bottom line would quickly reflect the loss. In a historic move, Sammy was allowed to sleep at the hotel with his colleagues, busting open the glass ceiling. Lena Horne and Marlene Dietrich followed suit, and the entire Strip opened up its doors. Segregation had dissipated, and everyone became equally welcome behind the glittering marquees.

"When our driver slid into the limousine drop-off at the Flamingo Hotel, he didn't stay to make sure we had a room; he knew we were welcome. Greeting us warmly, the valet took our bags and showed us to our suite. We were treated like royalty. Thank God, our time had come. We were there to make money for the casinos, and they reciprocated in kind. The bar was fully stocked, the room filled with flowers, and there was a huge fruit basket in the center of the living room. Opening up the curtains looking out across the desert, we felt like times were finally changing, at least in Las Vegas."

"Wayne Newton, often nicknamed Mr. Las Vegas, came by to catch our act and renew our friendship. Us tenors tend to stick together. I remember the very first time I had seen him perform at the Brooklyn Fox Rock and Roll Show back in New York. He got out there, in front of a huge crowd of teenagers, and sang his hit, "Danke Schoen." The young crowd booed him. He felt horrible; I guess his agent hadn't given him the heads up on what to expect.

"His dressing room was next to mine, and I quietly knocked on his door. He was seated with his head down, looking pretty gloomy. 'It's okay, man, you're really good, you can't go by that crowd. Don't let them get you down.' In Las Vegas, Wayne Newton was a big star, with his name on the mammoth marquees, playing the headliner rooms. It was just different at this venue." One evening, Anthony and the group were performing in a lounge in Las Vegas, and one of the guys overheard a couple talking about The Checkmates, who were playing directly across the street at Caesar's. After the group had finished the show, they trotted over to the packed Nero's Nook and saw the Checkmates performing.

"They were tearing up the crowd; everyone came to see this group. We sat there stunned. We were under the impression that the Las Vegas crowds wanted to hear Broadway and pop songs, not our fifties and sixties music. We were just singing, but The Checkmates, they were performing, and it was to a sold-out room."

The next morning the guys met for breakfast, which in Las Vegas time meant the stroke of noon, and had a discussion. "Did you see those guys last night, they were unbelievable. I think they are taking our audience away? We can't let that happen, right?" After a quick meeting of the minds, they got back into the trenches, turned their show around, and started performing what they performed best: their own music, with lots of R&B groove. The entertainment director located a room to rehearse in, and Anthony called in the band, handing out the scores to their songs. After adding the choreography, styled by Matt Maddox, they were ready to rumble.

It took more than one performance, but word spread quickly in the bourgeoning town, and Little Anthony and The Imperials took their seats of royalty, riding the high road of fame. "We went back to dancing, rhythm and blues, and pumping it, and we became the new darlings of Las Vegas. We extended our stay in the city, and migrated over to the Sahara at the Casbah lounge, performed for a couple of weeks, and flew home in time for the holidays."

The guys would continue touring, hitting the cities in Florida. The most memorable stop was at The Bachelor's Three nightclub in Fort Lauderdale, which was partially owned by Joe Namath, Anthony's football hero. Anthony never missed watching a game, screaming and yelling as Joe would pull back for a long throw; then seconds later, the fans would scream "Touchdown!" That was Joe Willie, the best football player in the tri-state area. With all his fame, and his love for warm weather, the football player invested in a nightclub in Fort Lauderdale, booking all the latest and greatest entertainers

"My only thought was if I was going to meet my hero. I couldn't wait until our car stopped and dropped us in front of the club. When I saw our names on the marquee, I just kept dreaming I would see my hero. Since we were booked for a week, I was hopeful he would be at one of our shows."

On that Saturday evening, after their last show had been performed, Anthony strolled over to the bar and there he was in the flesh: Joe Namath! Joe walked toward Anthony, "You're looking for the ladies? Me too. Glad to have you here; we've had a packed house the entire week." The two had a couple of drinks together, laughed and talked, but were separated as several gorgeous women surrounded Joe. Joe walked out the front door with a woman on each arm, and Anthony got the crumbs – but since they came in the form of a magnificent amber-skinned woman, the crumbs dropping from Joe were pretty good. Anthony never saw his hero again, although the group worked the club for three more years.

CHAPTER 15

Returning home to Brooklyn for a few days of rest, they continued to rehearse a few new songs for their engagement at the El Flambé Hotel in the heart of San Juan, Puerto Rico. At the time, that was the place where the entire Eastern Seaboard vacationed, and the nightclubs were teaming with life as the best acts were flown in from around the world to entertain the crowds and keep the casinos filled with guests. The drug lords were everywhere, supplying anyone who had cash with the crème de la crème of drugs.

Through word of mouth, Anthony discovered Rashid's Disco Club in Old San Juan, where several cordoned-off rooms held quick clandestine deals exchanging cash for drugs. Chino, one of the barbacks, offered to show The Imperials the ropes. He took them to local clubs, where they partied until the sun rose. Wearing a pass around his neck, Chino stood at the back of the stage watching their performance and afterwards, he piled the singers into a van. He drove down narrow, dimly lit streets on the outskirts of downtown, and stopped at a small, private club. The women were exquisite, as were the drugs, and the rum-infused drinks. "It was one of the most erotic encounters I had ever had. Between the drugs, the exotic sex, and the rum, I was flying; I was barely able to get up until the sound check the following afternoon. The next night, Chino was standing backstage, but I let the others go; in the morning I was going to see my daughter Liza, and I didn't want to be stoned or hung over."

"Years ago when Melba, Liza's mother, knew I wasn't in any position to get married, she escaped from New York with our daughter, and left Liza to live with her grandparents in Puerto Rico; my granddaughter had been living a quiet life in the hills outside San Juan. Melba returned to New York."

Anthony rented a small, rugged car, pulled the directions out of his pocket, and headed for Catalina, a township at the base of the rainforest. As he was driving up the steep incline, the car choked as he negotiated the sharp curves, through the thick tree-lined road. It was quiet except for the chirps of parrots, and the wind rustling through the leaves on the towering palm trees. Hearing the sound of goats, he knew he had arrived.

Melba wanted Liza to see a totally different side of life, and she knew that her grandparents could be trusted to give her that quiet life. They had purchased a small home, with enough land to sustain a garden and a couple of pets, which turned out to be baby goats. Liza ran out of the house, threw her arms around his waist; he picked her up, hugging and kissing her cheek. Smiling, the grandmother offered a hug, and thanked him for sending support money. Taking his hand, Liza showed Anthony around the yard and the garden, and then the grandmother set out a pitcher and poured fresh fruit drinks for them. The life Melba had chosen for her daughter wore well on her, as she embodied a slower-paced, calmer culture. She was as smart as she was beautiful, with a sweet loving disposition. Anthony was bursting with pride as he gazed upon his daughter; she was so full of life, happy, and so busy. He pushed her on the swing, played games, walked through the dense forest, and sat down for their first real meal together.

The sun crossed the sky; dusk had arrived, and it was time to drive back to the hotel, and prepare for the show. He kissed them reluctantly, pulled the car into gear, and slowly drove down the curves. Just as he was about to reach the base of the main highway, he spied something moving out of the corner of his eye. He was on the main thoroughfare, where cars raced in all directions. The lagoon on the west side of the street had turned an inky blue, as the sun dipped further into the horizon.

Anthony was driving slowly, savoring the memories of the afternoon, when the something he had seen came closer. It was an elderly man, stumbling onto the roadway. The old man stopped and glared at the car, and then turned around to head back to the lagoon, but it was too late. Anthony felt a thump, white coconut milk spilled over the windshield, and the elderly man was hurled fifteen feet into the air. Startled, Anthony spun the car around; it flipped onto the side of the highway, smashing into a light pole. He killed the engine, got out of the car, and was aghast as he stared down at the lifeless man lying at the base of the headlights. "What just happened?" he screamed, as witnesses yelled out he had hit Mr. Ortiz. "I was in total shock, I didn't see him until it was too late, and the old man was just standing in the road."

The cops arrived on the scene within minutes, grabbed Anthony, and took him to safety. Numb and in shock, he kept repeating, "I didn't see him; he was there, and then he wasn't." The sixty-year-old drunk was dead before he hit the ground, and Anthony was paralyzed with fear. It was nightmarish; nothing remotely like that had happened to him, and he had no idea how to handle the situation. Don Taylor, their road manager, bolted down to the police station to bail Anthony out of jail. Don held a wad of cash that the hotel manager had given him to guarantee Anthony's safe return to the theater.

"I had to work that night. The show had to go on, so I summoned all my courage and we put on a great performance. In the morning it was all over the newspapers about the death. My daughter and her grandparents heard it on the local news. Word spread back home to the states; it was all over the news in New York. I felt doomed. The hotel was so worried about my safety that they hired a bodyguard to stay with me twenty-four hours a day. It didn't hurt the show; there was never an empty seat in the audience, and people were applauding as loudly as ever. They must have known it wasn't my fault, or they felt sorry for me, but the fans continued their support." In the morning, Don knocked on Anthony's door and told him to get dressed, that they were headed to court. What the District Attorney hadn't counted on was the hotel's influence in obtaining the ex-governor of Puerto Rico to act as the defendant's attorney. Dressed in a simple white shirt, khaki pants, and leather sandals, Anthony, along with his attorney and road manager, somberly walked into the courtroom. The attorney loved Little Anthony and the Imperials, and was keenly aware of how much they added to the economy of the city. There was no way he was going to allow the DA to punish a young man for an accident, and the attorney was smart enough to know it wouldn't bode well if justice wasn't served. Puerto Rico, a seemingly step-child of America, the attorney was determined to conduct the case as professionally as if he were in the middle of Manhattan.

No, this wasn't going to be an eye for an eye, not when the elderly man was drunk, senile, and had wandered onto a busy highway. He was still clutching the coconut milk as he lay in the street. According to the court records, the old man was drunk. The DA presented his case, and the trial would commence in a couple of days.

"I went back to the scene and they measured the skid marks to prove that I wasn't speeding. My attorney gathered several witnesses and obtained the autopsy report, which showed clearly that the old man was completely wasted. Through it all, I was numb; I couldn't believe such a thing could happen to me. I kept playing the scene over and over in my mind, and never understood what made that man just stop, stare, and reverse his steps. The windshield was coated with milk, and when I looked down at his face, I couldn't cope with the awful memory. That night the guys brought me some great coke to help ease the pain, but I was in no mood to go out partying. The hotel wanted me to stay in my room, watched by a trusty bodyguard. It was so weird: the next four days were spent in the courtroom, and then I would come back to the hotel room, dress, and put on a show."

"This man," shouted the DA, pointing in Anthony's direction, "deliberately killed an innocent victim. He knew him, and he wanted him dead, and now this young man should pay for his mistake; he is a cold-blooded murderer!" Unnerved, Anthony sat shaking with fear as the court interpreter translated the accusations, while his attorney kept insisting things would turn out well. After the DA had presented his findings, which were sketchy and lacking substance, it was time for the ex-governor to go to work. Presenting the physical evidence, he proved the car wasn't speeding; presenting several witnesses, he proved the victim had been drinking most of the afternoon; presenting the autopsy report, he showed the high level of drugs in the victim's body. Lastly he disproved any motive, or the fact that it was intentional, especially since it was Anthony's first visit to the city; he had no idea who the elderly man was.

The judge, who was also keenly aware of how his bread was

buttered, and the fact that the DA had put together a farce of a case, grabbed his gavel, banged it down on the desk, and dismissed the case. "I was still in shock, but my attorney rejoiced as I walked freely out of the courthouse. Farmer's, who held the insurance policy on the rented car, dropped me, forever. If that's the worst punishment I took from the case, that would have been easy, but the dreams plague me to this very day. I wanted to build a bridge across the highway to the lagoon, as that old man was not the only person to die there at the hands of a car driver, but it never happened. Years later I returned to the city and the scene of the accident, and I was happy to see a bridge had finally been constructed. When the truth came out, I was embraced by the city, and we were invited back on several more occasions to perform. Although the other guys weren't involved, they felt sorry for me; but still, I had created a situation that tarnished our reputation. We were one for all and all for one, and what happened to me hurt us all." The rest of the week went without incident, but they were most happy when the door of their jet slammed shut and they were in the blue skies on their way home to New York.

Don Taylor, road manager and nursemaid to the crew, began preparing the next tour, the first stop of which was on the pristine island of Bermuda. The group had taken extra pains in preparing, with new, sparkling white costumes, dance steps, and fresh songs; they wanted to knock the stuffy audience over. Playing in the high-class resorts was so much more fun. During the day, they had use of the resort facilities, and at night, after they performed, they had access to the best of what the island offered: women and drugs.

The serene, gently rolling mounds on world-class golfing links were only surpassed by the sounds of the swelling ocean waves, rolling gently to shore. Between horseback riding, aquatics sports, boats, fishing, sunbathing on endless miles of beaches, and access to the gyms and spa, their days were blissfully filled. Meeting at Forty Thieves nightclub, they performed the obligatory sound check. From the corner of the room, a man walked over and introduced himself as captain of the Skip Jack, of an atomic submarine. The captain had seen the group perform, and had hoped to run into them during the day at the nightclub. The next day, the entire group was escorted onto the ship and given the grand tour.

There was hardly a place left on earth where Anthony wouldn't run into a former lover and so was the case at the Forty Thieves nightclub. When his former lover had opened up the entertainment section of the local newspaper, and spotted Little Anthony and The Imperials were slated to perform, she purchased a ticket, making sure she sat in the front row. Dressed in her most provocative cocktail sheath, she left a note on the refrigerator stating that she had gone to the movies with her girlfriends. She had done well for herself, and married the local constable, who kept order on the tiny island. She was drawn to Anthony, like a bee to a flower, an alcoholic to beer; she was plainly obsessed. That night, before the show began, she was able to convince the security guard to allow her near the dressing rooms; after all, she was the constable's wife, and what harm could she do? When Anthony answered the knock on the door, his eyes lit up, she was as beautiful as ever, even with a few extra pounds. No matter. He drew her into his small room, kissed her, and they met back in his dressing room directly after the show, rekindling a strong memory. "I have to leave," she said, quickly gathering her shoes as she opened the door. "How about coming to my home for dinner tomorrow afternoon? Bring the guys, it'll be fun." Handing him the address, she kissed him once more, and raced home before the last movie had ended. She needed an alibi.

After lunch, Clarence, Kenny, Sammy, and Anthony were on rented motor scooters and driving on the left-hand side of the road as they approached the constable's home. Introducing her husband as the head honcho of the island, she winked at her lover, and then gave the guests a tour of the house. In the backroom was a gleaming oak pool table, and Sammy was thrilled to join the constable in a friendly game. Sammy was an expert at pool, and forgot his manners, soundly beating his host at every game. This began a slow simmer in the cantankerous husband, who was annoyed at his losses, and by the end of the evening, he had figured out that Anthony had bedded his wife, making him even madder.

So wrapped up in pursuing his former lover, when the group departed, Anthony left his wallet on the coffee table in the center of the living room. Inside were the remnants of a smoked joint; it was less than an inch long, but there it was, stuck in between his American Express and Macy's credit card. The constable picked up the wallet, discovered the illicit tip of the joint, and decided he would get his revenge; nobody screwed his wife and got away with it.

The next morning there was a knock on Anthony's door, and there stood the constable. At first Anthony thought he wanted to thank them for coming to his home, but his smile was instantly replaced with an irate scowl, "What do we have here?" the constable questioned as he barged into the hotel room, where he began opening drawers and shaking out articles of clothing. The constable and his assistant ransacked the room until they found a couple of joints, and then went into Clarence, Sammy, and Kenny's rooms, repeating the drill until they had found at least one joint in every room. The assistant handcuffed the three singers, threw them into a police car, and then threw them into a small jail cell.

Again, it was Anthony who was to blame; he had gotten his

group into another pickle. They were paraded into an airless cell, rancid from the smell of urine. In the corner sat a desolate American who had tried to throw himself off a cruise ship; the ship's captain didn't know what to do with the passenger, so when the ship docked at Bermuda, he called the constable and put the young man in jail, until a relative could retrieve his sorry soul. At least for the suicidal young guy, things perked up in his lonely cell when he was surrounded by world famous singers.

"Another fine mess you got us into," said Clarence as he plunked himself to the cement floor. "Now what?" There was no room to pace, so they were mute as each thought how they would recover from this untidy situation. The problem was, it was Saturday morning, and the judge wouldn't appear until Monday morning. They stuck out the remainder of the weekend in the confines of the cell. All day long, the cops came and peered into the cell to see what the famous singers were doing. Everyone was miserable beyond belief, and they missed their show.

"I have to pee," said Sammy. "I have this crowd. I can't pee with a crowd."

"So don't pee," said Clarence.

"But I have to pee. Hey, guard!" yelled Sammy, "Do you think I could have a private place to pee?" His answer came in the form of loud laughter from the crowd of fans that had gathered in the outer office. Word spread quickly that the singers were in lock-up, and people came to gawk at them in the tiny cell.

"That will teach you guys a lesson," retorted the on-duty cop. "You don't come to our island and smoke dope. Now settle down, and if you pee in your pants, that's just fine with me."

"Okay, guys, could you turn your heads?" Sammy morosely asked. Don Taylor arrived early Monday morning, springing the group out of jail, and taking them safely back to their hotel rooms. The judge fined them each three hundred dollars, slapped them on the wrist, and banned them from the island for a year. Don never uttered an admonishing word; they had gone through hell, and he didn't need to add any flames to the fire.

"I know you are miserable," began Don, "but Ernest is more miserable. While you guys were sequestered, he was riding on one of those rented scooters and got hit by a truck; he is in real bad shape."

Don drove them directly to the hospital, and after a quick visit with the guys, Ernest was medevaced to Staten Island, New York. He was in critical condition: both hips were broken, his spine was cracked, his legs and arms were severely bruised; it took him nine months to recover. Kenny took over his part, singing back-up, until Ernest had gone through months of rehabilitation and was pronounced sound enough to return to the group. Although their arrest hit the newspapers, and was another embarrassment for the families of the famous singers, when the guys compared their embarrassment to Ernest's situation, they were thankful. That accident could have been any one of them – they had all rented scooters.

Lying in a hospital in Staten Island, they plied the ailing biker with the finest hashish money could buy. They lit up tightly rolled joints after sneaking into the bathroom late at night, in order to ease the boredom and pain. Ernest had a constant trail of family and friends visiting, bearing gifts of food and flowers, but when one of The Imperials showed up, he knew it was going to be a high time.

"I think Bermuda was just bad luck, and since we were thrown off the island for at least a year, we won't be returning for a long time." That drew a rare chuckle form Ernest.

CHAPTER 16

Sammy, Clarence, Ernest, Anthony, and Kenny were in the depths of rehearsal. Matt, their choreographer, was putting them through the paces with a new dance routine, but was weary of Anthony's knees and Ernest's precarious situation. "No crazy stunts for the next few months until you guys are strong enough to handle the high kicks and splits. I will have to treat you like a bunch of old men. You have got to warm up every day; keep your muscles moving, and they will become part of a well-oiled machine, just like your car. You want it to run, you have to warm it up and keep it lubricated," he advised.

When they had finished the rigorous practice, they walked a couple of blocks to Andrew's Coffee Shop, known for its great coffee, and cheap sandwiches. Seated at a booth, Sammy began to complain bitterly about the weather. "I'm sick of the cold. Matt wants us to warm up our muscles, so I'll tell you how I am going to warm up mine: I'm moving to California. I can't stand another winter tromping through the snow, rushing through horrible weather trying to get to our performances. You guys remember all those wonderful times we had on the West Coast? The beaches? The warm sun in February? Well, I want to do more than remember it, I want to live it. Anyone want to join me?" Shocked, they remained silent as they mulled over Sammy's sudden pronouncement. "We don't have to live in the same town. Once we have a show rehearsed, we're on a tour doing the same thing for weeks or months at a time. This can work, I have no doubt!" The guys sat around the table, drinking coffee, eating their sandwiches, and pondering every word Sammy had uttered. "You know, my friend, you have a great argument. With my trick knee, it would be great to never have to worry about slipping on the ice, and my kids would love it. But my wife, Judy...I don't know. Her whole family is here in New York, and she has never left them. It would be asking a lot of her to make the big move, but hell, why not! Tonight I will ask the question, and get back to you guys. We all know that the music industry is making the move out West, and there is Las Vegas, a town that has endless opportunities for us. I say we all think long and hard about this prospect. Sammy, we have to give you the credit for being the one with the courage to make the move," said Anthony.

A week later, Anthony, Judy, Tony, and Andre were standing anxiously at the airport waiting to board a jet that would take them to the other side of the country. Judy looked down at her ticket. It read "one way." Swallowing hard, she grabbed the boys' hands, and took her seat in first class. When the stewardess slammed the door shut, she felt her heart leap out of her chest, but it was too late to go back. She worried about her future, unable to share in her husband's joy. She knew he was unfaithful, and that he would probably be unfaithful in the future. She knew she couldn't compete with those blonde haired, blue-eyed movie queens, who would do anything for a piece of a star, especially one as famous as her husband.

The real estate agent met them at the airport, with a long shiny white limousine to take them to their new home in sunny Los

Angeles. As they drove into the circular driveway, Judy's trepidations fell aside when she gazed at the exquisite two-story home. The agent handed Anthony the keys, who turned and gave them to Judy, "It's all yours now. I love you, and I want you to love our new lives out here. I promise everything is going to work out, and we will be really happy." The boys sprang into house, running from room to room, and then screamed joyfully when they glimpsed the huge swimming pool in the center of the back yard. There was no doubt that this was paradise. Judy just prayed that every day would be this happy and content.

"I was making a lot of money. The gigs and tours were plentiful, the records were selling, and our futures were bright. We went on shopping sprees, buying stuff for the kids and the house, and trips to Hawaii. We were living the big life of Hollywood movie stars. The party invitations flooded our mailbox. It seemed as though someone was always celebrating something, and in Hollywood, they always did it in a big way. As soon as I began going to those l parties, I was back to my old ways, cheating on my wife. I couldn't resist those beautiful women. I had never seen so many beautiful women in my life, they were everywhere I turned. With the warm weather they had beautiful tans, and wore skimpy clothing. They were incredibly sexy, and they were willing to have sex with me. I just couldn't say no."

Judy tossed her silk Chanel bag onto the whitewashed oak dresser and began a tirade: "I saw you gawking at that woman, and then you disappeared for an hour. Where the hell were you? You just left me alone in that huge home. I didn't know a soul, and you up and left me. I can only guess where you went, and what you did. I saw that smile on that blonde's face when she came over to shake your hand. You can't fool me, do you think I'm stupid? Having sex with another woman, and right under my nose? I thought things might be different when we moved out here, that you would treat me well and stop the running around, but that didn't happen!"

"I have given you everything: jewelry, a beautiful home, a car, expensive clothes – and all you can do is complain?" Anthony answered back.

"Here, you can have this back," she screamed as she ripped off the silk dress, tearing it into shreds, "Take it." She threw the pieces into the air and slammed the door to the bathroom; she fell asleep to the track of "Tears on My Pillow." The very person who sang that song was the one who created those tears that night. Judy felt as alone as alone could get. With no family and few friends, she had no cushion to support her needs, and she knew she couldn't go on living like this: it was just too hurtful.

In the morning Anthony felt a twitch in his vocal chords; could it be he was so enraged from Judy's haranguing that it had immobilized him? Coughing, he felt horribly ill, and could barely talk to the children. His blood ran cold; was there something wrong with his voice? He called Dr. Charles Snyder, a trusted doctor, who specialized in throat and mouth problems. He sat nervously in the waiting room until the nurse walked him back to the examination room. "You a smoker?" Dr. Snyder questioned, while gently examining his throat. Dr. Snyder was considered the throat doctor of the stars.

"Well, yes, doc, I have been smoking since I was sixteen."

"Then today is your lucky day, since today, you are going to quit smoking if you ever want to sing again. You have a node on your vocal cords, and it is there because you smoke. If you keep smoking you will have no career. The node is not large enough to operate on, and you will be fine; that is, if you STOP smoking." He then wrote down an address and sent Anthony to the Schick Institute to be cured of his smoking addiction.

"When I walked into the institute, it was clean, peaceful, and quiet. The nurse then took me to another room that was filled with cigarette butts from the floor to the ceiling. It was disgusting, and it stank. That was my introduction to quitting the habit. They used the simple Pavlovian method of shock treatments. When I saw a pack of cigarettes, they shocked me. Then they would show me pictures, or hand me a pack, or even light one up in front of me, and shock me each time. After smoking over two packs a day, I finally quit, and quit for good. It took another month or so, but my voice came back, which was comforting, and most reassuring. At least I could answer Judy's screaming, handle the kids, and reach all those high notes. I was cured and I never looked at another cigarette."

The California sun enticed Don, the road manager, and several of the band members to follow the same path out west. That first New Year's Eve, everyone in the group was invited to a lavish black tie bash at a private home, where, for once, they didn't have to perform. Dressed in sleek Italian ensembles, Anthony and Judy walked into the warm, subdued glow of a Mediterranean style mansion, which sat on top of a hill overlooking the mountains.

The party was at Don Taylor's home. Monica, his wife, introduced the couple to several guests standing around the massive living room. After an hour of grazing and drinking, the music escalated into an upbeat tempo. Anthony took Judy's hand, grabbed her waist, and twirled her around and around, until she could barely stand. Drunk on three glasses of champagne, she took a seat near the bar, while he found his way to the bathroom.

Those California women were very athletic. In addition to their great beauty, they had perfect bodies, and were in fabulous physical condition. Anthony made a mental note to make sure he hit the gym every day, otherwise he would never have the stamina for the anticipated lusty years to come. His lover adjusted his bowtie, slapped his bottom, and reminded him he had left a miffed wife at the bar. Self-consciously touching his bowtie, Anthony found Judy still seated at the bar, nursing a large flute of champagne.

"Please, let's stay until midnight, and then I promise we will leave."

He gave his wife a perfunctory kiss at the stroke of midnight, and they left the mansion while the sounds of "Auld Lang Syne" flooded the room. Sober as a church mouse, Anthony grabbed the wheel of the car, anticipating another raging diatribe from his sullen wife. Yes, he knew he had done wrong, and he deserved whatever punishment was about to come his way, but instead, Judy was silent. He had finally broken down her will, had destroyed her ego, her love, her sense of value. It was death of a marriage through humiliation. No matter how he tried to rationalize the growing apart as the country bumpkin marrying the city slicker, he had been an awful husband, and deserved to suffer for his crimes. That night, as his eyes refused to shut, he could hear her cry herself to sleep. What was he doing? The house, his two beautiful children, the love of a wonderful woman – did he really need to toss it aside for a few rolls in the hay?

In the morning, she dressed, grabbed the camera off the top of the dresser, got the kids off to school, and then ran a bunch of errands. "Later that afternoon I was home, taking a swim in the pool, and making appointments with a producer for the next series of tours. The phone rang, and Judy picked it up: the photos were ready. Inviting me to run an errand with her, and then pick up the kids from school, was a rarity, and I was happy to accompany her. Judy went to pay for the photos, while I walked over to the candy aisle, picking up huge bars of chocolate. I inserted the keys into the ignition and was backing out of a tight parking spot when I felt a smack on my face. I thought I had hit a car, but it was Judy."

"You jerk! The clerk handed me these lovely pictures of our trip to Hawaii, and these racy photos of one of your girlfriends were inside the envelope. How could you! Wasn't it enough you go with these girls under my nose and have sex with them, but then to take pictures of them is insane! I can't stand it anymore! All the money, the clothes, this bright shiny Cadillac, can't make up for your cheating," she cried as she tore the photos into a thousand pieces scattering them into the air. "See those pieces? That is how I feel. My heart has been ripped into a million pieces and it's too late, it can't be put back together." After picking up the kids, they drove home in silence, as Anthony thought about his life. He was miserable with Judy, although he knew he was to blame for the demise of the marriage. He felt like no matter what he did, it would never be enough to make amends for his cheating. The life inside the walls of his home had become more like a prison than a sanctuary, and he didn't want to live like that.

He made up his mind: he was leaving. He composed a letter filled with regrets, and longing for the love they once knew; for a time when they had few material possessions, but a home filled with love; a time when they shared their lives spiritually and unselfishly. Love had died, and it was senseless that they remain together. He folded the letter into a cream colored envelope and placed it on her night table. He threw some clothing and musical paraphernalia into his car, kissed his boys good-bye, and drove across the desert floor into Las Vegas.

"A voice inside my head kept a running mantra through the three hundred mile drive, 'you're not fulfilled, I have a plan.' I had to get away; I needed to start over. It was too overwhelming, the fights and the constant bad feelings. I wanted a fresh start, a place I could go to where everything was different, and a place that would have lots for me to do. Las Vegas was the perfect spot." He located an apartment near the center of town, called his friends and family, and gave them the news his marriage was over, and that now, he would be living in the desert. After a cooling off period, he and Judy began to talk, and he began visiting the kids. They never got back together, and they never stopped loving each other. Eventually, Judy moved back to New York, while her sons remained in California. Tony and Andre received a call from their mother, she had been diagnosed with bladder cancer, the prognosis was terminal. When she notified her two sons, they insisted she move out to California so they could be with her. Tony was at the airport gate with a wheel chair, and startled at her condition. Her face was ashen, her hair lifeless, and her arms thin and frail. Hugging her, he feared he would have little time to be with her on this earth. Judy stayed a week with Tony, but she required more care than he was able to give and he and Andre moved her into an assisted living home just two blocks away. The two sons came and went each day, spending as much quality time as they possibly could. Tony made a solemn vow to his mom that he wouldn't let her die alone. He would be there for her always. Tony kept his promise. It was one in the morning when he received the call that Judy was not doing well and wouldn't last the night. Dressing quickly, he took a seat at her bedside, held her hand and watched his mom until four in the morning when she took her last breath. On the day before Judy died, she was holding a white leather bible, and as she lost consciousness, a photo of Anthony fell out of the book resting on her heart.

Anthony didn't forget his two sons, he just needed his freedom. "The fighting really got to Andre and me," said Tony, Anthony's second son. "Dad would come home, and mom would have been drinking, and then they would yell and scream at each other. Andre and I would bury our heads in our pillows, but we could still hear them yelling at each other. We were frightened; we didn't know what was going to happen, and when dad walked out on us, we were really terrified.

"Although we were really young, we knew our mom wasn't in the best shape and that the fights weren't just dad's fault. When he left us, and all we had was our mom, who had turned into an alcoholic, we didn't know how we would survive. Eventually, mom got a job as a secretary, and somehow, there was always food on the table, and Andre and I had new clothing for school. Dad would call the house, and Andre would run and grab the phone out of my hand. He was the oldest and really missed Dad terribly. There were so many occasions when my brother hung up the phone, smiling from ear-to-ear, bragging 'Dad is coming this weekend, and he promised to take us to Disneyland'.

"But the problem was, Dad didn't come home, and those trips to Disneyland never happened. After an endless series of broken promises, Andre's hopes vanished, his heart crushed one too many times. Andre and I loved each other, and counted on each other. For a long time it seemed as though that was all we had. Dad's absence never bothered me, perhaps because he was never around when I was young, but for Andre, the effect of dad's absence left a deep scar that would take years to heal," said Tony.

A gig was on the horizon for the month of July in Lake Tahoe at the Sahara Hotel. In trying to make amends, Anthony called Judy and arranged for the entire family to spend the month together. He knew he had a lot of making up to do, and perhaps this would prove to Andre and Tony that he loved them dearly and hadn't forgotten them. He met up with Judy and the kids, and they packed up the car, including the family dog and cat, and drove 480 miles up the coastline and over to Lake Tahoe.

"The trip seemed to take forever; someone always needed something and the dog and cat had to be let out as well. When we arrived at the rented home, it was worth the trip. The kids and I began to bond as I took them to the lake, the tennis courts, shopping, and the movies. Plus, some of the other entertainers had brought their children, and my two boys had plenty of friends to play with. Things weren't cool with me and Judy, but she was civil to me and never caused a ripple in the harmony of the situation. I think her love for our children outweighed any ugly feelings she was harboring for me. I was so thankful and happy for that month with my kids, they enriched my life and I was so proud of the way they were growing up, in spite of me not being around. Judy was a wonderful loving and caring mother and I was forever thankful to her for always being there for our kids. I was missing in action, but she stepped up to the plate and raised our two beautiful sons with genuine love and compassion."

CHAPTER 17

Before they were off and running, the group assembled in a recording studio cutting an album far different than most of the music they had made in the past. Leaving the pop world, they cut an R&B album which sold well, but didn't make it to the top 40. "The Loneliest House on the Block" was the single released from the album; bluesy and soulful, it reflected diversity and added another dimension to their pop repertoire. It was just another notch, proving and sustaining their talents. Don kept the group busy up and down the West Coast touring with Ike and Tina Turner, the hottest couple in show business. Thom Bell, produced and wrote these new bluesy songs and for AFCO Embassy Records. His lyricist was the famous Linda Creed.

"We opened their shows, and it was electric. Ike and Tina were so hot on stage, they exploded with energy and the audiences went crazy, screaming and cheering. There was never an empty seat, and we played in some huge venues. I'll never forget that night when I first met Sonny and Cher at Ike and Tina Turner's show; she was unbelievably beautiful." The Cow Palace in San Francisco was one of the largest places we had ever performed at; it seemed as though the filled seats went on forever. In spite of all the people, I was able to meet the most famous couple in the entire place.

"With that packed house, our share of the take was substantial. In New York I had purchased a black leather suit. I guess I wanted to look a little like Ike. As I was walking across the street to the House of pancakes, a police car pulled over."

"The cop yelled, 'What you doing here, boy?' "I shuddered; what the hell? I'm just walking down a city street. Doesn't the cop know who I am? But wait, that shouldn't matter. I'm not doing anything wrong, I'm simply walking. I could have, and maybe should have, told him that I was a famous person and was going to have my photo taken for millions around the world to see, but I wouldn't give that white cop any satisfaction. I could have been one of those people who sat at the drugstores in the South begging for equal rights, but that had come and gone, and those laws were in place. What right did this white policeman have chiding me?

"I kept walking, and after two blocks, he and his partner turned on their siren and sped away. When I reflect on that day, I realize that I was dressed for the photo shoot, in expensive clothing, and a brand new leather jacket. I guess I didn't fit into the mold of the neighborhood. Racism hit me again; I realized it wasn't over, it was just a lot more subtle."

The photographer gathered the four men, taking a picture that would be seen by millions, one of the most artistic, dramatic shots ever released of Little Anthony and The Imperials. Anthony was not smiling; the photographer captured a sober, thoughtful, haunting look: the uncensored purity of a pensive artist.

Straight from the shoot, Don had booked the guys at a week-long performance in Mexico. Another trip to the airport, and Anthony, Clarence, Kenny, Sammy, and Harold were bound for Mexico City. The Imperials sometimes changed singers, and this time Harold joined the group to make a full quartet. At least this time they avoided the rumblings of the bus, and the headaches of wondering where their next meal would be eaten. They discovered while chatting on the plane that none of them spoke Spanish, although throughout their childhoods, growing up in the projects, they had gleaned an understanding of a few choice phrases. As the plane glided to the tarmac, they viewed the huge panorama of the city. Over a mile high, with millions of people sprawled across miles of land, this was the biggest metropolitan area they had every performed at. They eventually found their luggage in the long, crowded corridors of the airport, and then waited for the limousine driver to dispatch all the bags and instruments into the deep trunk. While driving to the Camino Real Hotel, they were amazed at the size of the city. "I'm sure there are more than enough people living here to fill the seats for this week," joked Anthony.

The polite desk clerk handed each of the singers the keys to their rooms. He snapped his fingers and five valets appeared, each carrying a set of bags. Because of the altitude, Don gave them a full day to rest before the first performance: they needed to learn how to catch their breath. The next day, the guys met for a sound check and introduced themselves to the lounge act performing adjacent to the showroom: Sunny Girls of Sweden, three upbeat women, who sounded similar to ABBA, but the all-girl group was younger, and each was stunningly beautiful. The girls immediately bonded with the guys, who were all horse lovers, suggested a joint outing. Early the next morning the two groups met at the lobby, and were whisked away to a dude ranch, where, according to the concierge, they would have the finest horseback ride of their lives.

The hotel van comfortably accommodated the singers as they drove an hour into the Mexican desert. Opening up the door, the driver promised to return later that afternoon and bring them safely home. Anthony, who had become a vigilant traveler, placed several pesos in his hand to ensure the driver's return.

They walked up to the rustic stables, kicking up layers of dust, and admired the beauty of the horses. This was going to be a great day! An elderly man stepped out from behind the barn, bowed, and held out his hand to receive payment. After he had meticulously counted the money, he bowed again, and called over three ranch hands, who secured all the riders onto their trusty steeds. Atop the horse, Anthony adjusted his black felt cowboy hat, securing it tightly, in case a breeze suddenly cropped up, grabbed the reins, and took the last place in the procession.

The sky was crystal clear as the sun slowly arched directly overhead. After being on the trail for a couple of hours, the singers became extremely thirsty, and in the distance, they saw an old Indian village. Dismounting, they slowly walked around the village, shocked at how primitive the Indians lived. The women were cleaning the clothes at the edge of the river using large smooth stones, just as they had done over a century ago. It was almost as if they had stepped back in time to a hundred years prior. The homes were adobe huts; there was no refrigeration, at least none that they could see. They brought the horses to the edge of the river, and the steeds dunked their mouths into the muddy water. Anthony looked around for a place to purchase a drink as an old native man approached the group. "Hey Black cowboys, (he said in Spanish), would you like a taste of my special drink?" he asked in a thick Spanish accent. The old man had learned just enough English to entice the tourists to pull some pesos out of their pockets.

"Sure," said Kenny and Harold, who were dying of thirst. Offering the old Mexican a few pesos, everyone in the group was treated to a few squirts of mescal from the tattered leather pouch slung over his shoulder. Instantly, everyone was as high as a kite, and in dire need of water. Seeing the hand motions they were making, the old man shuffled over to one of the huts, opened up an ice chest with a picture of Coca Cola on the top, and handed each person a soda, but he had failed to let them know that there was no ice in the ice chest. "Better than nothing," said Anthony as they quickly drained the hot cans. After handing out more pesos to an elderly woman for use of the bathrooms, the riders mounted their horses. In spite of the sodas, many of them were so drunk from the old man's concoction, they couldn't sit upright in their saddles. The cavalcade of riders slowly departed the village. Twisting his head around, Anthony looked back, and saw many of the women and kids laughing at them. A shiny object caught his eye. At the top of all those primitive roofs were television antennas. Guess they weren't so backwards after all.

After another mile or two, and one more look up at the sky, they realized the afternoon was quickly fading, and they were quite lost. They passed some young children herding goats. One of them yelled out, "Bandits," and he turned and pointed his finger in the direction the horses were headed. Anthony, who was still at the back of the pack, remembered the advice from the old Indian. "Follow me," Anthony yelled, "We are turning the horses around." As soon as he tightened the reins and turned his horse around, the others followed suit, and at once all of the animals changed from a lethargic walk to an all-out canter. Hanging tightly onto the reins, still feeling the effects of the mescal, the bobbling heads and jangling butts clung on for dear life. No one fell off the horses, and they made it back to the stables in under an hour.

When they finally dismounted, Anthony turned to the guide, and thanked him for his advice. "When you said to turn the horses around, you were right; they sure knew their way back, but boy, did they go fast!" The hotel van had just arrived; the driver knew the drill. By handing out ice-cold glasses of water, he was sure to extract an extra-large tip from these gringos.

As the van pulled up to the circular driveway of the luxurious Camino Real, a simultaneous sigh of relief was uttered by the tired horseback riders. The guys waddled to their rooms, took showers and prepared for the evening performance. The hotel was one of the most prestigious in the city, and it attracted the upper echelon of the populace. Because of the tight security, it also attracted political leaders, and high profile business entrepreneurs. That evening Sylvester, one of the wealthiest business leaders in the city took a front row seat at the show. He had a passion for Anthony and the group, and after the show, they met to chat and share in the refreshment of a potent joint. As they talked, Anthony was surprised to find out that Sylvester, was the son of the man who created the coffee growing bean process that was sold and used to make Maxwell House Coffee. Not only was Sylvester very rich, but powerful; he had married the President of Mexico's daughter. "He knew we had a love for great weed and this guy was so powerful he told us when we reached the border, no one would bother us. We sat around talking for a while and then he began to open up and tell us that he was very depressed and he didn't want to live anymore. Sylvester told us that because he loved our music, he wouldn't kill himself. He returned to a couple more shows, and tossed flowers on the stage as a show of appreciation. None of us believed he was that depressed that he would kill himself, he seemed to have everything, money, power, prestige, brains, and health. When we were heading back to the states, we got a call from his friend Alex Masucci, whose brother was with the President of Fantasia Records. All Alex said was 'he did it.' I asked him what he meant, and then Alex explained that Sylvester had killed himself. All of us were shocked. We had spent time with this guy, and he seemed to have everything, then pow, just like that, he was gone. It put a damper on the rest of the day, but it also made us realize how powerful our music was, at least temporarily, it put off Sylvester's demise."

Don Taylor had planned the Nassau trip carefully, booking the rooms, obtaining the band, preparing the stage, and making sure there was plenty of publicity, so that all the seats would be filled. Yes, he had done his job perfectly, with zest and meticulous attention to detail. He had started at the bottom as valet to the group, and through the years, watching, learning, and listening, he became their trusted road manager. What he hadn't planned on was a fight that ensued before his very eyes, unraveling his precious years of devoted work. "Clarence, I'm sick of you always being late, running around and not showing up at rehearsals."

"And I'm sick of you making excuses; you can't not show up for a gig, or miss rehearsals and still expect to give the audience our best."

"Yes, and I'm sick and tired of hearing you guys squabble about every damn little detail." Between Bobby Wade, (who had taken the place of Sammy), Harold, Clarence, and Anthony, the bickering continued for over an hour until Anthony stood up and announced that he was leaving the group.

"Maybe we need a break; with all this constant travelling, maybe we need a vacation from each other." The four looked at each other, finished up the gig, and when they gathered at the airport, each had a ticket in a different direction. Nobody spoke, offered a last hug, or said a word of encouragement. They silently rolled their luggage down the long corridor, and somberly boarded their respective flights. "The fight was over nothing, nothing at all. The guys seemed to be sick of each other. At first I didn't feel badly that I was the one who stood up first and said I was leaving, because at that moment it seemed like the right thing to do. It was, in fact, the dumb thing to do. I was leaving the group when things were heading south, making it even harder for me to be successful. It had been a while since we had cut a new record, and the money wasn't coming like it had in the past. There was a lot of tension, and I could feel it, and I didn't want to be surrounded by a constant worry that the guys would blow up."

Redd had run into Bill Cosby at the lobby at the Hilton in Las Vegas. They were all friends and colleagues, and had gravitated toward each other as their careers escalated. Being forthcoming, Bill had mentioned that "Your boy (Don Taylor) has spent a lot of money at the baccarat tables, and I would make sure your singers check their bank accounts. Either Don is making a whole lot of money as a road manager, or those singers of yours are getting robbed."

Redd didn't want to be responsible for Don's demise, but neither could he sit back and do nothing, when he knew what was going on. It was the job of the road manager to collect the money, and make sure it got into the right hands, and from where Redd sat, he knew where the money was going. Since they were fighting off and on for two days, the singers had never bothered with Don, who had been missing in action; they were too wrapped up in their problems. Redd told Sammy that he thought that Don was gambling a lot, he saw him drop thirty-five thousand, gambling at Caesars Palace.

"You know guys, we have been so busy fighting, they none of us realized Don has been gone for two days." After a short explanation of the situation, and a quick check of their bank accounts, they decided to find their manager, and have a pow-wow. Sammy grabbed a chair, and signaled for Don to have a seat.

"What have you done with our money?" asked Sammy, "Because I checked, and we haven't been paid for the last week." Don's suntanned face began to brighten as his heart beat faster, and the blood rushed to his head. "I, I," he stuttered, "I got robbed. Yes, it was one night ago. I had the money, yes, I had put it in a drawer in my hotel room, and later, when I returned, I opened the drawer and all the money had disappeared."

"Is that so?" said Sammy, "Because I sure didn't see any police report." He was bluffing. "So what really happened to our money?" Again Don kept to his story, but the singers knew he was lying. "Well your story is bullshit. You have lied to us for the last time, and you have stolen from us for the last time," screamed Sammy. Don left the room. He vowed he would return all of the money that was missing. If nothing else, for several days the guys had quelled their infighting and joined forces. It was years later, when Anthony would find out that on just one night at the baccarat tables, Don had dropped over thirty-five thousand dollars – money that belonged to the group. They realized how hard it must have been for Redd to rat out Don, but they grew to appreciate the fact that his loyalty lay with the singers. Redd was a performer and had the same thing happened to him, he would have been infuriated and would have appreciated someone watching his back.

CHAPTER 18

Living out west opened many doors to Anthony who had a proclivity and a passion for acting. They scattered in all directions, and each member of the group sought out a new style of living. Anthony decided it was better to return to Southern California, where he could be near his kids. If he needed to sing either as a solo act or with the group, it was as simple as boarding a plane. After decompressing from his marriage to Judy, he decided to seek an alternative and acting was just the perfect outlet. Because Anthony was serious about an acting career, he drove to the Valley and enrolled in David Alexander's acting classes. It was an intimate setting where he could polish up his acting skills. One his second visit, he met John Zenda, a well-known character actor, and after several shared classes, the two became fast friends. They never went out for competing roles, which solidified their friendship even more. John's talent emanated from the concept of imagery method acting, the ability to completely take over and immerse himself in a role. To be able to do this, the acting teacher explained how to go deeply within your personal psyche and visit your inner self. In one class, the teacher instructed the students to remember a sad moment in their memory, and then bring that scene to the surface and make the students believe you. Once they had learned to do this from their own world, the future characters' lives they would be expected to act would be easy for a discerning audience to interpret. The classes centered around this concept, and although Anthony was already quite good at this, the classes polished up his presentations, and would later go on to help him land several roles. The program was expensive, but the knowledge and contacts more than made it worthwhile.

"One morning, our teacher told us to pick an animal, it didn't matter what, and become that animal. I picked a big tiger, and began pacing and becoming the tiger. In real life, the scene would have been humiliating, but not in acting class. We had to make our colleagues believe us, and that was pretty hard to do. Besides acting, we did what I considered menial labor; we moved props, learned what backstage and front stage meant, worked on lighting and sound equipment and set changes. Our teacher's philosophy was that if we wanted to act, then we needed to understand the entire process from the floor up." David Alexander was the acting coach who truly believed in Anthony's talent, so much so that he introduced him to Merna Eisenberg, the top agent in the business. It was right after his first performance that she offered him the opportunity to join her agency; she loved what he could do on that stage. Anthony read for *Slow Dance on the Killing Grounds*, and got the part about a man who was a serial killer, about as deep and as intense as any role he would ever land. Jack Lemmon was invited to the showcase at David Alexander's acting studio, and said, "I don't know who you are, but you are one hell of an actor."

"I became that person, dark, foreboding, and mysterious. The problem was shaking off this image when I left the theater and entered the front door of my home. It was hard to do. Many nights I carried that persona home. That first night's performance, the theater was packed. The lights dimmed, and I began acting. You could hear a pin drop throughout the entire first scene. When the curtain dropped after the first act, the crowd came to life, applauding loudly. Damn! I did it, and they loved me." The show played for two months before closing, but it played to a full crowd every night, and Anthony's phone began ringing for other roles.

Merna sent him out to read for *Sistuhs*, a play comprised of several vignettes, but rather than landing the lead, he was offered the job as the understudy to the lead. Being a comedy, it was a welcome respite from his last role. It didn't take more than a couple performances until Anthony was moved from understudy into the lead role. "I played a pimp in one of the segments, and I reached into my memory to a guy named Nat, who had once sold me drugs in New York City. Using imagery, I fell into that character and when the scene was over, even the other actors clapped for me. The show lasted three months, with two matinees each week, and there was never an empty seat. I loved it. I loved pretending to be other people, and apparently I was quite believable."

Word had it of a new film in production, and auditions were being held for roles about the Tuskegee Airmen. *Contact 303*'s script was a history of the brave Black men who were crack pilots, who were never given the opportunity to fly the bigger, more prestigious planes. Originally crop dusters, the Black pilots entertained small country families with aerial shows, performing dangerous stunts that wowed and excited the small gathering of fans. The news of their talent spread, and the military offered them a chance to fly during the war, giving them raggedy, outdated planes to practice with. When war finally broke out, every talented man was inducted into the service, and there was a Black unit just for the Tuskegee men. Known as the "Red Tails," they put their skills to work escorting huge bombers entering enemy territory in Europe. The history books agreed on the bravery and the immense courage the pilots demonstrated, flying over a hundred missions and never losing a plane or a life.

Anthony was chomping at the bit to play the role of one of the airmen; it would be his first big break on a nationally released film. The cast read as a who's who in the film industry: Henry Fonda, Chad Everett, and Billy D. Williams, and he wanted to be a part of this history making movie. He scouted army-navy stores, and finally purchased a jumpsuit, reminiscent of the uniforms worn by the original flyers, and submersed his mind into the character.

The audition hall was crammed with Black actors, all patiently waiting to read for the part. An hour into the auditions, they called Anthony's name. They handed him the script; he nervously scanned his lines, and took a deep breath. When given his lines, he remembered the concept of imagery, and dove deeply into the role. Having studied with David Alexander, he had fine-tuned his acting skills through the concepts embodied in psychodrama, which gave him the confidence he needed on the set, in front of world-class actors. The audition used a three camera shoot, so they could observe him from every angle.

Walking onto the stage, Anthony stood silently. The room went pitch black, and then a voice filled the void, the lights slowly came on, and the director yelled out, "Roll it, action," and Anthony read the part. He poured his heart and soul into the part, and when the scene was over it was so quiet, all that could be heard was the sound of the director breathing. Leaving the studio, Anthony stopped for a chili dog on his way home. He hoped he had done enough to land the role.

That afternoon, Merna called with the wonderful news: he had been offered the part. Wildly happy, he jumped for joy; it was a dream come true. This was a principal role; he would be listed on the credits, and this film would serve to springboard his career as a legitimate actor.

Because of the need for large rustic land to film the flying scenes, the studio hired a van and took the actors two hours east, into the desert. One day Tony, the youngest son, was off from school, and convinced his dad to take him to the filming. As they arrived on the set, the eight-year-old's eyes lit up when he spied the planes, the props, and the special effects. Henry Fonda was seated in his specially marked canvas chair, and yelled out, "Whose kid is that?" Tony came flying over to his side, introduced himself, and then was invited to be Mr. Fonda's script boy for the day, something he would never forget. After several weeks on the set, an announcement was made that the producers were shutting down the movie. The studio had a new president, and he didn't want to release the film. Disheartened, the actors collected their last paychecks, walked off the set, and were chauffeured back to Los Angeles.

Merna called, filled with apologies; it was rare that a movie so deep into production was suddenly cancelled, but she promised she would find him another job, as she knew he had the talent and the drive. After hanging up the phone, he was sullen. A part like that came around once in a lifetime; it would have catapulted him into another realm of stardom, but now that dream was shattered. All he could do was do what he did best: sing. A couple of weeks went by and he was surprised he hadn't heard from Merna, who called him often, even if she had nothing to say. She liked to keep in touch. Anxious, Anthony called Merna and was told she was couldn't be reached. A month later he received a call that she had died of cancer.

It was sudden and devastating. As he stood among the large crowd at Woodlawn Cemetery, his tears were shared by many other young actors whose careers she had helped build.

Anthony drove home to his Redondo Beach apartment. "I became severely depressed; I saw my big chance as my only chance. 'What kind of a God are you? Where were you when I needed you?'

"That child in Brooklyn, who had yelled out my name and stopped me from walking into the street and killing myself, was gone. There was no one left who could pick up the pieces of my life. 'Is there anyone out there? God, did you desert me? did you leave me alone in my sorrow?'

"Putting my head down, I cried, and I cried, and I cried, until a puddle of tears had formed on the floor. I took a deep breath, and I felt sudden warmth spread across the back of my neck, and then it caressed me. I stopped crying, and I waited, and listened. In the austere quiet of the apartment, God came to me. I felt him touch me; I felt his presence in the room. 'I love you', God said as his warmth touched my face and my heart.

"I got up and the warmth evaporated, but I felt like a boulder had been lifted off of my heart. A joy filled me and I felt alive and filled with energy. It was okay to begin again, to wash away the sins of my past, and take another path in life; it was okay with God that I start over. Stunned, I walked around the apartment trying to grasp what had just happened, as the sense of complete joy continued.

"Later that afternoon, I had a meeting with my old friend Ken Lasarouth. I got in my car, flipping the station to the latest rock sounds when the voice of a pastor caught my ear. He was pontificating about being born again; that was exactly how I was feeling. Was God trying to speak to me through others? Knocking on Ken's door, I yelled hello, and let myself in. My friend, who always had a stash of the finest variety of marijuana, was sitting on his bed with a bible in his hand. What the hell? 'Ken, what happened to you? You're sitting here reading a bible?'"

"I've changed, Anthony; I've stopped the drugs and I'm clean," he said as he held the bible high in the air. "This is where my inspiration comes from now, not from a toke, or a smoke." In a heavy Jamaican accent, he pontificated about Jesus, how he had seen the light and that Jesus had become his drug of choice. Yes, he still might be handling the goods, but he was no longer partaking. "I'm taking in Jesus' love and living like he says to," Ken said as he put his head down. He began reading passages. Anthony shook his head in utter disbelief and walked back to his car "What's happening? Am I just imagining all of this change? Or is this a sign? Is God trying to tell me something?"

"After an hour or two, I returned home and I saw the bible my mother-in-law had given me laying on the desk. I sat down and grabbed it, and began reading. I didn't know who to talk to, but something happened to me that day that was so right, that was so extraordinary, that I could never explain it. I had turned around; I had clarity of purpose, and a sense of wisdom overcame me. I saw things differently: colors were clearer, my sense of smell and taste more acute, and I heard things more precisely. It was as if my entire mind and body had become finely tuned instrument."

In 1980, the next role Anthony auditioned for and landed the role as the drummer in *The Drummer*, a radical play about Black power. Playing the lead in a theater-in-the-round performance took extra practice, as he had to rehearse his lines to people seated in every direction. The play ran only two weeks to a sold-out audience, but the pay was meager, as was the recognition.

That afternoon he packed up for a trip to Miami. He was playing at the Lighthouse, one of the hottest nightclubs on the beach. This sense of joy sustained him as he performed seamlessly with the musicians. After the show, the requisite visit from the cartel drug lords began with a familiar knock on his hotel room door. Two large Cuban men stood outside, and taking a few furtive glances, entered the singer's room. They gave Anthony the finest cocaine money could buy, and the two men left as quickly and quietly as they had arrived.

He set the drugs at the edge of the table, and instead of tearing open the bag, he held back. "From the bedroom of the hotel room I looked out the window, and saw the moon shining brightly on the water. It was huge and lit up the entire sky. I looked down at the pile of cocaine, and then back at the moon. I stood mute; it was now or never. I had to change my ways. God had provided the sign, he had come to me, and I wasn't going to let him down. I picked up the bag of cocaine. Opened it up, and I flushed the drugs down the toilet. My addiction was gone.

"I looked back at the moon, and a wisp of cloud passed over the center. It looked like the moon was smiling at me. It was at that moment I knew there was a God, and that he had truly embraced me, and he truly loved me. I became at peace with myself, and unafraid of life. I never ever felt another lonely day, and the joy I felt on that day has remained with me ever since. I wondered if there were other people who had this born-again sensation, so I began studying different religions. I couldn't believe I was the only person on earth who had been touched by God."

After Merna died, and acting gigs had whittled down to nothing, he obtained a new booking agent and set back out on the road singing. His agent booked him at a small supper club in South

Carolina, which was a new beginning for the solo artist. The small marquee read "Little Anthony," but the audience had expected The Imperials and they were not happy. A four hundred seat club was only filled with eight-five people. The audience wasn't happy, the club owner wasn't happy, and Anthony sure wasn't happy. To make matters worse, the owner of the club took his photo and placed it in the center of a toilet bowl, a low point in Anthony's career.

After that he did a couple more gigs in the area, none of which were terribly successful, and then he flew up to Detroit. It was a Saturday night in the heart of Motown and his agent had booked him at a supper club, which was just above dive status. The musicians had arrived late minus one horn player, for the sound check, but there was nothing Anthony could do. He would improvise, and pray the music was on the right beat and in the right key. The tiny dressing room had a cracked mirror, cigarette butts littered the cement floor, and two small lights framed the mirror. The men's room was just as dingy and dirty, but for the moment he would overlook all of that and concentrate on the show.

He checked the back of the tuxedo, buttoned his double breasted worsted wool jacket, snapped the heels of his shoes together, and walked confidently onto the stage. The band was ready, and had warmed up the audience with a melody of the classic songs. He grabbed the microphone and began crooning a romantic ballad. The audience, or lack of it, was replete with empty chairs. Groups of people were seated in a haphazard fashion throughout the club, making it appear even emptier that it already was. The waiters were bustling around the floor collecting dirty dishes, tossing them onto huge, overfilled trays, and spilling them loudly into the kitchen sink. The sounds of the ranting chef rang out through the side kitchen doors, as the scantily clad cocktail waitresses pushed more liquor onto the few customers.

Anthony would sing through the mortification and the humiliation. Anthony didn't disappoint; he did his best, but the smattering of applause did little to warm the cockles of his heart. That night there was no encore. Rather he walked back to the dressing room angry, hurt, and filled with disgust. His heart was pounding loudly, and he was filled with frustration and rage. This was not the life he deserved. Things had to change; he would never do another performance in that rat hole again. He punched a hole in the wall and screamed out that he would never return.

Anthony took a taxi to Brooklyn, to do a series of nightclubs, mostly financed through underworld money. The itinerary read The Brown Derby Club in Bay Ridge, Brooklyn, and that was where his taxi was headed. "I knew nothing about the club, other than I was going to get paid for a four- night engagement. The moment the taxi dropped me off, I sensed this wasn't the typical place. The signs of the mob were everywhere.

"When I walked into the entrance I saw the toughest looking guys I had ever run into. They all looked like linebackers for the Pittsburgh Steelers; no one was under three hundred pounds. I was carrying my tux in a garment bag, and I needed a place to change into my costume. A couple of guys pointed to the back until I finally ended up in the kitchen. I could smell the garlic, the large pots of marinara sauce were bubbling on top of the stove. Waiters were running around carrying plates filled with pasta and sauce oozing over the sides. I looked around and there was no dressing room, so I asked one of the cooks where the dressing room was located. 'You dress here,' he said.

"'Here?' I answered, 'But this isn't a dressing room.'

"'Well,' the cook said, 'this is where you get dressed.' I was infuriated and refused to change my clothes in the middle of all that turmoil. I walked out onto the stage and complained bitterly to one of the band members. I told him that I didn't deserve to be treated in such a shabby way. He then told me that Mrs. John Gotti, his mother, was in the house that night, and that she loved my music. Someone must have said something because a few minutes later, two bouncers came up to me and told me that I would have my dressing room.

"They pulled up in a limousine, took me one block west, and handed me the key to a motel room. 'This is where you will dress this week, sir,' said one of the bouncers. 'We will wait for you outside and take you back to the restaurant.' I have to admit, I was really nervous, but sure enough when I was safely returned to the nightclub, and stood beside the band, there was Mrs. Gotti, right in the center table, smiling and applauding each song. The two bouncers, who at first were incredibly tough with me, but then later super kind and polite to me, proved how powerful Mrs. Gotti's influence was.

"I will never forget: a couple of months later, when my wife Linda and I were at an airport, and those same two guys saw me and yelled across the corridors, 'Hey Anthony.' When I looked over and saw who it was, I instantly put my head down and kept walking.

"Curious, Linda asked who those guys were and I said, 'Honey, you don't really want to know. I just kept on walking.

"I realized that I needed to change the act and I remembered a simple phrase a fan had said to me: 'Just go out and sing; close your eye and give it all you got.' I thought about this long and hard, and began looking for someone who could help make that happen. Steve Welch, a brilliant conductor, and creative arranger began to work with me. He had worked with Pat Boone, and understood what I needed to sound good. It was a match made in heaven. I completely changed my act. Back in Los Angles I continued studying with John Zenda, who coached me, introduced me to many professional actors.

"He inspired me and taught me the art of performance singing; it was a completely different ballgame. I bought elegant clothes, and Steve rearranged the music using a full orchestra. I made my act simple and classy. I would walk out on the stage, bow, and then sing songs from the heart. The audience was in awe, and they embraced me back into their hearts again. I did sing 'Tears on My Pillow,' but it had been rearranged for a single voice. My new theme song became 'Cold As Ice.' I was chic, cool, sensual, and in vogue. I became the highest-paid performer.

"My agent rethought, and revamped the venues selecting only the crème de la crème nightclubs, theaters and supper clubs. I toured from Canada down to Mexico City, and my one man shows were sold out. I discovered the difference between recording stars and performance stars, and I became a performance star. Acting helped me add the theatrics I needed to hold the audience's attention. I found out it wasn't so much what I sang, but it was how I sang, and that was what John had taught me how to do."

The one man shows were high energy, filled with contemporary songs that Steve had rearranged to fit his style. Wanting to sing from the heart, Anthony selected only those lyrics that had meaning and were a part of his journey of life. Every song was a separate piece of art, and every song moved the audience. As the months unfolded into years, his performances became legendary. There were other venues that weren't so exclusive, but still fun, and they put Anthony's solo act back into his fan's memories. He toured with Richard Nadar Oldies Show, and Dick Clark's shows which played across the country.

Anthony's manager called with a welcome gig, so it was back to Manhattan for a week run at the Waldorf Astoria, one of the most exclusive hotels in the city. There was a message at the front desk that he had made plans for the afternoon for the following day: they would be going to the races. Smiling, Anthony called his mom; she had a passion for the horse races and given the opportunity, he was going to include her. Anthony's agent knew he was a lover of horses and had arranged the next day to be invited back to the stables to meet Angel Cordero, a famous jokey. In spite of the winter months, the horses ran. Anthony and Elizabeth hopped into a taxi and spent the afternoon betting on the horses. While walking back to the horse filled stables, they met Angel. Elizabeth was most interested in worming out information as to which horse would take home the honors. She would place her bets on his expert choices, but he had little to give. Suffice it to say, they bet on Angel that afternoon, and in that one race, they were winners. Anthony invited Angel to the show the following evening. Angel brought a stunning blonde as his date, although she was foot taller than him.

Opulent was the best description of the Waldorf Hotel, as everywhere one looked, it was decorated luxuriously: red velvet upholstered banquettes anchored the thickly tapestried walls, thousands of tiny crystals hung from chandeliers, mirrors framed in brushed gold hung throughout the hallway entering the elevator bank. The showroom copied the extravagant style, with plush seating, roomy booths, and softly dimmed lighting. The wait staff went through the room silently as they set large glasses filled with the finest alcohol on small marble tables. The only sound in the room came from Anthony's voice as he belted out song after song.

It was a favorite place for performers when they weren't performing, so every night, the room was packed with stars, many of whom came over after the performance to offer congratulations "Redd Foxx was in the house that Friday evening and after my show ended, we walked across the avenue, took the elevator to the Rainbow Room. It was a spectacular view and I was quite impressed.

"It was a lot of fun playing such a diversity of places, and singing to such a wide range of people. One night I would be singing in an exclusive nightclub with a full orchestra, and a couple days later, I would be with the Shirelles.

"One of the most interesting and fun gigs was in Sparks, Nevada, at the biggest casino in the small town. I shared the stage with Siegfried and Roy, the world famous magicians. They had an elephant and made it disappear in front of the audience, but because I was backstage I saw how the trick was done and to this day, I am sworn to secrecy. I have to say that was the one night I knew I had been upstaged by something bigger than me: an elephant!"

CHAPTER 19

Brenda, Linda's twin sister, had insisted on dragging her from Los Angeles to Las Vegas to watch her boyfriend perform at one of the lounge acts on the Strip. "Why don't we just stay home and go to the local bars?" Linda protested. "I really don't want to drive three hundred miles in the heat, for one of your one night stands!"

"Oh, you know he is just more than a one night stand. I really love the guy, and I know he loves me. Besides, he has lots of friends, and you never know who you can meet. Come on, it will be lots of fun," cajoled Brenda. Since Linda had nothing better on her plate that weekend, the twin sisters coordinated their outfits down to the very color of their underwear, filled the tank with gas, and sped across the series of rolling mountains and into the high desert valley. After driving north for a while on the Strip, Brenda slid the dusty car up to the valet at the Sahara Hotel, grabbed the ticket, and the two headed for the lounge. The lines at the Sahara Hotel's theater snaked through the velvet ropes into the labyrinth of slot machines, where customers waited to be seated for the second show of the night. There were two reserved seats in the second row for the second show, seats waiting for the twins.

Leonard, a handsome Black jazz singer, opened the show,

grabbing the microphone and caressing it as he starred directly into Brenda's smiling face. When he turned to cue the band, Brenda nudged her sister. "See, I told you he loves me." That was a fight Linda would lose; she could see the twinkle and longing in her sister's eyes. She knew her sister was in love, and she couldn't help but be a bit jealous. That was one thing the two of them vowed never to share: the love of the same man. From the first time they began dating, sharing a man was taboo; each had to fend for herself, but that didn't mean they wouldn't help the other. So that night, Brenda was determined to make good, and help Linda find a date. Leonard turned his head back around, and broke into a wide smile as his eyes connected with Brenda. She, (actually, they) was the most beautiful woman in the audience. Many other people arched their necks toward the second row, to get a glimpse at the two beauties. Leonard was a back-up singer for the Sonny Turner group. Leonard's sleek dance moves and deep bluesy voice had mesmerized Brenda. and she fell helplessly under his spell. The group took their final bows, and the emcee introduced the next act: Shecky Greene, an insanely funny comedian. After a thirty minute set, the comedian departed the stage with the audience in stitches. When the laughter died down, the emcee announced the headlining act, Little Anthony and The Imperials. Anthony was laughing so hard he was afraid he would blow the opening song. "You knocked them dead again, Shecky. I just sing the same songs, but you come up with a lot racier material for each show. I just hope they pay attention to me, after you just bowled them over."

A loud drumroll jarred the chattering twins as they returned their attention to the stage. With the confidence of a mountain lion, Anthony and The Imperials strutted out, and began an hour of singing, dancing, and telling off-color jokes. Linda never took her eyes off of the lead singer. She was completely mesmerized by his performance, and found herself inexplicably drawn to him. She was sure it was just the music, and the way he moved; what she did know for sure, was as soon as he left the stage, that would be the last she would ever see of him. The stage crew overdid the output of the vapor machine, enveloping the theater with thick air, but in the dim, Anthony saw her seated in the second row. A stunning blonde, she was so beautiful she appeared ethereal, as the haze bounced off her face. Her brown eyes pierced through the air, closing the distance between the two. It was as if he were singing to one person, a person whose name he didn't know. "Please Say You Want Me" came to mind and he turned to his music director to cue up the song, not included in that night's play list. Looking directly at the stranger, he sang as if it were the last song he would ever sing, and when he finished, she was so overcome with emotion that tears were streaming down her face. Taking her hand, Brenda led her sister backstage where Leonard smothered Brenda with kisses. He then turned to Linda and began to laugh, "I sure hope I kissed the right sister!" Annoyed, Linda hardly took that as a compliment. Shouldn't he be able to detect the difference between the two, or did all white women appear the same to him?

"Leonard Beal knocked on my dressing room, and introduced me to his latest squeeze, Brenda. She had a twin sister, and suggested we all go out for a drink. When he presented Linda, my heart stopped cold: she was that outrageously elusive woman in the second row. I was drawn to her like every other chick I had met, thinking this was just another notch on my bedpost. Up close, she was even more beautiful than when our eyes first met, with long flowing blond hair, a voluptuous shape, and an endless pair of legs. She was about as perfect as perfect gets."

"Where would you like to go sweetie?" asked Leonard. "Oh yes, and Anthony asked if he could come along with us tonight. Is that okay with you, Linda?" She was pleasantly surprised that The Anthony would want to be with her. Before she could answer, he held out his arm, she laced her arm through his, and off they went.

"Now that our dates are settled, let's go have some fun," announced Leonard, who knew the Strip like the back of his hand. Starting at a street level lounge, they grabbed some drinks, talked, and then took a cab to the top floor of an in vogue nightclub, where bottle service started at five hundred bucks. But neither Leonard nor Anthony paid the entrance fee; quite the contrary. Since they were stars, the clubs welcomed them with open arms. After stepping into the mirrored private elevator, they got off at roof level, which provided a panoramic view of the entire city. It was breathtaking. Selecting a small table near the edge of the window, the guys ordered drinks and a few appetizers, and then snagged the women and headed for the dance floor. It was near dawn when the twins were dropped off at their hotel room, and after several kisses, their dates departed, promising to call in the morning. The twins shed their shoes and cocktail dresses, and fell into a deep sleep.

Brenda picked up the phone. It was Leonard on the other end, and from the hour on the clock, the girls had slept through the morning. "Sweetie, it's late, and we working girls; we have to get back to Los Angeles. I'll catch you next weekend," she said tossing the phone aside. Shoving her sister, Brenda announced the afternoon had arrived and it was time to head home. Like Cinderella, they had to be back in their beds before midnight. Monday, they both had to rise early for their jobs. Filling the car with gas, they took turns driving west as fast as the sedan and speed limit would allow. "That Anthony is quite the gentleman, and to tell you the truth, I can't stop thinking about him. He is so handsome, talented, kind and…"

"Well now, from where I sit, it sounds like you have a crush on this guy," said Brenda.

"Do you think it odd or strange that I would fall for a Black man? What do you think our parents would say? But then, you seem to be in love with Leonard, and his color doesn't bother you."

"I love Leonard, I love everything about him. He could be green or pink, for all I care, I love him, his mind, his heart, his soul, and his fine body. So don't think I am one to judge who you fall in love with."

Linda thought about this long and hard, but wondered if Anthony would ever call her again. She had to do something that would capture his attention, something other girls wouldn't do. When she got home she sat down and composed a long letter thanking him for the evening, trying to lay the groundwork for future dates. She dropped it in the mail, and was hopeful he would respond. It was Thursday afternoon when Brenda announced she was headed back to Sin City, and Linda had yet to hear a word from Anthony. "Nah, you go by yourself, I'll stay home and play some golf and tennis, and keep completely sober," she moaned. The ringing phone startled Linda. She bounced over the lounge chair and smiled when she heard Anthony's voice on the other end. "Two weeks had passed, and although Linda was on my mind, other women had taken her place in my bed. Upon opening the mailbox, I saw a letter from Linda, and thought, 'How odd.' No woman had ever written me a letter thanking me for the time we had together. It was filled with respect and an admiration of my talent, and she asked to see me again. Curious, I called her and we made a date for dinner that weekend."

"I just got your letter today and was amazed that you would

actually send me a letter. Listen, Leonard told me Brenda's returning for the weekend; can you please spend Saturday with me? I would like to get to know you. I have to admit you are quite different from anyone else. What do you say?" At this early juncture in their relationship she wasn't sure how to play this thing out. Should she go, or should she stay home and mope, or should she play hard-to-get, or jump at the chance to be with him? The choice seemed obvious to her: "I'll see you Saturday, but how about some quiet time?"

"Then quiet time it shall be," Anthony responded as they both gently hung up the phones in great anticipation of their first official date.

"Do you think Leonard cheats on you?" asked Linda, as the car sped over miles of desert highway.

"I told you, we love each other, and I trust him. I know there are always women around him, tempting him, calling and pursuing him, because of who he is and what he does, but I believe in him. Without trust, our relationship wouldn't last another day. It is possible to have a relationship with an entertainer; a good relationship, and an honest one, it just takes a little extra work and a whole lot of faith."

Linda pondered this as she pulled the sedan into a motel a half block from the Strip. Cheaper and not as luxurious as the one the weekend before, it would do for their two night stay. They changed into matching red cocktail dresses, and walked ten minutes to the Sahara lounge. Sitting in the same reserved seats as the week before, second row, stage left, they anxiously waited for the performance to begin. When Anthony spied Linda in her brilliant dress, a smile crossed his face and he sang one of the ballads to her.

The girls joined their guys at the dressing rooms but after, they split in different directions: Brenda and Leonard went to an after-hours party, while Linda and Anthony went out for a quiet romantic dinner.

"Her beauty took my breath away; she was intoxicating, and I wanted her, but that night she turned me down. She wanted us to really get to know each other. Although she had been to my show, she hadn't a clue who I was, and the impact my group had upon the music industry. She just loved my music, and took me for what I was: a simple human being. After our last kiss that night, I began to take the relationship seriously. I was falling in love, and didn't want to lose her." Relating his story and his passions, Anthony unabashedly told Linda about his life, and after several patient hours, she told a portion of her story. By the end of the date, a genuine meeting of the minds had taken place. They understood each other, and found out they wanted the same things. Anthony was in the final moments of his second marriage to Judy, and the divorce was almost finalized. He wasn't about to hide this from Linda. She was too sweet and too caring for him to sustain a lie. He laid all his cards on the table, and Linda willingly picked them up. She accepted him, his flaws, his talents, but most of all, his sterling heart and his ability to foster a love of such depth that nothing could undo it. That was the love she was seeking, and that was the love he offered. When he kissed her good night, the king of sex never even tried to enter her hotel room. There would be plenty of that in the future. For the moment, he had to win her trust and her heart.

He had to come up with something, since he didn't want to be without her. "How about a game of tennis tomorrow morning?" he suggested. Surprised, she agreed to meet in the hotel lobby at eight in the morning, which gave them three hours of sleep. After taking a quick shower, she closed her eyes for a catnap, and dreamed about this unusual man she was falling in love with. In the morning, when the elevator doors opened, she saw that he was standing in the corner of the lobby with his eyes pointed in her direction. Dressed in shorts and a white polo tee, he was ready for a romp on the local courts. Linda laughed at his boney knees. It was the first time she had seen them – he was always dressed for a night on the town. Strolling onto an empty court, they spent the morning batting the bright yellow tennis balls back and forth, until he was exhausted. Anthony wasn't ready to say good-bye so he suggested a movie and later that afternoon they saw *The Towering Inferno*, which was not one of those romantic date movies, but nonetheless, they had a great time. Back at her hotel, they kissed good-bye, and she disappeared into the elevator, leaving him wondering when he would ever see her again.

Linda was as naïve as she was beautiful, and had a wholesomeness he had never witnessed in other women. When he dropped her off at the hotel, he made a promise to call, and then kissed her longingly. "You aren't like any of the other girls I date. I see something special in you, and I want to see you again. Can you come back next weekend?" Giggling, she said she would wait for his call.

When she opened the hotel room, Brenda was in tears; she and Leonard had split and she was beside herself. "He cheated, just like all those other singers. They all cheat." Linda felt her blood run cold; just as she was discovering a new love, her twin was bailing out of a relationship. Linda feared this was the way it would end for her. Their trip home to California was filled with extremes: Linda was falling in love, and Brenda was falling out of love. "I promise, I will help you find someone," said Linda. "I owe you for fixing me up with Anthony, and words can't express how much I love that man. It's like we were meant to be. I love everything about him."

"Yes, just wait until he cheats," said Brenda, "and then you won't feel the same way." Linda refused to allow that statement to get the best of her. She believed in Anthony, so she just let it slide. Her next project was to find a nice fit for her sister. Considering all the men that Anthony knew, that shouldn't be such a tall task. She would ask him the next time they spoke.

"The following week, I had a short gig, and then I was going to meet up with my kids in Florida and fly them with me to the Bahamas. I probably shouldn't have, but I asked Linda to meet me and my two kids in Florida. When we picked up Liza and Tony at the airport, they were surprised and not too happy that I was with another woman, but by the time the trip had ended, they had fallen in love with her. She was patient, kind, understanding, with natural motherly instincts. Perhaps because she was a teacher and truly loved kids, my own children sensed this, and warmed up to her immediately." They spent a couple of days walking the beaches, enjoying the fresh air, playing tennis, and swimming in the ocean. They had two adjoining rooms, and Linda showed Tony and Liza how to knock on the interior door if they needed anything, and she made sure they were safely tucked into their beds at night before cozying up with her lover. "Kids come first," she said as Anthony nodded his head, waiting impatiently for her to lie beside him. Satisfied the children were safe, and the windows locked and shuttered, she closed the door, turned, and smiled as she crawled into the king size bed.

He put his arm around her and felt unusually content. He had a woman that he loved, and two perfect children in the next room. Could it be that he was finally growing up? That the pure sense of parenthood, and emulating an ideal husband, was something he could finally aspire to becoming? Looking at Linda, with her deep inner beauty, he decided that maybe she had cast a spell on him, and had thrown a hex on his womanizing days. Maybe she was just the one he had been searching for his entire life? Shrugging his shoulders, he held her tightly. He was not about to let this woman get away.

The light breezes from the ocean floated gently through the room, billowing the thin curtains. It was as if the island were enchanted, imbued with a sense of calm and serenity that carried to its visitors. It was more than just the weather and the beauty of the islands that attracted vacationers, it was the sense of total relaxation, and the chance to let the mind rest. With Linda in his arms, he had finally found nirvana.

When they returned, Anthony made a big decision: longing for California and the potential acting jobs, he pulled up roots from Las Vegas, and they rented an apartment in Redondo Beach. It was sheer heaven as the couple bound their lives together. She spent each day teaching her young students, and he ran around town auditioning and continuing music gigs. After several months of bliss, Linda announced she was pregnant, and although Anthony was happy, he had never divorced Judy. Linda never asked for anything, but her wholesome values, combined with his church upbringing, directed Anthony into the proper decision. He obtained a lawyer, and finally Judy and he were officially over. She kept the house, but she was more than willing to share custody of the children. Judy wasn't bitter, and she knew the kids loved him. She wasn't about to hold her children hostage to get back at their dad for his bad behavior. She was better than that.

After a year of living with Anthony, and lying to her parents, telling them she was living with her twin sister, Linda decided to face her mom and dad with the truth. "I want you to meet my parents. I think it's time, and I promise they won't bite," announced Linda. They arranged for a mid-week dinner, and Linda extracted a promise that her dad would be civil. When the couple arrived, Anthony noticed that the smells from the kitchen were much different from the Gourdine household: less potent, heralding a lighter fare filled with fresh vegetables, no red meat, and the scent of freshly picked flowers.

Linda had ceased drinking the moment she guessed she was pregnant, and Anthony wanted all his senses clear for this tension filled evening, so for the moment, he refrained from alcohol, which was a good thing, since neither of her parents drank. Anthony understood her father's point of view, and he was there to defend his love for their daughter, which would take all his concentration. One word said the wrong way could spark an explosion of hate, so he remained as quiet as he could, which for him was a feat in itself. The women went to the kitchen, leaving the men alone in the den.

Anthony nervously sat in the contemporary southern California home: a world famous singing star sat nose-to-nose with Linda's fuming dad. Had the tables been turned and it was his own daughter, pregnant, coming to meet him for the first time, Anthony would have already had his gun polished, locked, and loaded. He had to give her father some space and a whole lot of time for all of this to be digested. If her parents would accept him at first glance, then he would be as naïve as they would be disingenuous.

"I understand how none of this situation is acceptable to you, but know that I truly love your daughter and I will always take care of her. I get that it's hard for you to take me into your family, but I do love her."

"No, you haven't a clue," her dad retorted, "I've spent my entire life taking care of my wife and four daughters and I'm not giving my blessing to a marriage that is sure to end in a bucketful of tears. You entertainers are all alike, jumping from bed to bed, and I don't want Linda's heart to be broken. Look around you, son. We are a conservative family raised in the Deep South, and one of my daughters marrying a Black man, even in this day and age, is damn hard for me to swallow. How will it be for your kids? Your family, your friends? Have you really thought this thing through?

"When it comes right down to it, it's not the color of your skin that grates me, it's what you do. With all those women constantly after you, and being on the road, I don't see how you could possibly remain faithful. I can picture Linda surprising you at a concert, and finding you with another woman. All I see is her heart being broken. I didn't raise my girls, love them and sacrifice for them, to see a guy come along and destroy all that their mom and I struggled to make good. So no, you don't get it!" Flipping on the television set, he turned his head away, and remained close to mute the rest of the very long evening.

Shaken, Anthony got up and strolled to the backyard. A pitcher of sweet ice tea sat on the table and he helped himself to a large glass and starred into space. "You're pregnant, aren't you?" quizzed her mother. A tear dripped down Linda's face, verifying her mom's intuition, and then her mother hugged her tightly. "It will all work out, it always does. And if you two love each other as much as you say you do, then it's a marriage made in heaven."

Linda's mom was forgiving, but not convinced this would be any kind of a real relationship. True, Anthony's track record was poor, and he had a lot to live down, but Linda was so different from anyone. It was more than love, it was true companionship. They did everything from making love to playing softball. He had found a woman who actually shared his passion for sports. Not only did she teach gym, but she coached girls' softball and zealously enjoyed the outdoor life. All those attributes bonded their love, but wouldn't prove enough of an argument to sway Linda's dad. He just shook his head incredulously, remaining civil while he waited for the meal.

Linda and her mom joined Anthony outside, and from the look on his face, it was obvious he had been beaten down. "He got to you," said her mom. "That doesn't surprise me. He is a tough guy, and when it comes to his girls, he is overly protective. I doubt I can change his mind, but I will tell you who can: the two of you. Given some time, he will eventually see the light. He has tunnel vision, and all he can see is Linda getting hurt somewhere along the road. Anthony, prove him wrong. If you love each other, it will work out, and one day he will finally give in, and accept you. Right now, all he sees is an impossible future with so many hurdles, that you have lost before you begin. Prove him wrong, make this marriage last." She put her arms around Anthony and cried.

"Dinner is ready; please, everyone, let's sit down." She filled three crystal glasses with healthy portions of iced tea and then raised her glass. "We have a lot to celebrate," she announced. "We are about to become grandparents!" With tears running down her cheeks she kissed her daughter and Anthony. The dad, shocked by the announcement, vehemently returned his untouched glass to the table.

"You're pregnant? I should've guessed. That's all you musicians know how to do, jump from bed to bed. You took advantage of my daughter, my love, my child, the apple of my eye. How could you? Get the hell out of my home!" he screamed. Linda looked pleadingly into her mother's eyes, as the three of them shed tears of remorse. As the couple left, they heard her dad yelling out that he wouldn't be there for the wedding. Linda's once jubilant mood had turned deeply melancholy. "Gosh, that went well," Anthony snickered. Turning to her, he took her trembling hand and said, "I'll make you a promise that one day your dad will like me." On the drive home, there was nothing he could say or do that would make things better. Her father would never give his blessing to their marriage. "Time, just give it some time, eventually he'll come around. You and I both know that my first couple of marriages didn't last, and right now he is probably worrying that I will hurt you, or leave you; or worse, cheat on you. I love you, and you will just have to trust me."

"My dad is overly protective. With four girls in the household, almost all I remember him doing was work, there were a lot of mouths to feed, and we were all ambitious and needy. I was the only athlete among my sisters, and some of the rare time my dad spent with me was coming to my softball games. I know he would've loved a son, but I was the closest he got. The rare times he came to see me play really made me feel special. He didn't go to my high school or college graduation, yet he would show up at my ballgames. I guess that was what was meaningful to him.

"I know he loved us, he was so reserved; he hardly ever kissed or hugged us. As we all sat around the dinner table, he would say little; he would just listen, and when a decision was to be made, he would finally speak. He was quiet, maybe a little too distant, but that was how he coped with life. In so many ways, you are the opposite of my dad, and for that I am grateful. Being afraid to show love, or to voice your thoughts, is not how I see our marriage. Frankly, I don't see how we will ever run out of conversation," she said.

When Anthony got word from his attorney the divorce was final, he purchased a sparkling diamond engagement ring, and planned a romantic evening. He was going to make their relationship official. The past several months were the happiest he had ever spent. The love they shared each day made his life full and complete. She really did make him a better person, he knew that, and he knew he never wanted that feeling to leave. The restaurant was a block off the beach overlooking the ocean. The sun was drifting into the horizon, and the ocean breezes calm and soothing. He ordered two sodas, gazed into her piercing eyes, gathered the love churning inside his heart, and asked her to marry him. The tears of joy spilling down her cheeks was the answer he had hoped for, and she leaned across the table to kiss him soundly on the lips. "I love you, and I shall love you forever. You are the only woman I will ever need." As he slipped the ring onto her finger, she was overcome with happiness. "I love you too, and I know we will be together forever," she said, staring down at the ring, "It's beautiful, just like you."

Coming from a family of five children, Linda had the philosophy that hard work and sacrifice will see you to your goals. What little the family had was shared among the siblings, so Linda wore a lot of hand-me-downs. She was low maintenance, and her needs were modest. She asked for nothing, having learned at a very early age to make do with what she had; and for what she had, she was grateful. Her father was a redneck in the true sense of his ideologies while her mother was open-minded and open-hearted. When Linda broke the news to her mom that Anthony had made it official, had given her a ring, her father was livid. But her mother came to love him, and embraced him into the family.

They were married in Culver City at a small rec room at the Rain Tree Apartments. Both mothers attended the wedding, while her father stood his ground by boycotting the marriage. Walking down the aisle in a simple gown, Linda glowed radiantly as she took Anthony's hand, and they exchanged vows. They toasted by drinking sodas, and when their son was born shortly after, they all shared the same last name. Linda delivered Casey on New Year's Day in 1977, but things went wrong, and he was in an incubator for two long weeks before the newly married couple could bring the baby home. They doted on him, and proceeded to have two more sons: Damon in 1978, and Daniel in 1980. They wanted a girl and they eventually adopted a precious infant, Sarah, born in 1982. The family was complete: four children and a matched set of loving parents.

"We met Sarah when she was three months old, through a California state adoption agency. Five months later, Linda and I returned to the agency and picked up our baby girl, all wrapped up in a pink blanket."

Sarah became immersed in the household, loved and treated the same as the three boys. Her only distinguishing characteristic was that she was a girl, fascinated by dolls and dresses. As Sarah's life became part of the family routine, there never seemed to be the right time or place to broach the topic of adoption, and for years, they completely avoided the topic, failing to realize that Sarah would eventually find out; it had escaped Linda and Anthony's minds. The problem was that they had three other sons, who, somewhere along the way, unleashed the secret on their sister. Young and perhaps afraid, she harbored this secret, never acknowledging that she was aware of the fact that she was adopted. But what she questioned was why her parents had kept this a secret: if all the boys knew, and her parents knew, why didn't they tell her?

"Regret is my response to my little girl. I talk about redemption, and this was another notch on that ladder to changing my life, and putting everything in order. Time escaped us and we simply never brought up the subject, and apparently we were naïve to think that our three sons would hold the secret. If we didn't see any difference in our love for Sarah, then why should they? As the years progressed, she had behavior problems; she began acting out, and things at home began to get stressful. Instead of confiding in Linda and me, Sarah became attached to Casey, the oldest brother. She absolutely worshipped the ground he walked on and when he began modeling, she hung a huge poster of him on her wall.

"Finally when she was twelve, Linda and I sat our daughter down and explained that we picked her because we loved her. She was as much part of our family as any of our three sons. Looking back on this, I know we waited too long, and that we should have had this conversation years ago. Parents make mistakes and this was a big one. Had we realized this was bothering our daughter, that it worried her, we would have told her much earlier. Having kids is hard and adding the word adoption into the mix just made it harder."

Having such a large brood, they began searching for the perfect home, and found a large ranch house in Palos Verdes on five sprawling acres. It was an idyllic place to raise a family. The empty barn was later filled with two horses, Tag and Willow, and the kids spent every free minute riding and playing with the horses.

"I became a cowboy, taking care of the horses; that was a brand-new experience for me. It was fun, but a lot of work. I had no idea how much money and time it took to keep horses healthy and alive. I found out the hard way that I had to maintain the gates, or the horses would get out. One day, I got a call from the sheriff that one of my horses was walking downtown in the middle of the street. Tag had chewed through the gate, and let himself out. I started running down the yard, into the street, and yelling out 'Tag, Tag, come home baby.' But the horse was stubborn, and ignored my calls so I just kept running until I finally caught up to him. I reached up and pulled the hair on his mane, which slowed him down, and then I whispered, 'Tag, please come home.' The horse turned his head, propped up his ears, and then slowly followed my lead back to the barn. A couple of years later, when the kids grew to be teens, and were no longer interested in the horses, I sold them to a real cowboy, who really knew how to take care of them."

When Anthony wasn't playing cowboy, Linda would throw on a pair of boots, and take the kids hiking on the long walking trails carved throughout the rolling hills, or down to the pool for a refreshing dip. There was never any lack of things to do. She encouraged the kids to enjoy the outdoors, and as the boys got older, they picked up these cues rigorously.

"There were times when Anthony was on the road a lot, but it didn't bother me," admitted Linda. "Somehow things always seemed to work out. I kept busy with our four kids, my job, and running the household. Anthony is a family man, and family always was (and still is) his priority. We never pushed the children to become singers, because although we were able to demonstrate to them the glamorous side of the business, getting to that place isn't so glamorous.

"I remember one Christmas I bought Casey a set of drums. He was only five years old, but I guess I wanted to test out Anthony's genes. Casey was banging away and the noise was so bad that Anthony made me take them back. I think he had no patience, but mostly, he couldn't stand the discord; if music was to be played, it had to be good."

That same Christmas, Anthony had arranged for Linda's mom to watch the children. He was giving his wife a proper honeymoon: they were going to Hawaii. "When we landed in Oahu, I was wiser, older, and very much in love with my wife. It seemed natural to do things the right way. We were staying in a condo, overlooking the ocean, and it was as beautiful as the first time I came to the resort. It was just me and Linda, and it was all I needed. I took her everywhere, and when I met old friends, she was by my side. I felt so wonderful sharing all this beauty with my wife, giving her a little piece of what I had experienced years earlier. This spirit inside me wanted to do right by her. I had screwed up really badly with Judy, and I felt guilty for all the heartache I had caused her, and I wasn't about to repeat that with Linda. I loved her so much, I wanted her to be as happy as I was.

"Peggy Lee's "Is That All There Is" became my theme song, reminding me each day, how precious love is, and how I would never destroy the love Linda and I shared together. I would never be that callous man, nor would I ever disrespect the mother of my children. I didn't feel the need to run around in the evenings, drinking, toking, taking drugs, or smoking. Those days had ended when I felt God's presence at my first Redondo Beach apartment. His love had guided me to find Linda, whose was a sacred love that I cherished. I was content to sit on the balcony, hold her tightly, and watch the sunsets. I thanked God that He had brought me such love, and I made a promise: that I would never take her for granted, or do anything that would hurt her, ever."

CHAPTER 20

Linda's twin sister, Brenda, had a beautiful blonde daughter, who had caught the acting bug at an early age. She was singing, dancing, and acting and Linda's kids wanted to do the same. They begged their parents for a chance to delve into the business, so Linda signed Casey, Damon, Daniel, and Sarah with Century Artists agency. After the requisite tryouts, when the ink was barely dry on the contracts, the kids were summoned to endless gigs. They played parts in a plethora of television movies, commercials, and screenplays.

"The children absolutely loved the work. I think, in large part, it was to make their father proud. In the early morning, the phone would ring, requesting one or more of the kids to sets. I would call the school, explain their absence, and off we would go. Anthony purchased one of those huge vans so the kids could ride in comfort and not be bored. There was room for games, space to change their clothes, and even a small video that played cartoons and movies. When we arrived on the sets, there was always a teacher who would tutor them in between scenes. Because of their age, I had to remain on the sets, but it was fun watching the other actors, the stage crew, and the director producing shows that would be seen by millions.

"I remember one morning waking Daniel up early for his part as a peanut on an AT&T ad. He turned to me and said, 'Work, work, work, that's all I do.' I laughed, because I knew he loved his jobs, loved the work, and loved being around the sets. When Anthony would return from his gigs, he would take the kids, and I would return to my classes. I have to admit, my principal was more than understanding and generous; our kids always came first and she respected that.

"We discovered a secret to keeping the kids in line and out of the drug scene: we kept them constantly busy. If they weren't acting, then they were playing soccer, competing in gymnastics, tennis, baseball, track, and football. There was always something being tossed around the backyard and the house was always filled with the neighbor's kids," said Linda. Between Linda's career as a gym teacher and Anthony's passion for sports, all three boys actively participated in high school sports, and all shared a passion for football. Often on the road, Anthony often missed games, but when he could arrange it, as soon as the plane would touch the earth, if one of the kids was playing that day, he would make that his first stop. In high school, each boy joined a team, and each played throughout the school year. From fall football through spring baseball, there was always some practice or game to attend. Linda's calendar was so filled with her kid's activities, she often felt like she needed a clone, especially when two separate games collided at the same time. She was always in a quandary as to which to go to. Had Anthony been home, the problem would have been easily resolved, with each parent going separately to the games, but him being home was rare. Sometimes Linda became so frustrated trying to be fair and equal with all her kids that she would flip a coin to decide which event to attend. The love and passion continued for all three sons, as one by one each entered college at San Diego State University.

The excitement of watching their kids play football at the college level was much different than high school. It was a happening, complete with tailgate parties, bouncing cheerleaders, marching bands, and fantastic halftime shows. Anthony recalled, "I was asked to sing the national anthem at one of the home games, and I was very honored. There I was, with my son on the field dressed in uniform, holding his helmet underneath his arm, while I sang. I don't think I ever experienced a more profoundly proud moment."

Life continued for the Gourdines on a celestial plateau. Money was flooding their bank accounts as he worked on the road, and the music continued selling. That joyful revelation he had experienced in Redondo Beach rested complacently inside his heart and soul. He never bedded another woman, and he never took another drug. But as the years progressed, business did begin to slow down, and they eventually sold the ranch and moved to smaller quarters. Linda never complained. She had everything in the world she ever wanted: Anthony's love and four exuberant children. Leaving a big home for a smaller one didn't faze her in the least.

They packed up the last of the baseball equipment, and then quickly unpacked it in another comfortable home, settling on a smaller piece of property. Although Anthony would never admit it to his kids, he was sick and tired of taking care of those horses, and at the new home, he was thankful that the only large space was the garage. His Brooklyn roots held no love for farming and ranching. He was, at heart, a city-slicker.

Anthony's agent was always barraged with phone calls for an acting job here or there, a music gig in town or on the road, but when religious leaders found out about Anthony's revelation, he was called upon to give testament to his story, to tell the world that God truly touched us and lived within us. "I was invited on TBN, Pat Robert's show, and various other Christian ministry shows to talk about my meeting with God. When I would walk on the stage, people would look: is that Anthony the singer? If he could become one with God, then maybe I could. I would tell the congregation my story, and they would listen, and believe. They had faith, and believed every word. I remembered my Aunt Bessie telling me I should become a preacher, and there I was, in front of a vast audience, telling them how I embraced God. It was surreal. When I said the words, I couldn't believe they were coming from my mouth."

Trinity Broadcasting Network, owned by Paul and Jan Crouch, also invited Anthony to come onto their program and give his testimonial. But when their guest appeared, what poured from his mouth was not exactly what the Christian station anticipated he would be saying, and it sure wasn't what the word of their God would have wanted him to admit. Anthony, dressed in his Sunday best, was escorted to a state of the art dressing room, with plenty of make-up and hairstylists, to insure his person was as perfect as it could be when he spoke to millions of people around the globe. His pants were sharply pressed, his shoes shiny, and his white shirt pristine. He was ready, willing, and eager to help spread the word of God, but Anthony would do it his way.

After a warm round of applause, Paul handed his guest the microphone, and stood off to the side of where Anthony's epiphany would be unfolded. "I know people talk about drugs, but I have to tell you, I can't lie, I had a great time sinning. It was fun getting high, and tripping to places I could only get to on those drugs. Getting stoned before a show, now that was not only fun, but challenging, as I sang my way through the evening. Afterwards, we would all continue partying until early in the morning. There wasn't a drug I didn't try. Yes, at the time it was a hell of a lot of fun. I thought I was invincible, that nothing I did, smoked, or ingested could harm me. But here I stand today, God showed me the light."

Anthony was sitting in the reception room with the other patrons when two huge bodyguards quickly escorted him to the executive office. Unbeknownst to Anthony, the phones of the ministry had begun ringing off the hook, and people were calling in, praising the mutinous confession. He cooled his heels while seated in a huge leather chair until one of the head honchos of the studio took a seat on the other side of the desk. He felt like a little kid who had been summoned to the principal's office for bad behavior. Apparently, the viewers had responded in an unprecedented manner, and instead of throwing Anthony's admissions to the lions, they found his truths refreshing, real, and honest. "They loved me so much, I was invited back on three different occasions. They told me I was refreshing; I guess the wages of sin sit differently for those who make a living on television ratings."

Shortly after those revelations, Anthony's faith would be tested time and again, by the deaths of family members. In the early 1980s, he lost his dad, his brothers Elliot, Sonny, and Donald, several aunts, and finally his mother, Elizabeth. It seemed as though all he was doing was flying across the country to attend funerals and sob at wakes. "In 1980, my brother Elliot died of alcoholism; he was only in his early forties. I used to drive my car up to the top of the Palos Verde and cry out, 'My brother is dead,' and then I would walk back to the car and drive home. His passing broke my heart and sapped the energy from my soul; and then a year later, Donald, my brother, died of heroin addiction. Two years later my dad died, followed by Aunt Shortie; in 1987, Sonny, my oldest brother, died of an enlarged heart. "Sonny was a tough guy from the streets, but he carried his problems so deeply that he was unable to cope. He joined the army, worked his way up to Staff Sergeant, but his eyesight was poor so he left the service. When he returned home he was unhappy and couldn't focus; there was a disconnect that took him years to comprehend. Although Thomas had raised Sonny as his own son, there was an underlying subtle resentment; raising a child that he had not fathered sometimes waved its ugly head in the form of undue punishments, and Sonny sensed this resentment. I believed that Sonny died before he had the chance to come to terms with Dad's feelings.

"The decade of death ended in 1990 when my mother passed away."

"I'll never forget: I was on the plane coming back from New York, and Steve Welch, an old friend and conductor, was also on the plane. We shared the trip across the country together. During an uneventful ride, we talked about the business, our families, and about how many times I had made this long trip. So many problems with my family: sickness, and too many deaths.

"While I was in the middle of humming a new melody, the captain's voice came over the speaker, explaining that the hydraulics for the flaps had failed, and that we should all prepare for a crash landing. Steve and I looked at each other, and noticed an immediate mood change in the cabin: the air was tense.

"I dropped my head: "Lord, whatever it is, I'm at peace with it." The pilot's voice was calm as he explained he was three years short of retirement and he had been flying these big DC 10s for a long time. 'I'm not going to lose this plane, or anyone inside it; we are going to get down safely. Please listen to your crew, while I and my co-pilot get this bird out of the sky.' Steve's head hung down too while we both waited for the imminent crash.

"We could see the runway lined with emergency vehicles, fire trucks, and piles of foam. Less than a minute before we hit the tarmac, the flaps miraculously opened up, and we landed without a scratch. Everyone was clapping and cheering and when we left the plane, the pilot stood by the door, so we shook his hand and thanked him for keeping his promise. I was in no hurry to get back on a plane for a while, didn't want to tempt God's blessing."

"Anthony, I would like you and your family to come for dinner," Elizabeth weakly requested. "Just one last time, let's have the family all together and I will make your favorite foods." Anthony gathered his brood and flew into La Guardia. They stayed at the closest hotel to the projects. Anthony's family was way too big to squeeze into the modest apartment he had grown up in, and they didn't want to overwhelm Elizabeth with so many young boys running around. When Anthony's mom opened up the front door, he was shocked by her face: she had aged. With her body slightly slumped and her demeanor lacking that once jubilant posture it was clear she was unwell, and at that moment, he realized why she had summoned him.

Linda knew immediately that Elizabeth was sick, and had quickly picked up on the purpose for this visit, so she hugged her mother-in-law, told her sons to behave, hung up her jacket, and began helping in the kitchen. The intoxicating smells of soul food permeated the air, taking Anthony back to happier times when his father and all of his brothers sat around the dining table telling jokes, laughing and enjoying being together.

"Dad, your home is so small," remarked Casey. "Son, when you are young, everything looks so big, but you're right, now it all looks so small. I don't know how Ma could've have made all those meals in such a tiny kitchen, but we made do." As platter after platter of food was placed on the dining table, the family grabbed plates, and sat in every seat available in the apartment. There were porgies, ribs, coleslaw, macaroni and cheese, collard greens, roasted ham, and fried tomatoes, all Southern favorites. Every inch of the home was filled with chatter, laughter, reminiscing, and love; they all sensed why they had come together, and they were determined to fill the home with joy, if only for one more time. Linda was definitely the odd woman out, being the only white person in the room, but she didn't care – the thought never crossed her mind. Family was all that mattered to her, and boy, did she find that with the Gourdines.

Elizabeth leaned over and told her youngest son, "She's (Linda) got it," which translated to, Linda was the right person for her son. Taking Linda's hand, she led her to her bedroom, sat her down, and began pulling out boxes, packages, and envelopes. "I want you to know where everything is so when I die, all of it will fall into the right hands. I sense that you have a deep love for my son, and I also sense that the two of you will last until God's will set you apart."

After making a full explanation, Elizabeth returned all the items back to their original places, making sure that Linda kept track of her future inheritance. Clinging tightly to Linda, Elizabeth extracted a promise that when the time came, Linda would make sure everything would be properly taken care of, since Anthony would be too emotional to handle such matters. "Hell, he was devastated when he found out that Thomas was Santa Claus, how do you think he is going to handle my death?" she joked.

When his mother reappeared in the hallway, Anthony went over, hugged her, and bemoaned the fact that he never purchased his mom a real home. He was sorry, and asked her to forgive him. "Forgive you – are you nuts?!" she said. "For all those wonderful times you gave me and Thomas I am forever grateful. The trips to Puerto Rico, to Los Angeles, Las Vegas, and Aruba, I would have done none of that without you. I love you, and all I ever wanted was your love in return, not material things. You have given me more love than any mother could hope to have. I know your life wasn't perfect, and your dad and I mopped up many of your mistakes, but that's part of being a parent. Our love for you and your brothers has been unconditional. You were born out of love, and we lived our lives to share that love. From where I stand, I think it has all worked out very well. So, no, you don't need to fret about a big old house that I never wanted. I'm fine just the way things are." She hugged and kissed him, drying a few sentimental tears that were running down her face. Six months later, it didn't come as a shock to Linda when a cousin called to tell her Elizabeth had passed away. The couple took plane, and Anthony made a solemn promise: it was his last flight to go to a family funeral. He had cried so many tears that he had run dry. With his mother's death, he needed to take back his life. With every death, a part of him ended up in the grave, and now with his mom in her final resting place, it was time for Anthony to pull himself out of all those graves and give himself solely to the living. He became the patriarch of the family, and the engine that would keep the Gourdine name flourishing.

"The decade of death left me feeling very strange and one day I decided to go to a Christian psychologist. He sat me down, listened to the tale of my entire family extinguishing within a short period of time and then handed over some simple advice.

"'Did you ever just cry?' he asked.

"As I sat there, I thought about that simple statement. My family was dying off so fast, I never had a chance to properly grieve; I just kept going from one funeral to another. In the psychologist's office, I began to cry, and that began four years of coming to terms with the loss of my beloved family.

"I had been so close to my brothers, Sonny and Donald; and Elliot used to take me fishing and to the baseball games. He taught me a lot about the game. I began thinking deeply about every member of my family, remembering the times we shared together, and I wept for each one of them. There were many days when I felt lonely, and missed my family so much I could feel my heart aching. I would have given anything to be able to call my parents on the phone and let them know that I was alive and well, that I have a beautiful family, and am still singing and performing. Yes, I know they would have loved to hear that."

CHAPTER 21

With a new agent, Anthony began auditioning for every acting role that became available. When a part came up for *The Jazz Set*, he wanted to dazzle the director with something so unusual that it would get him the role in the production. Standing patiently in line, he adjusted his costume. Walking confidently onto stage, he acted a scene from *Julius Caesar,* speaking with an English accent. It did what he had hoped it would: startled the director. He was offered the part the same day, and played to a packed house for a one month run. With critics and directors from across the country seated in the audience, he piqued their interest and he was asked to come to New York and work off-Broadway. But the money wasn't that great, and he wasn't going to uproot his family, so he reluctantly turned down the part. Between singing gigs and sporadic acting jobs, Anthony was able to support his family as the kids grew into their teens.

"There was a veteran actor on *Jazz Set* who had been on the Hollywood scene for two decades trying to make a name for himself, and damned if he didn't like me. No matter what I did or said, he was just plain mean to me. I guess he felt that he had been working so hard, and here comes this singer who hadn't paid his dues, and gets this big part.

"One day, I was sitting by myself reading the Bible, and he walked over to me and announced that I was encroaching on the other actors. At the time, I had no idea what he meant. I came to rehearsals, never missed a live performance, and this guy was giving me a hard time. The cast was small, and we were close, except for this guy, so I decided to turn my cheek, and invite him to our home for Thanksgiving dinner.

"When the doorbell rang, and he was standing in the foyer of our home, I was shocked. I couldn't believe he would show up. We fed him, he played with our kids, shared a few glasses of wine, and the next night, he was a different man. When I returned to my dressing room for the Friday night performance, he came over and hugged me, thanked me for dinner, and we have been friends ever since. If I took away one lesson from this, I would have to say that showing respect to those who pave the way for you is important; without their talent, I wouldn't be where I am today." Anthony's love for acting overshadowed his love for singing, but the disappointments were daunting. His agent sent him to MGM studios to audition for a large part in a Robert De Niro movie, and he was called back three times for the part, but the writer's strike hit the movie industry, shutting the entire business down. Hollywood came to a screeching halt. Although he was disappointed, he had learned to take things in stride; something else would turn up, and he always had his music.

A couple weeks after the shutdown, his agent sent him out for a role in new play that had been completed well before the writer's strike: *Are You Looking?* Anthony had to laugh as he read his lines; he was to play the part of a drug dealer. "Reading is so important. I learned how to sight read, that is, look at the words on a page and turn them into a story, even if I had never rehearsed the lines before."

Ed Harris, one of the actors on the set, was so enthralled with Anthony's talent, that Anthony was hired on the spot. For four months, the Gene Danoski Theater was filled with patrons coming to see the new drama. "One night, my mind just went blank. Ed was so attuned to my dialogue that he fed me my first line, and the rest of the play went off perfectly. After the last bows, I went to his dressing room and thanked him for helping me out. He said it happened to everyone, including himself." In the audience was Sally Field, and Buddy Ebsen, of The Beverly Hillbillies. Sally came up to the dressing room to see Ed Harris (I was sharing the room with him). Sally said, "Ed you were so wonderful," and turning to Anthony, she said, "And you, you were one bad sucker."

"I became so immersed in the role, it was as if it were preordained. People came knocking on my dressing room telling me how much they loved the show, and how believable I was. That spring, I won best supporting actor for live theater. Not bad for a Brooklyn kid."

Before the play ended, Anthony's agent handed him an offer to do an off-Broadway play, but it would mean a reduction in pay, and months being away from home. Despite chomping at the bit for the opportunity, he turned it down. His life was in California with his wife and family, and they came first.

Years later, he returned to the Big Apple but it was in the form of a short gig, at an exclusive supper club. The intimate ninety seat night club was located below street level, like one of those prohibition era nightclubs, with tight security at the front door. The production included dancers, Brenda's daughter, Wendy, a full band, and moving songs like "Lady in Red," one of Anthony's favorite. Anthony followed Peggy Lee's show, and so had to be able to stand up to a fickle, critical, city crowd – not an easy task, but the audience overwhelmingly loved Anthony, the show, and the music, and the theater was booked solid for a month.

The owner, a theatrical diva, was openly gay, and decided to take Anthony and Linda out for an evening, to give them a glimpse into how the other half lives. Proud of his world-class entertainer, he wanted to show him off to his friends. One evening, after the performance, the three hopped into a black limousine, driving to the red light district, a tiny section of lower Manhattan that catered to the sexual fantasies of the superrich. As clandestine as the supper club was, entrée into this gay club was even more rigid. They flashed a pass and entered into the surreal world of men who morphed into women, cross-dressers, and gay men.

The interior lights were dim, with flashing lights above the dance floor, and the prevailing color was red. The plush carpet led to a highly polished oak dance floor flanked on either side by glass and steel bars. Two sets of Lucite stairs coiled up the walls leading to several private rooms on the second floor, and another opulent bar. "Everyone was dressed up in tuxedos and evening dresses, with tons of make-up and jewelry. I didn't know who was a woman or a man, until I later found out everyone was a man! The guys were so beautiful; I've rarely seen women look that beautiful. I was absolutely fascinated by all those people and Linda was so stunned she walked around speechless."

Paradoxically the next evening Bill Parcells, along with a couple of other football coaches, came to the show. "After the performance he walked up and told me he loved me, and he owned all of my records. He looked at me, and said I sweated and worked just as hard as his players on the field. I was truly in heaven, especially when he asked if I would like to go to the game. Does a hog love slop? The next day Bill called his friends at the newspaper and touted my show as one of the best he had ever seen. Those glorifying reviews helped keep the seats filled and my reputation as a solo act soaring.

"Upon returning to Los Angeles, I met Bill the night before the big Sunday game at the Disneyland Hotel in Anaheim. I took my son, Tony, with me, who is also a football fanatic and proved it every day as a high school football coach with a winning team. When we walked into the suite, our mouths were hanging open, as we met sportscaster John Madden, who was also there. Later, Bill took several tickets from his pocket, and handed them to me. One of the biggest thrills of my life was standing at the edge of the playing field, right alongside the players. I felt like I was part of the game. My family was safely seated in the stadium, but I had the best seat in the house. I was on the sidelines of the playing field, watching the Rams in the Los Angeles Coliseum."

It felt so natural, with Tony, his second eldest son, sitting by his side on a short plane ride up to San Francisco. Tony was really excited; this was the first time he would sing live with his dad. It was just one duet, but in the back of his mind, he had hoped this would lead to a career in music.

"When I was six years old, I got a few friends together and we made up a band, lip-synching to the latest rock and roll stars. Our parents were so supportive; they bought us matching costumes. We went on all those talent shows in elementary school but then my interest fizzled out when I put on a football uniform," said Tony.

That evening, they wore black tuxedos, and Anthony performed a one-man show at the Fairmont Hotel. "We did a Luther Vandross song, and I thought it sounded pretty good; at least, the audience applauded loudly, and for me that was enough gratification," said Tony. "After the show we had dinner at the top of the hotel. People congratulated me and told me I was the next Little Anthony. I knew it had been such a long time since dad had sang with The Imperials, and when he walked onto the stage, it was just him, alone. I thought for just one night, when I sang with him, he would remember how he had felt when he had the group to support him.

"I watched dad grow strong and confident throughout the years and tonight, when we sang together, I finally realized how gifted and talented he really is. As hard as I tried, I would never have the gifts my dad has been blessed with. In my heart of hearts, I knew I could never reach that standard and after I returned home, I became a football coach at Franklin High School. That was where my real passion lay and that was where I knew I would become successful."

As much as Anthony loved doing those challenging acting jobs, music was his first calling. Linda had grabbed the phone; ugh, it was seven in the morning, too early for conversations. "This is Dick Fox, is Anthony available?" Shaking Anthony gently, she pointed to the phone, and told her sleepy husband who was on the line.

"How are you?" Dick asked. "I'm sorry to call so early, I kind of forgot the three hour time difference, but I was a bit anxious to talk with you. I'm doing a show back in New York called 'The Legends' and I want you to come back and be a part of the show. I want you to sing again as Little Anthony and The Imperials. Could you do this once? This is going to be a rip roaring show. Everyone who has ever been famous will be on the show. It's already sold out. Please, we would love to have you and the guys together, at least one more time." When Dick added in the contract payment, free flight, and four-star hotel, the offer was too sweet to pass over. Anthony had just performed with the New Editions, and was feeling his oats as a rock star. Tossing aside his classy image, he let the rock and roll in him bubble to the surface for a short stint with the ravenously popular boy band. But reality sunk in.

Later that day, when he knew his colleagues had arisen, Anthony called Clarence, who was back singing as the Imperials throughout Las Vegas, and told him about the chance to sing on the show. Harold, who had a stellar tenor voice and an ear for perfect harmony, often interspersing with Sammy, jumped for joy; he loved Anthony. Anthony called Ernest's daughter, who contacted him in Europe and Ernest then called Anthony. Sammy then contacted me, although he had been singing with O'Jays for the past sixteen years.

It would be one night in New York, but their fans would get a chance to see them back together. They would be supported by the best rock and roll band in the business, E Street Band. Once they had all agreed, Anthony contacted Ernest, who was traveling Europe with the Platters. It took ten days to track Ernest down, but once he finally got him on the phone and gave him the date, Ernest was quick to say yes. His tour had wound down and he would be in the States the following day.

"It's a one night gig and I want you to come with me." The look in his eyes, and the added lilt in his gait, told Linda this wouldn't be another one night gig. Since the moment he had received the call, she could sense an excitement and anticipation of getting back with the guys. So she packed two sets of bags and they boarded the plane for the East Coast. They met at the theater, where the guys shook hands and hugged. It had been a long time since they had been together on one stage. "It felt like I was home. We had all gotten a little older, but everyone was the same person."

"Since this is a one night gig, let's rent some tuxes and then we can go on our way right after the show," suggested Sammy. They grabbed two taxis and sped to the closest costume rental store, in an obscure corner off Broadway. Laughing and joking, they made fun of each other, and how they had each changed throughout the years.

"This night will be fun, and with the best band in America, we should have the crowd jumping in their seats," said Clarence. They knew the songs; they could sing them in their sleep, "Shimmy Shimmy Ko Ko Bop," "Going Out of My Head," and "Tears on My Pillow." They were a monstrous hit, singing as expertly as the day each of these was recorded.

"In 1958 when we first started, Richard Barrett came up with the idea to paint our shoes and gloves with iridescent paint, and it glowed in the dark when hit with a special light. It affected people so much, that the audience remembered it. At this this performance in front of fourteen thousand people, we duplicated the iridescent look, and it blew the audience out! We were so excited that the audience loved this, when the next song was cued, I gave the guys a signal and we tried to replicate the splits that went with the choreography to "I'm Alright," written by Sam Cook. But when Sammy went down to do his split, his body locked, Clarence's leg swelled up, and the audience went bonkers."

A week later Anthony received a call from Dick Clark's office, who had seen the Legends show and had fallen in love with the group all over again. He asked them to perform on his 40th anniversary show. The guys returned their rented tuxes, deciding to go to a tailor and purchase new suits. "I don't know," said Sammy, "That is a lot of money to spend on another one night stand." Not one to cause any discord, Sammy pulled out some cash, and joined his fellow singers, "I'm sure I will have a place to wear this," he rationalized.

Dick Clark was thrilled when he saw the group walk into his studio. He provided every comfort, giving them dressing rooms and all the rehearsal time they needed. This was his big anniversary show and he knew groups like Little Anthony and the Imperials would make it a hit, and grab those sacred ratings points.

The time had come, and it was Little Anthony and the Imperials at center stage. They sang two songs, took quick bows, and walked off the stage. At the end of the production, and after Dick Clark's voracious applause for all the performers, Anthony suggested the group go celebrate. Once seated at a local bar, the buoyant atmosphere continued; they were smiling, jovial, and whatever tensions they had carried in the past had vanished. It was if they had a case of amnesia, as they reminisced about the good times and wonderment of their music. It was magic, they were magic, and perhaps it was time to begin again.

"What would you guys think about getting back together – and I don't mean for just one of these special shows, I mean for real. Go out sing our songs, make the big money, see our names back on the marquees. I don't know about you, but I'm not ready to hang it up. I think the best years of our lives are ahead," suggested Anthony, who had grown much stronger and independent. After hashing out their individual thoughts, they came to a meeting of the minds, and got back together. Ernest, Sammy, Clarence, and Anthony began touring.

"I guess buying those new suits was worth the money," laughed Sammy. They recruited their old road manager, Ernie Martinelli. They notified their individual agents, and the phones began to ring; gigs were booked in venues across the country.

"We knew the industry had changed, but our music was in great demand, and people not only wanted to hear the music, but see us perform. Life evolved and so did we, as we began packing our bags saying good-bye to our families, and heading out on the road.

Sometimes we were the sole headliners, and sometimes we shared the stage with survivor groups who had begun with us and had withstood the test of time. We were strong enough to command an audience on our own, and didn't need others to share the billing.

"One of the major reasons we had survived was the cessation of drugs. I wasn't the only one who had quit: Sammy and Ernest had stopped using, and it was only Clarence who clung to his addiction. Sometimes he would disappear, we couldn't find him and then he would reappear as if nothing had happened. We took our music seriously; it was our livelihood, and our families depended upon us. Sometimes he would disappear for days or even months at a time. That was crazy." The group was scheduled for a gig in Miami, at one of the dance clubs in South Beach, which was the hottest beach in the country, and commanded the hottest music in the country. They had prearranged a sound check at three in the afternoon, and had to strip off their bathing suits and replace them with cotton shorts. Bye, bye to sun and fun as they gathered to rehearse for the show. The stage hands were kind and helpful, even as Ernest barked out orders detailing placements of lights and microphones. The three singers milled around waiting for Clarence to show up. Each time the door to the lounge swung open, three sets of eyes looked up, but it was always nothing. Gazing at his watch, Ernie was annoyed. It was almost four in the afternoon, and Clarence still hadn't shown his face.

"I'll go look for him; you guys go ahead with your sound check until I get back," volunteered Anthony.

"We have to do something," said Sammy. "Look at us: working, rehearsing, and where is Clarence? I don't know, and frankly I don't care. I'm sick of him never showing up. We need everyone. I say it's time to give him the boot. We have been patient for a long time.

Look at the three of us; we knew when it was time to kick the drugs, or the drugs would kick us. It seems, for Clarence, the drugs have won. I think it's high time we replaced him."

"I agree with you," added Ernest. "It's not fair; the club expects all of us to show up. I for one don't want to disappoint our fans. It's not easy getting gigs, and if we don't all show up, it will really hurt our reputation. We need someone reliable."

"Okay. First let's decide who would take his place." With a loud sound they all screamed out Kenny's name: Kenny Seymour! "I will make the call as soon as we are finished up here, but how do we tell Clarence?"

"I say we do it together," suggested Sammy. "Then the decision looks like it was unanimous, and we are all angry." Later, Anthony returned to the rehearsal shaking his head. He hadn't located Clarence. Disgusted, they knew the show would go on without him, but they vowed this would be the very last time. They were all disgruntled.

After a late brunch on Sunday morning, they ruminated as to how they would break the news to Clarence. "He is probably so stoned, he won't know what we are saying," said Sammy. Walking into Anthony's room, they picked up the phone, sat on the bed, and called Clarence's home.

"Hello," said Brenda, Clarence's wife.

"It's us, Sammy, Ernest, and Anthony, and we need to talk to Clarence. "He's not here. Isn't he supposed to be with you guys?"

"Yes," they responded, "but he went off somewhere and we can't find him." Anthony took over the conversation, and broke the news that they had made a decision, and Clarence was ousted from the group. The drugs seemed to have overtaken his life and they needed a trusted partner. "Anthony, couldn't you give him another chance?"

she begged, and he simply answered no, he had had enough. The sounds of sobs permeated the air. There was nothing anyone could do. Clarence had dug his grave and was unable to get out. There were too many times when he hadn't shown up, or had been late, or been too stoned to perform. It was time to say a final good-bye. After they hung up the phone, silence filled the air. Anthony pondered Brenda's appeal.

Two years later, Clarence came knocking, but first he made a call to the manager, Ernie Martinelli. Ernie said nothing, simply shrugged his shoulders. "It's up to Anthony, not me."

Picking up the phone, Clarence called Anthony. "I'm clean and I want my job back. I swear to you it's different this time. I'm different. I went through rehab, and I have seen the light. I swear I will never disappoint you guys again," he sobbed. When Anthony contacted Sammy, Ernest, and Kenny, they were startled by Clarence's call, and were in no rush to believe his confession. The record had spoken for itself: too many lost years, too many no-shows. The group, with Kenny singing harmony, had been established, and for Kenny there was no turning back. The guys didn't want Clarence back in the group. Kenny had taken his place, reestablished himself as an Imperial, and there was no way he would open up the door and allow someone else to walk in and toss him aside. "No one knew what to think, but I loved Clarence, as did Sammy and Ernest, and we began to believe his story. I used to drive him from Los Angeles to a rehab center in Victorville, almost three hours. Clarence was determined to shake the demons, and come back to our group. For me, I was just determined to have him back in our lives, sober and sane."

Finally the time had arrived, and Clarence had proven he was clean, and back for good, Sammy, Ernest, and Anthony had another pow-wow. Was Clarence going to rejoin the group, because if so, Kenny was out. No one wanted to make that decision, but after days of soul searching, they decided to take Clarence back and oust Kenny.

"Man, that song, 'Breaking Up Is Hard To Do,' sure seems to fit this occasion," said Sammy as the three sat in a small coffee shop munching on burgers. "He is going to take it real bad. So much drama, so much heartache. I feel like we are breaking up with a girlfriend. All this love we share, it's going to be hard. This is one thing we have to do together."

"It's like the good, the bad, and the ugly," said Ernest "and this is definitely the ugly." They were not going to do this over the phone, so they met the next day for the heart-to-heart at a nondescript bar, off a side street. Sammy, Anthony, and Ernest arrived early to mull over their discussion. They wanted to let Kenny down easy. They had to remain steadfast, solidly together, as they began humming the tune to a Peaches and Herb song. "Thank God there is a song for every condition in our lives; let's just keep humming until he gets here."

Kenny was dressed in jeans and a simple black tee-shirt, with a smile covering his face. "What's up, guys, why all the secrecy? Are we going to rob a bank?" The tension was dense, as the singers waited for Sammy's opening line. Hesitatingly, Anthony looked directly into Kenny's eyes, and told him Clarence was rejoining the group, and that he was out. The smile on Kenny's face was instantly replaced with a remorseful dejected look, plainly he was shocked and heartbroken.

"I gave you guys my best, stepped in, and made it happen. The gigs never stopped coming, and you knew you could rely on me. Now you're giving me up for Clarence? The no-show guy, they guy who has left you hanging time after time. Shit, I can't believe you are throwing me out of the group."

Standing up, he forced an inner strength, turned around, and swore, "The next time you call me and tell me your druggie friend has gone off the wagon, I won't be coming back. I'm done, done forever!"

Once Kenny left, the three remorseful singers felt horrible; they had destroyed a man, a man they loved. "I just hope we have made the right decision," said Ernest, "because we know Kenny ain't ever coming back."

"This man practically invented four-part harmony, and taught us all how to sing. The arrangements, the songs he wrote," reminded Anthony. "I pray to God we are making the right decision." And Kenny never did come back, instead, he suffered a nervous breakdown, taking months to emotionally recover from the devastation. He was a true artist, and had a heavy hand in making the group successful. It was his superior arranging and writing, that sold millions of records and albums. How could they let him walk away? How could they treat him so badly? There was no answer, nor was there any solace, other than the guilt he was sure Anthony was feeling. Packing his bag, Kenny flew off to Luxemburg, singing with the Magic Platters. Eventually he made his home there, marrying wife number four. Along with singing, he taught music at the University of Luxemburg, and became very well known throughout the European city. Despite being an unlikely fit, he recorded vocals with Harvey Averne, a Latin music group. Although he never did any live performances with Harvey Averne, it was his voice on their records.

After years in Luxemburg, Kenny suffered a debilitating stroke, and eventually ended up in New York, at a nursing home on Long

Island. Mary, who had remarried, never lost her love or admiration, for his talent, and became his part-time caretaker until he passed away in 2012 at the age of 74.

"When Kenny died, it jolted me, and I realized it was never too late to change your life. I had written a couple of plays that had been performed at my church. Finally following my unfinished dreams, I enrolled at a local college to study screen writing, and directing. I got straight A's, and was accepted into both Yale and Columbia University. Not bad for a woman in her sixties! My goal is to write a play, putting all of Kenny's musical talent into a production of Little Anthony and The Imperials; that would a fitting tribute to Kenny's life, his talent, and the love we once shared."

"This is my chance to say something to Anthony," said Mary. "I love him very much. He was more than a friend, but a guru, always looking out for me. After I had my first child with Kenny, Anthony asked him if he was sending money home to support us. The thought had never entered Kenny's mind, who at times was very selfish. The next week, I received an envelope in the mail, filled with cash, and for all the times he was on the road, the money flowed into our household. I knew it was Anthony's doing, his thoughtfulness, sensitivity, and his consummate caring for others. I feel his music, and the songs that Teddy Randazzo wrote, are worthy of generations to come – certainly the stuff that makes a great Broadway play. I only hope that happens for Anthony, and I sure would like to be the one who makes that happen."

CHAPTER 22

The group was back on the Eastern Seaboard, working a theater in Newark, New Jersey, when Anthony received an unusual phone call from Paul Simon, half of the duo Simon and Garfunkel. Ten years prior Paul had written and produced a Broadway play, *The Capeman*, which was panned by the critics, and a colossal commercial failure. He was depressed over the failure, and the play closed shortly after opening. For some reason, ten years later Paul felt the need to resurrect the play, but now he needed to vastly improve the music and the opening. It was the music of Little Anthony's group that would change the past mistakes, bringing to light the message Paul wanted to convey.

At the time, the group was performing in downtown Newark, in one of the many concert halls. "Hey," yelled the stage director, "Paul Simon said he is here to see you." The legendary folk singer was escorted to their dressing room; he pulled up the only empty chair and offered Anthony a proposition. "I should retry *The Capeman*," he said, "Can I get some help from you guys?" As fast as Paul was explaining the plot. Anthony's mind was working, and in a few moments, he envisioned the opening scene. Pausing pensively, Paul nodded his head: yes, it would work.

Paul's liberal views brought to light the behavior of a teenager gone awry, who turned into a serial killer. He was eventually caught. The true story shines a light into the insane mind of the perpetrator, envisioning the hideous deeds through his eyes. It wasn't so much to cause sympathy for the murderer, but to create an understanding in the audience of what motivates a person to act in such an unforgiving way.

Paul's original music was a bit too maudlin, and adding Anthony's songs, particularly the one written by Ernest Wright, "Two Kinds of People in the World." provided the perfect balance. For two weeks, the play ran at the Brooklyn Academy of Music, and this time the reviews were excellent, redeeming his first efforts. The production began by simply dimming the theater lights. There was utter silence as the four men slowly walked onto the stage, pointed at imaginary landmarks, and then began singing a cappella. The critics fell in love with the play, vindicating Paul for his prior effort, and for that Paul was forever grateful to Anthony.

In March 2003, at Allentown, the four guys arrived at a modest downtown hotel, piled out of the car, rode the elevator to their floor, and said good night. Anthony was thinking about Linda and how he couldn't wait to wrap his arms around her taut body, and hmm did she have a great body. A sudden knock on the door snapped him out of his little fantasy, as he saw Clarence standing in the hallway with the most sullen expression he had ever worn.

"He's gone. God, I'm so sorry. Linda called me and asked me to tell you, as she didn't have the courage to do it over the phone," he cried.

Casey, their first born, was the apple of their eye, so gorgeous, healthy, and happy, a joyful spirit. They never dreamed he would die, and in such a senseless way. This child was going to be so dynamic, they believed, as he entered an esteemed private Christian elementary school. The oldest and brightest in the family, his teachers doted on him, instilling the ideals of Christianity, providing a solid spiritual and principled system of values. Casey's teachers warned him that once he left the confines of the nurturing school, life would become tougher and his value system would be put to the test time and time again.

With his character base so firmly engrained, when the time came, he would be able to make the right decisions, and not become corrupted by peer pressure. Casey had no plan; he was a young teen and he was unsure of what he wanted. The only thing he was sure of was his lack of musical talent. He just didn't have it' no matter how hard his parents tried to eke it out of him, it just wasn't there. "You can't teach talent, you either have it or you don't." Choosing the avenue of sports, Casey became proficient in baseball, soccer, and football, and won the hearts of his classmates, but he was always living under the shadow of his father's fame. He felt he would never be good enough in his parents' eyes and he tried too hard to win their approval. Exceedingly handsome and endowed with his mother's height, he modeled on the weekends, becoming the heartthrob of many young girls. What he may have lacked in singing talent was made up in his ability to move seamlessly down a runway while smiling imploringly at a crowd.

During one of the late fall football matches he took a tumble and blew out his left knee. Between his low tolerance for pain and the fact that the coaches wanted one of their star players back onto the field, he was prescribed painkillers and later steroids. Before anyone realized it, the young teen became addicted to drugs, his thinking becoming muddled and wrong. He hid it from Linda and Anthony, as children can do, but then a series of catastrophes began occurring, and it was obvious something was very wrong.

It was late in the fall season, the last Friday night football game, and Anthony had given Casey his car for the evening so he could celebrate with his teammates. Around midnight, when the couple was pacing the bedroom floor, the ominous ring of the phone shattered the tense household. Casey had been in a bad car crash and was in intensive care. Daniel, Damon, and Casey were all attending the University of San Diego, and the house was quiet except for Sarah. The couple rushed to the hospital and began a lengthy vigil, praying their first son would survive the crash. The car had been totaled, shortly after Casey had dropped off his last friend. Thank God there were no other casualties.

After a two week stint, Casey arrived home, battered, bruised, and emotionally defeated. Again, he had let down his parents, destroyed the car and almost himself. As Anthony sat for hours at a time trying to reconnect his son with his Christian values, he could only hope the tragedy would alter Casey's course. The accident, and the severe pain, put Casey right back onto the addiction of painkillers. He was back to square one, and his mind was a mess, unable to sustain clarity. It was weeks before Casey had the courage to get behind the wheel, but convinced he was better, Linda handed him the keys to her car. Casey opened the door on the side of the house, and the two cockers, Princess and Cody, scampered out, making a beeline to the thick grass near the edge of the driveway. But dogs are stupid, and Casey, tall and focused on trying to make it to a friend's house, didn't see one of the dogs race back to the back of the car. While slowly backing up, he heard a loud screech. He slammed on the brakes, turned off the engine, leaped out of the car, and found one of the cockers lying lifeless in a puddle of blood.

Casey was beyond consoling; he loved those two dogs, and now he was responsible for one of them dying. He would never shed enough tears to make it right. He was totally heartbroken.

"Why do we have to grow up?" he questioned his friend. Life had overwhelmed him and the only solace he could find was in a bottle of pills. He just couldn't figure out the world, and the harder he tried, the less he understood. Casey got caught in a web of spinning circles that he was unable to pull himself out of. Deeper and deeper he traveled, until he lost sight of the life he once had. At the end of winter break, Linda opened the mail and a large envelope with Casey's name was hand written in the center; the return address was from the university he had applied to. Tentatively she handed him the envelope, and he ripped it open and sprung an instant smile. "Congratulations, we are pleased to invite you to join the freshman class." Finally a cause for celebration occurred in the household, as he held that achievement in his hand. Linda was convinced this was a turning point and that Casey, now with a promising future, would come to see the light, stop using drugs, and turn out alright.

That late spring Casey was involved in yet another car crash, another totaled car, and another trip to the emergency room where they patched him together, kept watch over him for a week, and then returned him home with another set of painkillers. Again, Anthony sat by his son's bedside begging him to think about his life. Waving the acceptance letter in the air, he told him how proud they were and reminded Casey of the great future he was about to embark upon. "You hold the world in your hands, son. You are smart, handsome, a talented sportsman. If you stay the course, forget about the drugs, you will make it and make it big. I promise you." And it was off to college in the fall: taking courses, dating, studying, and continuing to take drugs. He met Shelia in one of his classes, one of the most beautiful girls he had ever laid eyes on. Obviously, she shared the same feelings and they dated exclusively for months. When word spread from a friend that Shelia had become pregnant, Casey was nowhere to be found.

"I can't be a dad," he yelled to his father. "Hell I'm just a kid myself. You always tell me I can't take care of myself, how am I supposed to take care of a kid?" As Casey lumbered up the steps, Anthony grabbed him by the sleeve.

"Casey, you have got to grow up, you have to step up to the plate and take responsibility for this."

He turned around at the top of the stairs, tears welling up in his eyes as he stared back into his father's eyes. "Dad, can't you love me, can't you just love me for me? I know I screwed up, but can't you just once overlook my errors, and simply love me?" he pleaded. "I know I'm a failure and I need you to know that I know I screwed up." Anthony and Linda were at wit's end trying to address the issue, sending him to rehab, initiating a family encounter, and providing individual therapy. Nothing seemed to work, but they had to continue living and they had to take care of the rest of their brood, so it was back to work for Linda and back on the road for Anthony. She kissed her husband goodbye, and prayed things would be smooth at home until he returned from his engagement.

Three Sundays later, Linda knocked on Casey's door, thinking maybe he would go to church with her or take the dog for a walk. After several minutes, she knocked again and when there was no answer, she gently opened up the door. Her heart stopped. She felt like she had taken her last breath. There was her son, her first born, sprawled out on the bed, foam drooling from his mouth, motionless.

She screamed wildly, bringing Daniel rushing out of his bedroom. He saw his brother and began mouth-to-mouth resuscitation as Linda frantically dialed emergency services. It was useless; he was gone. He had died in his sleep from too many painkillers. At the hospital, after the doctors confirmed Casey's death, Linda had the task of telling Anthony, a task so insurmountable that she wasn't able to do it. So she called his best friend and begged him to tell Anthony.

She could hear Clarence's voice close up, and the sound of sobs as he made the solemn promise. "God give me strength," he prayed, as he wiped his eyes and tapped on Anthony's door.

"I fell to the ground. I was covered in grief and in a state of shock. Clarence comforted me and then told the others, and they all came together, held me and comforted me until our plane landed in California."

"When the time came to bury Casey, it was our pastor, Bayles Conley, of Cottonwood Christian Center, in Cerritos, who helped us through the wrenching experience." The simple casket sat underneath the podium, gleaming from the morning sunrays bouncing off the highly polished wood. It was like God himself had come to help them bury their child. Holding his wife's hand, Anthony turned around and there was a sea of people inside the church, overflowing to the foyer.

"I never knew how many people loved our son. It was an amazing sight to see so many who had come to say a final good bye. The limousine procession had over twenty-five cars, one of the largest ever in the town, and it stopped traffic for a long time."

"As we stood at the grave, all I could think of was Casey's simple request: 'Dad can't you just love me?' Dear Casey I love you, and I will always love you. I know you didn't mean to kill yourself I know you didn't want to die. I wish I could have been there, I wish I could have stopped you. It's too late. Please know that I love you."

One of Casey's closest friends was Clark Hagen, who also went to Rolling Hills High School and shared a passion for football. Both were excellent players, and Clark went on to the University of Colorado, while Casey stayed closer to home at El Camino Junior College. From high school through college they had a devoted friendship that endured until the day Casey died.

Clark's parents were veterinarians and took care of the Gourdine's endless parade of dogs. When tragedy struck at Clark's household, in the form of both his brother and father dying in the same year, Anthony sang at their funerals. The two families communicated often and developed a strong friendship. When tragedy turned to the Gourdine household, it was Clark's mother, Doris, who provided a plot for Casey's funeral, supplying the stretch limousines and even the grave plot.

"I will be forever in their debt for helping us out emotionally when our son died. Later, our families drifted apart, but if I could look into Clark and Doris' eyes, I would profoundly thank them for coming to our aid when we needed it most. We were there when their tragedies occurred, but when Casey died, their help was so abundant that I could never repay that debt." Clark was living out his dreams: he had been drafted by the Pittsburgh Steelers in 1999.

Later that night, after family and friends had departed and it was just the two of them, Anthony and Linda clung to each other and cried. "Replaying Casey's request over and over in my mind, I didn't feel guilty; what I felt was ignorant. If I had just stopped and given him a hug, maybe that's all he would have needed. Maybe the solution was so simple that I couldn't comprehend that it was all he might have needed. Such a waste, a waste of a life that could have been so valuable."

"That night, after an hour of trying to get some sleep, I saw a light underneath our bedroom door. *Oh,* I thought, *it's just Casey using the bathroom.* He always got up at least once a night, and that night was no different, except I suddenly realized I had just buried him. I got out of bed and Casey was standing at the door just as clear as day. He waved to me, turned around, and walked away. The light in the bathroom went out. That was when I knew he was really gone, but I was convinced he had to tell me he was okay, and that he was now in the hands of the Lord. He was there, I saw him and I will never forget the look on his face: peaceful and at rest at last."

Sarah saw it too. Distraught, the youngest child tossed and turned in her bed and saw, out of the corner of her eye, streams of light crawling underneath her bedroom door. Those lights came from the bathroom she shared with Casey. Startled, she sat up in the bed, pulled back the covers, and opened up the door. There stood Casey as real as life; he was mute, but he came close to her, gave her a smile, and then waved goodbye. She reached her arms out to hold him, but in a flash he was gone.

She returned to bed, her mind replaying the scene over and over again. Was it real? Perhaps it was his spirit coming back to tell her he would be okay and to stop worrying. "I'll never forget you. Brother, I love you," she whispered in the dark, as she finally closed her eyes and slept. It had been a grueling day. Sarah never told anyone about this experience; it was between her and her oldest brother. She savored that sacred moment, keeping it to herself. It was all she had left of her brother.

"If I had to take one learning experience from this tragedy, I would tell parents to love their children unconditionally. Perhaps had Casey seen my love that way, things might have ended up a lot better." Linda went back to work, and Anthony went back to singing, as they both worked through the long and tedious grieving process.

CHAPTER 23

So many people had made the trek from the East Coast to the West Coast. The California sun and mild winters were too tempting for people like Murray the K. Anthony had found out the deejay was quite ill and paid him a visit. After he rang the doorbell and was shown to Murray's room, he was shocked at his condition. Murray's robust voice was weak, his hair gone, and he was skin and bones. Cancer had created its carnage, destroying a once vibrant man. They talked for hours, as there were years of catching up to do.

"I wish I would have done better by you," Murray admitted.

"Do you think I came here to complain to you? Quite the contrary, we were on your show plenty, and I do remember you playing our records. It was those damned Beatles who got in the way of our air time!"

Both laughed: Murray had his claim to fame by pushing the Beatles into unprecedented fame. "If we had to lose out to a group and that group was the Beatles, I have nothing to complain about." Once Anthony began talking with Murray, he couldn't stay away. All those memories, all the people they knew, and all his great stories to retell. As the visits continued, Anthony noticed a difference in the dying deejay. When he entered the room, Murray wore a broad smile and became infused with energy. For a brief time, he would forget his illness and live again.

"You've changed," Murray remarked, and that was the day that Anthony decided to share his revelation. Why not? Couldn't hurt. Maybe it would give Murray a new perspective. He was still alive, and as long as he was breathing, there was hope. After listening to what Murray had considered Anthony's confession, he stated, "I have lived a tough life. You know something? After listening to you, I think there is a God. Would you pray with me?" Surprised, Anthony took his frail hand and they prayed together.

"Do you think it matters that I'm a Jew and you are a Christian?" Murray asked. Anthony quickly answered that Jesus was a Jew who turned the whole world upside down and he did it without a press agent. "I want to feel God in my heart, to feel the joy you feel," Murray said, and then began to cry. Two days later, Anthony returned and was astonished to find Murray walking around his home, smiling, eating and talkative.

"The best thing I ever did in my life was pray with Murray. I couldn't stop his death, but all things are possible, I told him, if he embraced God. The love He bestows on all of us will get us through anything. At least when the time came, he went with love and joy in his heart. Somewhere in heaven the sounds of the music are playing, comforting his soul.

"My own voice is on loan from God. I believe and have faith in God and what he can do through us. I've learned to make everybody feel better. I truly love people and when I talk to them, they feel better, inspired, filled with hope. This love is so great, so overwhelming, that it can help people who are stuck and need to go another way. I'm wasn't called to be a preacher, nor do I intend to stand on any pulpit, but I have watched people do better in their lives by taking God into their hearts."

"As I meet people on my road of life, there are gatekeepers who point me in the right direction. I'm here today because of all those people and I believe that God has made that happen. I grew up a street kid, and got deeply involved with drugs. I knocked on darkened doors in the middle of Harlem to buy coke and weed from dealers. I knew the danger; I had many friends who had been killed by gang members, drug lords, or overdosing. If I wasn't taking hard drugs, I was drinking and smoking."

"But for some reason, God chose me to survive, to beat the odds and create my destiny. I see the second half of my life as much better than the first, and I feel like the richest man on earth. I know that time I spent with Murray helped him in his final days. I think he didn't feel as alone, nor as scared, in the final chapter of his life. If that is what faith and belief in the love of God is for, then for Murray it was a beautiful thing."

Clarence Collins became a thorn in Anthony's side. It was Clarence who initially inspired Anthony to join the group, but things went awry, particularly when Anthony's name was separated from the Imperials'. Clarence was no longer the leader, but part of the pack, and that didn't sit well in his mind. He believed he was the main man, the leader of the group, and that it should have been his name distinguished, as opposed to Anthony's. Angry, Clarence decided he would get his due reward and unbeknownst to Tracey, Ernest, and Nathaniel, in 1958, he copyrighted the name without their knowledge or permission.

When Clarence was very young, his mother died, leaving his father to raise him and several other children. Without the love and support of a nurturing mother, he became hardened and self-centered, which took a toll on his personal life. He was married to four different wives, including Anthony's sister-in-law Brenda (who is my wife's twin sister), and was unable to commit to anybody. He changed into a lone wolf. He was a troubled young man, who became spiteful as the years progressed.

Carrying a torch of disdain, he collected a few musicians and named the group "Little Anthony's Imperials." When Anthony found out about his treachery, he went nuts.

"I called the hotels and they pulled down the signs on the marquees, canceling all the performances. Clarence had lied to the booking agents and didn't have a legal leg to stand on. A big part of his problem was his inability to shake his drug habit, which began to cloud his thinking and further estrange him from his colleagues, friends, performers, and eventually his wife. We would fight and make up, and then fight again. It was a love-hate relationship.

"Clarence left to work in an investment company as a maintenance man and in a short while had begun climbing the ladder to success, but he wasn't happy and it wasn't where he belonged. Brenda, his wife, had been working at the company for a while, and when the position was posted, she put in an application, and he was instantly hired. At times it was awkward: Clarence had married Brenda, Linda's twin, which meant he was my brother-in-law – he was part of my family. How could I treat my own family badly? But Clarence had crossed too many lines in trying to destroy my name."

As he threw on a pair of jeans, Anthony said a prayer, and then he and Linda drove up the coast three hundred miles north of Los Angeles, to pay his off-and-on-again friend a visit. Clarence waved from the top of a ten foot ladder, and slowly descended as Anthony paced back and forth at the front of their home.

"What's up, man," he said as he hugged Anthony. "Do you want to talk? Come on in the house." Sweating from cleaning the gutters, Clarence opened the refrigerator and extracted three sodas, handing one each to Linda and Anthony. Linda knew this was a private conversation, so she made herself scarce and walked out to the backyard. Morgan Hills, was beautiful, and lush, there was plenty of scenery to occupy her time while the two men had their heart-to-heart.

Unbeknownst to Anthony, Clarence had called Ernie Martinelli, the group's manager, and asked about again returning to the group. Anthony knew Clarence well, and from the look on his face, it was painfully clear that he was hurting, and perhaps was very sorry for the problems he had caused. It took little convincing from Anthony to get him to tear off his apron and replace it with the fancy costumes of The Imperials. He was back, even if for a short while, but he was back. The one problem that had not been dealt with was his drug use. It was still going on and no matter how hard the others tried, he continued to use.

"I wanted to help him, make him feel important, so Clarence and I joined forces and created a marketing company called 'Imperial Plus.' But he became drunk with power, and when I made my son Tony my manager, Clarence was livid and walked away. I grieved but eventually I got over it until the lawsuit…" Maybe it was envy or greed, but whatever it was, Clarence thought he could control the rights to the name "Little Anthony and The Imperials." In 2010, Clarence's attorneys drafted a lawsuit demanding sole ownership to the rights to the name. With complaint in hand, he stood before a judge, who asked the simple question: "Clarence Collins, is that your name?"

"Yes," he responded. "Well then, what gives you the rights to the name? Are you Little Anthony? Are you all of The Imperials? Just who are you, then? Because you can't be more than one person," said the judge as she pounded the gavel on the oak desk. The case was dismissed and Clarence left the courtroom a broken man.

Turnabout is fair play and it was Anthony's turn to implement legal tactics. With the name copyrighted and the original Imperials (Sammy, Ernest, Nathaniel and Anthony) would all share equally in the name. "I'll never forget: we were singing at the 'M', the newest casino at the southern tip of the Strip, and Clarence tried to get an injunction prohibiting our name on the marquee and performing as Little Anthony and The Imperials. The injunction was squashed, and again he walked away a loser. Sometimes I think he has forgotten the love we all shared, our time together, or it just may be all those decades of drug use that has clouded his memory. I feel sorry for him and I feel sad. I think he lost his best friends and doesn't know how to make amends."

Anthony's year continued with revelations that would cast an irrevocable change in the landscape of his family. Linda's love and devotion never faltered, but she was keenly aware that her spouse was suave as a man could possibly be. After their marriage she would cast a blind eye at women who relentlessly flung themselves at her husband, but she had had no control over his behavior before he had placed the ring on her finger. Thus it came as no surprise when a young woman began searching social media seeking out her father and her siblings: Andre, Lisa, and Tony had been contacted by Faraga, who claimed to be their half-sister.

"At first I blew it off and explained to my kids that I had been accosted many times in the past with women saying I was the father of their child, but none of those accusations ever came to fruition. They were blatant lies. This time it seemed different. The child didn't contact me, but instead contacted my kids. She didn't want anything other than the chance to meet her biological dad. Faraga sent me an email filled with warm wishes and the date she was born. All she wanted was to meet her father, but was I the father? I wasn't convinced."

Faraga's mom was messed up from drugs, and had left her to be raised by her grandparents. With her mother in constant rehab, and elderly grandparents, she felt as if she had no lifelines or support system. If she could find her father, then maybe she would feel secure in knowing she had a family, or at least part of a family – and if she got lucky, someone to love her. She dreamed and she hoped that perhaps one day it would come true. She pestered her grandparents for years, but they would never divulge the identity of her biological father. They knew he was famous and for whatever reason, they felt like they needed to shelter their sweet granddaughter.

Her grandfather was nearing ninety; his heart was deteriorating and it was time he relinquished the secret. Lying listlessly on the bed, he drew Faraga near to him, took her hand, and whispered into her ear that Anthony Gourdine was her biological father, that he was famous. He also told her that he didn't want to create drama in her life, nor did he want it to seem as though she was asking for money. All he ever wanted for his granddaughter was to live a life of happiness and be content, but now, by sharing this secret, all that would be lost.

She was shaken and hardly knew how to respond, and before she had the chance to press further, he had released her hand and fallen comatose. That was all the information she would get, but that was all the information she would ever need.

"You would think my children would have been angry, but instead, most of them embraced the idea, and Lisa became so curious that she hopped on a train and met Faraga in York, Pennsylvania. The two girls had a DNA test performed and their genes matched at 99.9%, confirming the fact they were half-sisters.

The girls spent time together bonding, and upon Lisa's return home she announced to the rest of the family she had discovered another sibling. Anthony said, "When I looked at the photos, there was no doubt in my mind that she was a Gourdine; in so many ways she resembled my oldest brother, Sonny. The eyes, the high forehead – she was absolutely my off-spring. But now, I had to worry about Linda and the rest of my kids. I didn't want them to hate me. It drove me crazy trying to figure out when all this happened and with whom. Boy, did my Johnson get me into trouble!" I began mulling this over. I realized I had bedded hundreds, if not over a thousand, women, and anything was possible. But I had been married for so long, and had been, and still am to this day, completely faithful to my wife, so this had to have happened a long time ago. I began creating a timeline: Judy and I were married, but we had split up and I was out of the apartment living on my own for a while.

"One night I went to Small's Paradise, a happening nightclub in lower Harlem. Sammy Davis, Jr. was there surrounded by a circle of beautiful women and after he had made his choices, I was lucky enough to end up with a magnificent woman. After hours of drinking, dancing, and talking with friends, I took her back to my bachelor pad and that's the end of the story. I never saw or heard from her again. It was one of those one night stands where the law of averages was not in my favor. I never gave the incident a second thought. All I can remember was that she was a beautiful woman and we had a fantastic evening and maybe that lady was the one who conceived Faraga, but then, it also could have someone else. I have a great memory, but to extract just the right woman who gave birth would be impossible.

"When Lisa returned from York with the results of the DNA test and several photos, I was convinced. I knew that Faraga was my daughter and that I would welcome her into my home – but there were still my wife and other children to answer to.

"The first time I ever saw Faraga was in Baltimore where I was playing at The Chimes Theater for a major benefit. I got her a ticket and left it at the box office. After the show was over, she came back to the dressing room and the moment I laid eyes on her, I knew. Ernest was standing right beside me and he was shocked by the family resemblance. After all those years of never knowing, she has finally found a home with us. A few days later, I called Faraga and we talked for two hours. She told me about her life, and her husband. I invited them to visit us. Luckily, Linda was incredibly understanding; for her it was about setting another place at our crowded table, she was incredibly kind and accepting. A few months later, my secret daughter came to visit with Marcus, her spouse, and everyone embraced her with love and kindness. As the years have passed, we have remained close, so close that Faraga changed her name, making Gourdine her new middle name."

CHAPTER 24

On a warm lazy, Sunday afternoon, Linda grabbed a glass of ice tea, walked into the backyard with a copy of *The Las Vegas Review Journal,* and settled in for an hour of complete relaxation. Her cell phone rang, and she batted it away; the call could wait. Several moments later it rang again and this time she picked it up. Linda's relaxed face contorted into a pucker, her brow furrowed, and then she hastily clicked off the phone. "Tony! Tony is only forty, but he's had a heart attack and he is in the hospital," she screamed out loud. Tears rolled down her face in disbelief. "So young!"

Linda leaped up, checked Anthony's schedule, and immediately placed a call. He was on the road, and Linda knew she had to relay the news, but she knew she needed to pick the right moment. Tears kept clouding her vision; she couldn't believe this had happened to Tony. When she broke the news to Anthony, she wished she could have been there to help him cope with this horrible situation; he had lost one son, and now he was worried sick that he would lose another.

"I was on the road doing a gig. I felt helpless. I wanted to be there for my son. Images of Casey filled my mind: the casket, the funeral, the sick feeling in my heart. I found a quiet space and had a talk with God. My faith in the Lord was going to pull me through this. I believed He would get us all through this awful time."

"Okay guys," said Tony as he, Liz, and their two children jumped into the car, "It's off to Magic Mountain for a day filled with rides, junk food, and lots of waiting in line." He was so happy and so proud that he could be with his kids, and keep the promises he had made. His mind flashed back to the phone calls with his dad, when Anthony had promised trips and then never shown up. No, he would never be that dad, he would never repeat his father's mistakes. But in spite of all those broken promises, Tony loved his dad unconditionally.

Tony married at thirty, after having waited for the perfect soul mate, which he found in Liz. Both had a passion for sports, especially football. She was a statistician and he a coach; it was a marriage made in heaven. How many girls, especially beautiful, sweet, kind girls, had a passion for the game? None! Shortly after he caught her eye, they were married, and today, standing in line to purchase four tickets, Tony couldn't have been happier.

Just like his dad, he loved the rides, the scarier the better. He was a bring-it-on kind of guy. Starting with the most intense roller coaster, they boarded the Viper, and then the Batman ride, and every other exciting ride the park had to offer until dinnertime. While driving home, Tony smiled as he glanced in the rearview mirror and saw the children fast asleep. Liz prepared a simple meal, put the kids to sleep, and she and Tony lounged in front of the television. Tony rubbed his chest, attributing the pains to heartburn, closed his eyes and fell asleep.

The next morning he was at a conference for Aflac and in mid-morning, the chest pains returned – but this time they didn't go away. He pushed the wingback chair from the long conference table and stumbled to his car, and dialed 911 but the line was busy. Perplexed and terrified, he inserted the key into the ignition and drove onto the freeway. "I saw a sign for Sherman Oaks Hospital and headed for the emergency room. I opened the car door, collapsed to the ground, and in less than a minute two nurses rolled out a gurney and placed me on the bed. I handed them the keys to my car and they rushed me into the hospital. I'm sure I blacked out.

"When I woke up, Liz was staring at me with a concerned look on her face. 'What happened?' he said. Tears were dripping down her cheeks, and for once she seemed to be speechless." She took his hand and decided to let the doctors explain what had happened.

The doctor walked into the room, holding his chart. She was blunt; she had a strong message to deliver to this unsuspecting forty-year-old patient. "Mr. Gourdine, you have had a heart attack, but we have repaired your heart and put in stints so you can breathe and live a normal life. You will be okay but you must change your lifestyle and habits. The nurses will be in and give you a list of instructions. For the sake of your health and your wife, please follow every instruction. We will keep you here for a few days to monitor you. When you are ready to go home, you can return to your life but you must follow the rules."

Anthony called Liz, who had a perpetual stream of tears covering her cheeks, and sensed her fear. "Modern medicine is going to get all of us through this, son, you just have to believe."

Tony remained in the hospital for a few more days, and then returned home and followed the doctor's orders. He tossed out cartons of cigarettes, exercised, and ate properly, regaining his strength and health, but his fear of having another heart attack never left his mind. "Every night that I went to sleep, I was terrified I wouldn't wake up: I had a mind attack. One day, I sat down and wrote both my children death letters. I was afraid I would die and I wanted them to know how much I loved them." It was Anthony's belief in God that got him through that terrible time, and it was his belief in God that saved Tony's life: it just wasn't his time to leave this earth. Tony stayed on the righteous path, and nursed his body and mind back to health. He never smoked another cigarette. While he was in the hospital, Liz had thrown out every pack, replaced the beer with bottles of wine, red meat with chicken and fish, and purchased a treadmill. She was going to make him healthy even if it killed him!

Tony had been a successful high school football coach for years, passionate about sports to a fault, but after recuperating from his near death experience, he pondered other avenues. At the time, Selwyn Miller was managing his dad, and Anthony wasn't happy with Selywn at all. It seemed when Tony got together and chatted with his dad that Selwyn was the thorn in Anthony's side that he couldn't get out. So one day Tony boldly piped up and offered to take over a portion of Selwyn's position.

Initially, Tony was brought in as the road manager, but later, he took over the complete organization. "With a family member in charge of the money, I knew the money would stay within the family. Tony was someone I could wholly trust to take care of me and the group. Smart, sharp, quick, and adventurous, his cunning moves on the football field transferred well into managing our team. He listened, he learned, and he has been able to keep the business running smoothly and efficiently. I have to admit, when I overhear Tony talking on the phone and he says that he has to talk things over with his dad, I feel such a sense of pride. He truly understands me and gets it, he knows just what to do. I think all those years of coaching has taught him how to read people and how to make the score for the touchdown."

Having a life that was filled with a bustling household, sometimes it was overwhelming. "What's it like being married to Anthony, a world famous singer, who globetrots as if he were out to the store picking up a loaf of bread? It's exciting!" admitted Linda. "I love traveling with him and watching him perform, I love being able to expose our kids to this incredible world of entertaining. Because of Anthony's work, we were able to take our family to the Caribbean on luxury cruise ships where we were given suites and treated like royalty. Meeting incredible people and going incredible places has become our way of life and I love it. Sure, I miss him when he is on the road and I can't be there with him, but I've learned to balance the good with the bad, and there is a lot more good than bad.

"In the very beginning, when we were first married, I was worried about other women, but I kept my faith in my husband. One night we were at a night club, dancing and partying with several of his musician friends. He took my hand and walked me to the dance floor and after two songs this strange woman came over, pushed me out of the way and told me it was her turn to dance with Anthony. I was so furious! I turned and told her to bug off, he was my husband and she wasn't about to dance with him!

"Meeting stars, like Michael Jackson and his brothers, is one of my fondest memories. Anthony was asked to sing "Going Out Of My Head" at Liza Minnelli and David Gest's wedding. She wanted to dance with her new husband to one of her favorite songs. That wedding was the most amazing experience. It took place in New York City and lasted almost twenty-four hours. All the performers were flown in and provided with top notch accommodations. From the moment we landed, there was nonstop entertainment and activities for the guests. It was the most lavish wedding I had ever been to or could even imagine, and I was honored to be included in the prestigious guest list. What a party!

"There were times when I had to pinch myself, because I couldn't believe the life I was privy to. A while ago, Anthony was in a movie and I was on the set watching him act, when they needed an extra. So the director's assistant grabbed me, sent me to wardrobe and make-up, and I ended up playing a customer chatting with a bartender. It was an awful lot of fun. I began to understand how it was so easy to become obsessed with show business; play-acting someone else was quite an experience, in spite of the fact I had no lines."

Walking around their spacious Las Vegas home, she proudly points the array of awards her husband has won over the years. "We don't need a decorator, Anthony's awards fill up our shelves and our walls. Every time another award is hung on the wall, we rearrange the others to make it fit." In spite of the fact she lives with a rock star, Linda has stayed incredibly grounded. She still teaches and coaches high school kids, and has kept her own identity and sought her own goals. When her girls' team won a cheerleading award, she glowed with pride: her work meant something. She has touched the lives of thousands of kids throughout her years of teaching, and she intends to teach thousands more. Even though their four children have left the nest, situated within their own lives, they still keep her busy. There is always a birthday party to plan, another meal to cook, and another cause for celebration. Just keeping tabs on her husband's schedule, preparing him for the next gig, would be enough to tire most wives.

"Hey, honey," Linda hears Anthony yell out, "did you pick up my costume for tomorrow's show?" But before she can answer, the phone is ringing, or a text message has to be returned. "I wouldn't trade this life for anything. I love Anthony more than life itself."

Although most of the awards Linda proudly pointed out were from Anthony's brilliant career, many other plaques, citations, and statues were given as a gesture of appreciation for money he had helped raise for an army of charity organizations. "There were so many charities, I can't even remember – too many to count. I don't like to boast about what I did, because then it wouldn't feel right. But if I had to pick one of my favorite charities, it would be the Wounded Warriors, for the men who fought for our country and then returned home, broken and unable to get a job or have a normal life. They seemed to have been forgotten, yet we all owe them so much. So yes, I do a lot of concerts for these guys. When I am asked to talk here, or sing there, I just do it."

The awards strewn across Anthony's mantle, hung on the walls heading up the hall staircase, and stacked in a pile in his cluttered office are filled with a cavalcade of awards representing decades of his contribution to the music industry. They are a testament not only to his talent, and the impact his talent has had on the industry, but a tribute to his human spirit and the love and charity he has generously given to millions of people throughout his long and successful career.

In 2008 he received the Carolina Beach Music award for excellence in beach music. A unique sound that permeates down the Eastern Seaboard, from Virginia to Florida, it caters to the "shag" dance, a Southern rhythm-and-blues sound that was played in white suburbia.

"Jackie Wilson introduced the sound, a Black singer in all-white nightclubs and the music caught on like crazy. Soon we were all adding that beat into our new music. We became very successful, so much so that the music industry created an awards ceremony in

Myrtle Beach. The irony of this award is that when we began singing our way through the South, all we knew was segregation. Today, this award sitting on top of my fireplace, serves as a reminder of how far we have come. I know there is still plenty to do when it comes to prejudice, but this award is an acknowledgement of the great music we played, not the color of our skin. When they called to tell me about the award, I was truly happy. The committee flew us all down, put us up in the best hotels – hotels that were once segregated – and paid for meals in restaurants where we once weren't allowed a seat. It was worth the trip just to live to see all these changes."

That same year, 2008, it was Anthony's pleasure to give Teddy Randazzo the most prestigious award for song writers as Teddy was inducted, posthumously, into the Songwriter's Hall of Fame. "They gave me a script, and there was a teleprompter so I got all the words just right. What a night for Teddy! I was so proud to give him that award, he sure had earned it.

"There was a party after the presentations, and people were drinking, and having a lot of fun. In the corner I saw Dolly Parton, who I had always wanted to meet. George, our publicist, was at the presentation and when I told him how much I wanted to meet Dolly, he pulled me over and introduced me. She gave me a big hug and kiss, and told me she was happy to meet me. She is just a little bitty thing, barely five feet tall and a big set on her. I will never forget that night. Those award shows bring everyone together, people who haven't seen each other in years. Sometimes the ceremonies get a little too long, but seeing all the people and past friends, it's like a high school reunion. If I receive an invitation, I rarely turn them down."

In Los Angeles, he received the Soul of American Music award and years later, in Beverly Hills, he received the Heroes and Legend

Pacesetters award, which was given for outstanding achievements in show business. That night, on the illustrious stage, he shared awards with Smokey Robinson and Paul Rodriguez. The Make-a-Wish Foundation award sits next to the Lion's Club award for appreciation of services and contributions to their charities, and next to that stands the Doo Wop Hall of Fame award, which arrived in the mail. In 2002, the prestigious Black Music Award was added to the center of the mantle.

The Long Island Music Hall of Fame is host to the most iconic singers in America and to be honored with this award, you had to have lived in New York. Among the list of honorees are Billy Joel, George Gershwin, Tony Bennett, Neil Sedaka, Harry Chapin, and Cyndi Lauper.

"We walked the red carpet as hundreds of media people lined the entranceway, taking pictures and putting a microphone into our faces. It was a great night, one that I will never forget. I didn't know what to expect, but when I saw the size of the auditorium, I was shocked at the amount of people, famous people, who came out for that night and I am forever grateful." In September 2009, in St. Louis during the football season, he received the Sodexo Lifetime Achievement award. Representing a confederation of Black colleges, they honored outstanding Black leaders; some of the recipients were the Tuskegee Airmen, and the first Black bodyguard, (who was hired by Kennedy).

"After the presentation, Ernest, Robert, Clarence, and I had front row seats to the football game. We were treated beautifully as people came over and were showering us with love and attention. Being so loved by the Black population was an overpowering and humbling experience."

Holding up an unusually shaped, rather bland-looking award,

Anthony said, "This is my most valued award. It was given to me from *Food & Wine Magazine* for overall excellence in epicurean creation which best combines a careful balance of imagination and style. I won this for my Aunt Sara's shrimp patties, our family secret. To me cooking is like singing. I do it out of love and it gives me a chance to be creative in different ways other than through music.

"I guess through word of mouth, they found out about my hidden talent and asked me to come out and compete. From the moment I arrived, I was treated like royalty. They asked me what I was going to cook and then they purchased the ingredients and assigned me a local chef who would do the preparations. They told me to fax the chef the recipe, but I had no measurements, it was always a pinch of this and a handful of that. I learned to cook by watching my aunt, and she never measured anything.

"I met with a French chef and together we made the patties as she recorded the measurements. The recipe would eventually end up in the magazine. Once we had it down pat, we were ready for the competition. There was a large auditorium set up with complete mobile kitchens. The chef prepared the recipe while I stood overseeing the process in my clean suit. I didn't get my hands dirty. The smell was so wonderful that we had a line of people waiting to sample our appetizer. There were actors, football players, other famous chefs, and political leaders, all vying for the title. I looked around the huge room and there were no other lines, only at our booth. And guess what? I won!" Without a doubt, the highlight of Anthony's career was being inducted into the Rock and Roll Hall of Fame in 2009, the most prestigious award in the music industry next to the Grammys. The ingenious modern design of the Rock and Roll Hall of Fame Museum is a reflection of the artistry housed inside. Designed by Pei, it is a prism of triangular glass, appearing like an ancient pyramid, but made of out glass rather than stone. In 1998, Little Anthony and The Imperials were nominated for the award and lost, and for the next ten years it went the same way: The group would be nominated and then lose out to another star. It was the entrance of his publicist, George Dassinger, who finally made the nominating committee see the light. George had done his research, using the simple fact that Little Anthony had sold over twenty-two million singles. That fact alone was worth a lot of attention.

Sammy, Clarence, and Ernest, hadn't felt the need to hire a publicist, but Anthony had convinced them otherwise, that the music industry had evolved and this was a necessary step to insure their careers moved ahead. Meeting at their hotel in the bustling suburban town of Rutherford, New Jersey, they drank beers, ate thick steaks, and talked music business. He was head publicist for Reviver, as well as for a long list of recording artists, so they shook hands and became a team. "As long as you keep feeding us these delicious steaks, we'll keep coming back," said Anthony, who had a soft spot for excellent food.

George Dassinger was born in Queens, New York, and had a passion for music. When the time came to enter college, he selected Florida Southern College in Lakeland, Florida. He thought the change would offer expansive musical opportunities and increase his creative juices, but it did just the opposite. It had a regimented schedule and forced ROTC training, and he lasted one semester. He returned north and obtained his degree from Bloomfield College, in the bucolic setting of the northern New Jersey suburbs.

He lucked into the almost autonomous position as the deejay for the college radio channel. He spun whatever he wanted until one evening, he played a Jefferson Airplane song that had one unacceptable lyric. He was fired on the spot by the radio station manager who told him in no uncertain terms that the lyrics went against broadcast policy. Shocked, George fought back, but there was nothing for him to do but pick up his backpack and move on.

With a college degree, he wanted to set fire to the world with his passion or music, but all he landed was a dead end job at the postal service. He began interviewing musicians and singers and sending in columns to a music newspaper. One day he had scheduled an interview with Rod Stewart, which cut into his regular job and when George's boss found out, he opened up his private office and allowed his employee free reign for the interview. A few days later, George strutted into the office carrying a copy of the paper with the interview prominently printed on a column on the front page.

Later that week, George was invited into the boardroom of the head honchos of the postal service. There were several men sitting around smoking cigars, and drinking shots of whiskey. "George," began his boss, "I want you to leave here and don't look back. You have a promising future ahead of you and if you remain here, you will never see your dreams come true. Leave here today and never ever come back. Go and catch your dreams." Which is exactly what he did. He grabbed his coat, left the building, and forged ahead to his dreams.

Tall, thin, with a boyish handsome face and thick dark hair, his bubby personality and easygoing manner provided him with all the tools he needed to succeed. Up until his boss had given him his marching orders, he couldn't see it, but his boss surely could. A waste of a life and a career is what his boss saw the day he made him leave.

As George drove home, he pondered that last scene in the boardroom. Had he stayed, he would have ended up just like the rest of those guys. It's impossible to look at yourself objectively, but when those you respect, who have been around the block for several more decades, see talent, and push you in that direction, you feel like you should act on their advice.

On George's way up his career ladder, in the early 1980's, he became a Vice-President at Rogers and Cowan, and then several years later, he hopped over and became the Vice-President at Elektra Records in charge of Information Services. This decade served him well, giving him the experience and the network to attain his eventual goal. Public relations firms are mostly situated on upper Madison Avenue, and so he began his career promoting the C-list of singers. In a way that was great; since the talent was pretty much at the bottom of the barrel, anything he did would be an improvement. He started working for Henry Rogers, and nursed the clients to a higher position in the entertainment world. Laying public relations groundwork, the artists began selling more records and getting more gigs, and that was the proof of the pudding.

One day George's boss sat him down to tease an idea out for a problem client, namely the Remington Shaver Company. When the new guy on the block suggested using the owner of the company in the ads, Henry thought the idea so inspired that he turned to the other two employees in the room and fired them on the spot. George cringed, not wanting to be the reason anyone lost their jobs. "Son," said Henry, "You figured out in a minute what these guys couldn't in a couple of years."

The pitch to the shaving company was overwhelmingly accepted, filmed, and the increase in sales reinforced George's inspired thinking. "I got promoted, and was forced to go out and purchase suits, since they handed me more of the business clients. But my heart wasn't in it; I loved music, and I wanted to be surrounded by it.

So on Saturdays, I would meet with my C-list musicians, and during the week, I was with the entrepreneurs. For the moment, I was satisfied and so was my C-list. "Then a friend of mine, Ron Bienstock, an entertainment lawyer, gave me a call. He represented Anthony and The Imperials and suggested I meet with them. That night, the group was headlining at the Meadowlands Arena at a doo-wop show. Since I had a passion for music and loved their songs, I was all too happy to go. Ron specialized in entertainment law, and has taken on many high profile cases in his decades of practice, he was definitely an attorney I wanted on my side of the court."

"The next day, I met with Clarence and Anthony at the Renaissance Hotel restaurant and we discussed what I could offer them in terms of public relations. Clarence did all the talking while Anthony sat quietly, immersed in his bowl of chicken soup. My job was to persuade them to take what I had to offer and the idea was very clear to me: 'You guys have been in music for fifty years and we need to celebrate that and tell the world you have survived for five decades. You should rename your tour the 50th anniversary tour and I will help you promote this.' Anthony dropped his spoon and looked up, and I could clearly see he was excited about the idea."

Turning to Clarence, Anthony simply said, "George, I think you are that guy, that one person who sees what we need."

Within a few weeks after their first meeting, the group's name began to reappear in columns, newspapers, and blogs; album sales spiked, and deejays were receiving more requests. George's strategy was working and the music was given a fresh new look by the music industry. With his connections, George created Hall of Fame buzz. Could it be that after ten years of nominations, and ten years of disappointments, their time had finally arrive?

One of the most potent moves George made was to call Paul

Schaffer from David Letterman's Late Night Show. Dave loved "It Hurts So Bad," and welcomed the group to the show. They rearranged the song to an upbeat tempo and accompanied it with a full orchestra; it sounded fantastic. Dave went out of his way, walked across the stage, and thanked the group for their performance.

The next day, George called his newest clients and told them that the buzz was getting louder for the possibility of induction; Anthony went to Clarence's house the next afternoon at three, and waited for his call. Anthony did as their publicist asked, and arrived on time, patiently waiting for the call. Terry Stewart, who was responsible for constructing the Hall of Fame building, came on the line and congratulated Anthony and Clarence: they had won the nomination and would be inducted into the Hall of Fame. Clarence and Anthony jumped for joy, hugged each other, called Ernest, and then called George and thanked him for making this happen.

The induction was an entire happening, celebrated before, during, and after the defining moment when the award was secured in the owner's hands. Anthony arrived two days ahead of time, and was scheduled for an early morning talk show on Fox Channel 8. Well before his usual hour to rise, he made an exception to appear live with the early morning news panel. The commentators remarked how thrilled and honored they were to have Little Anthony with them that morning, on the day before the induction ceremony. He reminisced about the history of the group, saying, "I don't think anybody could have imagined that fifty years later we would be where we are, still singing to sold-out crowds and selling our music."

Sitting with a true legend, the interviewer was humbled and reverent. Little Anthony was truly a legend in his own time and she was there recording the historic moment. "This is bigger than the

Grammys; it's like saying I'm the best and it was one of the best nights of my life. We are the only singing group that had three decades of top-charted music. Although so many people consider us a doo-wop group, that is far from how our music can be defined. We can sing it all, from fifties to Broadway tunes to current songs, and when we perform, we give our audience a taste of all of the music." While standing in the wings prior to the induction, George was talking with Ron Wood of the Rolling Stones.

Ron walked over introduced himself to Anthony and then bent over, making a reverent deep bow. "Why are you bowing to me?" asked Anthony.

"'Tears on My Pillow' is one of my all-time favorites songs and it is an honor to meet you," said Ron.

"It is an honor to meet you as well, but that bow really threw me off. Thank you; and I'll tell you that I'm glad I can still sing 'Tears' the way it should be sung," said Anthony.

It was Smokey Robinson, with his eloquent style and sophisticated demeanor, who introduced the group. "When they called out, 'Little Anthony and The Imperials!' Sammy, Nathaniel, Clarence, Ernest, and me, walked onto the stage together to accept the award. I was overcome with emotion. So much had happened, good and bad, but that night on stage the five of us rejoiced together as the entire audience gave us a standing ovation. At the time we accepted the award, I failed to mention Tracey Lord's contribution to the group. After the show Tracey's wife approached me and asked why I hadn't mentioned Tracey. She was hurt and I realized that I had made an oversight because Tracey's great talent helped the group become successful. It may be a little late, but Tracey is not forgotten, his memory and friendship will forever be in my soul." The show was recorded and their induction, later put on youtube.

com, has become a permanent fixture on their website. "Weeks later, Kohl's had a private birthday party for the owner. We were entertaining and sitting in the first row was one my heroes, Yogi Berra. My wife, Linda, was talking to Carmen, Yogi's wife and said that my husband would love Yogi's autograph. Yogi overheard them and said it will be nice if I had a baseball. Terry Stewart, overheard the conversation and knew of a memorabilia store just around the corner. He strutted out, purchased a ball and he handed it to Yogi to sign for Anthony. Today, that is proudly sitting on the mantle of our home. After the performance, I just had to ask Yogi a question. In 1955, during the World Series, Jackie Robinson stole home base. Was he safe or was he out? Yogi turned to me with a grin and simply answered, 'Out!' I just had to know. When I was six, my dad had taken me to a baseball game and it was the first time I had seen Jackie Robinson play. I had never seen anyone run so fast so I believed that he was safe when he rounded the plate and slid into home base. That day, Yogi set me straight."

The accolades continued in the form of interviews, talk shows, and of course, an endless stream of gigs. Phil Roura, a *Daily News* Writer, interviewed Anthony in New York City. Titled "Years on their Pillow," the interview ran a full page.

"Relaxing in his desert home on a golf course near Las Vegas, Anthony Gourdine laughs at reaching the golden milestone. 'Fifty years? Yeah that's what they tell me.' But it doesn't feel that way. There is no place to think of time passing by if you have a youthful mind- and we have youthful minds. We are very fortunate and pleased to have a very dedicated following. They bring their children and they hear us and say, hey that's cool.' Gourdine chalks up the group's longevity to being able to respect each other. 'Even when we went our separate ways a couple of times, we never killed each other or beat each other up by saying horrible things. It's very rewarding to know that you have survived all those years over your peers.'"

On the flip side of their fiftieth anniversary, *Jet Contents* wrote the following: "'We survived for fifty years because we realize we are not hit recording artists of today. Beyoncé is today's recording artist. We know that and we understand that.' They have concentrated on becoming consummate concert performers and continue to travel all over the world singing their hits. 'We made the transformation into becoming performing artists. We are the real deal. We are very good at what we do as performing artists. We have developed a following; they come to be entertained, to hear those old songs. We have been blessed.'"

Steve Jones in *USA Today*'s half page article, "Little Anthony finds a way back to your hearts," wrote another prestigious article, with an accompanying color photo featuring Harold Jenkins, Ernest Wright, Clarence Collins, and Little Anthony, all dressed in printed jackets and cream colored linen pants. "Anthony Gourdine and his friends used to sing under the streetlights in Brooklyn's Fort Greene projects. 'What we did was follow our dream, I've been blessed by God for fifty years to do what I like to do and have people pay me for it. I've never worked a day in my life. People will tell me that I'm singing. Well, I tell them, that ain't work."

Todd Baptista, of *Goldmine Magazine*, wrote, "A lesson on defying categorization," which he explains musically is often daunting and dangerous. "While some artists can be easily slotted into various genres, many shudder at the process. Classify someone under blues and try to get their record played in a non-blues format. More than fifty years have passed since Little Anthony and the Imperials traveled from the Fort Greene neighborhood to record for George Goldner's top successful company, End Records. In that time the group has endured a host of categorizations- rock and roll, rhythm and blues, soul, vocal group, doo-wop and -ouch- oldies. 'That one hurts the worst,' agrees Anthony, now 69 and living in the Las Vegas suburb of Summerlin. 'It sounds like something old and dusty and moldy that you dragged out. Even doo wop shows, which we rarely do, because we're not a doo-wop group.' In 2009 Little Anthony and The Imperials continue to record and tour around the world." Jim Beckerman's two page article in *The Record* quotes a time and a place to see the R&B group: "Tuesday through Saturday at Feinsteins at Loews Regency, Park Avenue, Manhattan, jackets suggested." Entitled "Little Anthony: Longevity," the article welcomes home its prodigy. "Where did Little Anthony & the Imperials go right? Two years after they were inducted into the Rock and Roll Hall of Fame, the group is going where few 1950s R&B stars have gone before: playing to the supper-club set at $60 a ticket. If that doesn't impress, consider that most of their contemporaries- the lucky ones- are playing doo-wop nostalgia shows in Holiday Inn ballrooms, packaged with seven or eight other groups that maybe have one member of the original group.

"'We made it out business to be as sharp as we could as long as we could,' says Anthony whose falsetto was and is one of the best in the business. 'I've always said that we were once recording stars, but we became performing stars. We did a transition. Ninety-five percent of the artists that came out of our era did not. They live in the past. Longevity is when you keep reinventing yourself. That's the whole idea. That's the reason we've lasted for 53 years. The saddest thing to me in the world is to see a bunch of old dudes that keep on singing the same old songs. They're like 85, 90 years old, and they keep on doing the same old thing. I won't name names. But the great performers like Sammy Davis, Jr. understood that they were as good as their last performance. They were constantly changing and adding. By maintaining their vocal equipment and their energy level, they are putting on performances 53 years after their first hits that still surprises people who are expecting a typical 'oldies' show. We're known as a high energy act; I think people sometimes think we're going to roll up in wheelchairs or something."

In the Night Life & Entertainment section of *Coast*, August 2009: "You simply can't have a conversation about the hottest vocal groups to come out of New York without including Little Anthony and the Imperials. Lead singer Anthony Gourdine gave a voice to teenage passion back in the fifties and continues to push the boundaries of contemporary R & B today. I have to tell you that anyone who pigeonholes Anthony Gourdine as a blast from the past is missing the mark. His- and the group's- longevity in the business is due at least in part because they refused to let others define them. 'I've always followed by instinct…don't allow anyone to define me.' Unlike so many other 50's vocal groups relegated to anachronistic reunion shows or tours, Little Anthony and the Imperials celebrate their past without living it all over again. A tangible example of this is their 'You I'll Never Know' CD, released in 2008. Clearly a labor of love, it pays homage to the past even as it reaches the future."

The news stories continue to be printed and devoured by music lovers throughout the world. Hats off to George Dassinger for infusing just the perfect amount of public relations, reinstalling the Anthony back into the limelight and keeping him there. Anthony is history in the making and as his old and new music is played, future generations will be lucky enough to become familiar with all those beautiful tunes. Analyzing the spins on records around the globe, somewhere on earth every hour, a deejay is playing their music.

The Twenty-fifth anniversary of the Rock and Roll Hall of Fame was approaching, and initially, Anthony's group was not on the list of performers. Paul Simon walked into a production meeting and noticed that his friend wasn't on the program. Taking a stand, he turned to the production manager and said to count him out of the show. Billy Joel sided with Paul, and also said he refused to perform unless Anthony was included. The production manager, whose face had turned several shades of red, realized his extraordinary omission, and piped up that he could "fit Anthony into the show."

The night of the four-hour special, Anthony tugged on George's sleeve, "I feel real nervous, I haven't sung in such a huge venue in seven weeks." When he walked up to the microphone, and the music cued, Anthony's voice could be heard throughout the huge auditorium. After receiving a standing ovation, he was further convinced that everyone loved him and his music.

CHAPTER 25

In 2009 when so many accolades were showered upon the group, they couldn't and wouldn't allow anything or anybody to stand in their way of success. Clarence, sitting in his home studio, turned to Anthony and said "Listen to this: Harold's off key and he sounds bad." It wasn't just a one-time sour note as Anthony and Clarence replayed live performances, and then listened acutely to the last recording.

"What do you think? As for me, I think it's time for him to hang up the microphone, at least with our group," said Clarence.

Tearing away the headphones, Anthony concurred, "He's gotta go. It's time. We have a lot of gigs coming up, another album in the works, and everyone has to be on point. We can't let this slide no matter how much we love Harold."

Simultaneously, they both spat, "He has to go!"

Clarence punched in the number in his cell phone and made a date for the following day at Harold's home. A public place wouldn't do, nor would they want him coming to their homes only to drive away in utter despair.

"Harold was always that guy who jumped in whenever son~ was sick, or unable to perform. Boy, could he move on st?

nights he performed, we knew it would be a good time. He loved being up on that stage showing off his talents. He really got us to move; he knew how to use every inch of the stage, and how to play to the audience."

They rang Harold's doorbell, standing awkwardly at the front door. Who would start the conversation was left up in the air, but today was the day, and they knew the bad news had to be delivered. Harold's wide smile flashed as he opened the door, hugged his buddies, and then escorted them to the cozy living room of his apartment. The sky was cloudless, the sun warm, but the thoughts of Clarence and Anthony weighed heavily on their mind, and perfect weather wouldn't temper their bad news.

"Great to see you guys. How about a soda?" asked Harold. Shaking their heads, Clarence began a lengthy explanation as to the purpose of the visit, "Your pitch, it just wasn't it used to be. We are all getting old, and I know every day I thank God for continuing to allow me to sing, but sometimes it ends. Harold, for you and the group, I'm afraid it has ended. We need that three octave range, and we have to have perfect pitch."

Anthony piped up, adding his piece to the conversation, "Sorry, man, but it just isn't there anymore. With all these elaborate recording devices, and high technology equipment, every note can be heard and if you're off-pitch, it's picked up. We are all going to have to hang it up sometime and I only hope that when my time comes, I will know."

"This hurts, and it's killing us to have to tell you, but we are ırvivors, and we intend to keep the music playing. 1972, that's how · it's been, and it has been a great ride. I'm sorry, really sorry," ıthony. They stood up and walked out of Harold's apartment.

It wasn't until Anthony had slammed his car door and had traveled a few miles that he reflected on the conversation. Instead of plunging into sentimental thoughts, Anthony began singing some of Harold's favorite songs, a fitting tribute to a buddy who had jumped into help them out on hundreds of occasions.

In 2009, The Imperials were searching for a replacement voice and after numerous fruitless efforts, found their newest member, Robert DeBlanc. Coming from Louisiana, his voice reflected that rich R & B sound heard throughout the jazz venues in the deep South. A back-up singer for Aretha Franklin and Marvin Gaye, his résumé spoke worlds of his talents. Robert knew and understood the music, and had the pipes to match; it was a marriage made in heaven.

It all began with a frozen chicken, which may or may not have saved Anthony's life. Linda wrapped a towel around her bikini, grabbed a magazine, sunglasses, and her trusty bottle of suntan lotion, and prepared to sit by the pool in the late summer afternoon sun. Anthony was already in the water, swimming lap after lap, when she looked over and saw two chickens lying on the picnic table, where it appeared as though they too, were taking in the sun. "Hey Anthony what are those two chickens doing sitting on the table? Do you think they are going to sprout wings and fly?" she jested. "Gosh, hon, I was just defrosting them, and thought setting them out in these 110 degree temperatures would speed things along. Besides, that was how my Aunt Bessie defrosted a chicken."

"Are you nuts! First of all your Aunt Bessie never had a freezer that could hold two chickens, and second of all we will all get salmonella if you don't take those chickens inside and put them in a pot of water to properly defrost." In charge of cooking, but not of cleaning up, he dutifully climbed out of the pool, touched the sunbathed birds, testing to see how ready they were for their ultimate end at the mercy of the gas barbecue. They were still solid as a rock when he picked them up and plunged them into their bath of tepid water in the center of the sink. He strolled back out to the pool and finished his delightful afternoon swim. That night as they gathered around the dining table, Linda again admonished the chef for abusing the chickens and the fact that they could have all gotten food poisoning. Bowing his head, he promised never again to set another frozen piece of meat out in the open.

When the table was cleared, and the chickens were nothing but a few scattered bones on their empty plates, Linda had to admit that Anthony was a great cook; whatever he cooked turned to gold. Maybe his Aunt Bessie couldn't defrost, but she sure taught him how to cook.

"Do you need any help getting ready for the fair in California?" Linda asked as she placed the dishes into the dishwasher. "I wish I could go with you, but I promised my mom I would visit her and then I promised our daughter I would babysit our grandchild. I'll miss you and I will sure miss all that great food at the fair." Even though she was stuffed from the meal, it didn't stop her mouth from watering just thinking about the cotton candy, the corn dogs, and the endless parade of foods cooked in large, deep-fat fryers. It seemed as though every year they invented new foods to fry, and each was better than the last. Anthony said, "I can't think of food, to tell the truth; lately my appetite is not what it used to be." Linda took a look at his stomach; from the size of his stomach, it didn't look like he had lost any weight; in fact, just the opposite.

"I think I will take a little nap." Within ten minutes he was sound asleep on the leather sofa. Funny, Linda thought as she kicked on the dishwasher, he never took a nap after dinner, usually he took an hour walk around the golf course after the players had retired for the day.

Packed and ready to go, the next morning he headed out to California. His first stop was at a charity benefit for Pat Boone at a lush golf course in the suburbs of Los Angeles. Dressed in madras shorts, a yellow, knit, short-sleeved shirt, and white cap, he was sure to do himself proud; at least he looked the part of a savvy scratch golfer.

"I was driven around in a golf cart with a couple other guys and I was so tired I could barely walk to the tee. I felt like I couldn't catch my breath." After the tournament ended, he walked to his car and drove south down Highway 1. He was to meet up with the group for their gig at the county fair. "Oh do I miss the smell of the water, and the jogging on the beaches. There is nothing like California, but I still feel awful," he thought, as his distended stomach ached and hardened. "I just need to get up on that stage and sing, and I'll be just fine."

He pulled into the motel, grabbed his room key, checked in at the front desk, and called all of The Imperials to meet at the registration desk by six that afternoon; they were scheduled to go on at eight o'clock. Although they were unable to have a real sound check, they needed to arrive early and figure out the audio so they came off as professionally as possible. From decades of experience, they knew that fair sites had deplorable acoustics, but if they had an hour of listening to other groups singing before them, their attuned ears could guide the way.

Sure enough, the reverberations were bad, so they decided to cut short lingering notes and runs, and move the microphones away from their mouths after two beats, to cut down on the echo. It worked like a charm; the music, especially the ballads, sounded much better than the two previous groups. Making those few adjustments, the music sounded almost as good as if they were inside at an arena. With only fifteen songs in the set, they were on and off the stage in under two hours, and although Anthony thought he would feel on top of the world, his stomach still ached. Gathered at the back of the stage were Julie Barette, the road manager, Tony, Robert, Ernest, and Clarence, who were anxiously waiting to take in all the fair had to offer. "You guys ready for some of that great food waiting for us on the midway?" asked Tony, who shared the same passion for food as his dad.

"I just want to go back to my room. I really am feeling worse." But even lying on the bed and taking an aspirin, he never got better and finally, he was writhing with pain. Grabbing his cell, he called the only person who knew just what to do. "Linda, I feel awful, I'm in so much pain and..."

"Listen to me. You call 911 right now and get yourself into a hospital. I'm at mom's house and I can meet you in a couple of hours but you are not to wait, do you understand?" she bellowed.

"Yes." The ambulance arrived within ten minutes, carting the star to the nearest hospital, Scripps Memorial, where a staff of doctors and nurses was prepared for their famous patient. They took his vitals, and saw an escalated fever signaling infection, so they hooked up IVs and an EKG. Any first year intern could have easily diagnosed his problem: appendicitis. After he signed the authorization forms, the nurses rushed him two stories up to the operating room, where they performed an emergency appendectomy.

Linda arrived within two hours, received an update from the staff, and then paced the small waiting room until the young, on-duty surgeon walked through the swinging doors. There was a latent smile underneath her mask as she announced the patient's surgery went well, but he had a massive infection throughout his intestines and he required heavy-duty antibiotics. She didn't sugarcoat Anthony's prognosis, and it wasn't favorable.

While he was in surgery they received results from two blood tests, one determining that along with the busted appendicitis, he also had an E. coli infection that had spread throughout his lower internal organs. "We are doing all we can for him, we just have to hope those drugs are strong enough to get rid of the E. coli. He is a strong man, with a sound heart, but he will need a lot of rest in the next few days."

Linda sat down on the sofa and began to cry endless tears. He could die, she thought; there was no way she could say this out loud. When they finally wheeled him out of surgery and into the hospital room, she was curled up on the chair next to the bed. He opened up his eyes to acknowledge her presence and then fell back to sleep. "He is in a lot of pain," explained the nurse. "I suggest you go home and get some sleep."

"No, I'm not leaving this hospital without my husband. When he is ready to leave, then so will I," she said adamantly. It was almost daybreak when she finally closed her eyes after spending the last couple of hours watching her husband's breath, waiting to see if he would open up his eyes again. Still too early to call the family, she finally gave in and slept until she heard the sound of the nurses attending to Anthony.

The hospital, aware of its famous patient, had given him a suite with a bed for Linda. The nurses changed the IV, took vital signs, rearranged the sheets, propped up the pillows, and brought Linda the breakfast they knew the patient wouldn't and couldn't eat. Later that day she phoned the children and her mom, telling them the news, promising them an update on his condition. With just two days of clothing, she was ill prepared for the long haul ahead. Shopping for essentials was added to her to-do list, but only until reinforcements arrived and she felt comfortable enough to leave her husband's bedside.

Tony, the oldest son, arrived later that evening, filled with anxiety and grave concern which escalated each time he looked into Linda's eyes. Watching his exuberant dad lying on the hospital bed, inert and sleeping, scared him. Tony shared the vigil so Linda could eat and take a shower. The long day rolled into evening and by the next morning, Anthony finally opened his eyes. Still drugged from the operation, he was in a fog and in pain. Linda explained what had happened, and that he would have to wait for the drugs to do their work. She never let on how serious his condition was; there would be plenty of time later, after he was home, for that conversation. For the moment, she was there to raise his spirits and make damn sure he stayed alive.

No one was allowed to visit him, not even his buddies; the last thing he needed was to be exposed to outside germs. By the time the third day rolled around, his pain had increased and the surgeons insisted on inserting a breathing tube down his throat. It would only be for a day, they promised, but without it, he may not survive. Anthony was absolutely terrified: what if that tube destroyed his vocal cords? Then he would have nothing. No, he didn't want that in the worst way, but between the doctors and Linda, he gave in. He was too weak and in too much pain to fight. The tube was inserted and remained there for almost two weeks while all of his nutrition came through the means of a feeding tube.

"Come on, sweetheart, I will walk with you, remember what your doctor said, you must get up and walk several times a day," Linda pleaded. Being still in so much pain, rather than follow orders, he preferred to simply lie in the bed. At her wit's end, she phoned Damon, who had moved to Seattle, and the next morning he was at his father's side. He had made his dad get out of bed and they were slowly walking the corridors. Three weeks later, Anthony and Linda finally emerged from the hospital. He was a lucky one, surviving a devastating infection that killed most patients. The staff at Scripps Memorial had done their job superbly. "God wanted me to live. It wasn't my time to go."

When they finally arrived home, she threw a cotton blanket onto the leather sofa, and he gently sat down. "My throat feels so dry and I'm afraid my voice…"

"Now, just stay quiet," Linda ordered as she set a glass of water on the table, handed him the remote, and began scurrying around the home, cleaning, and preparing soft foods for him to eat. The cell phone rang, and as he went to answer, Linda grabbed it out of his hands. He was to save his voice, and get back his strength. It was Tony, calling to see how he was doing, and testing the waters to see if he should call off a huge concert scheduled for the second weekend in August 2013. Taking back his phone, Anthony said, "Son, I feel like I have lost a month out of my life, and I know I'm weak, but I'm going to make sure I play that concert. I've got the best nurse in the world to take care of me."

"I'll be there to visit you at the end of the week and we shall talk about it then. Dad, just do what you are supposed to and get well."

The healing process was slow and arduous as Anthony began regaining his strength and his voice. When Linda deemed him psychologically strong enough, she fully explained the severity of his illness and that he could have died.

"You always got on me about making sure the kitchen and the

food was clean, I see you're right. I've learned my lesson the hard way. But what I can't figure out is why no one else got sick?"

"Remember your habit of licking the food you're working with? How you put your fingers on the food and taste it even though, especially in this case, the food wasn't cooked? Well that's probably what happened. We all ate the cooked food, but you inadvertently tasted it raw after it had been soaking in the sun. For the life of me, I don't know where you picked up that habit, but it almost did you in!" She held him tightly for several minutes as they both realized how dangerously close he had come to losing his life. "Now, we have to get you better if you are to play to a sold out crowd at the Cannery."

Because of the stitches in his stomach, he remained on the sofa for another two weeks until he was allowed to walk the two flights of steps to their bedroom. Placing one lightweight blanket on top of her snoring husband, Linda flipped off the television, and silently lumbered upstairs. Later that night Tony called: he would arrive early the following afternoon and they would discuss a game plan. He was his father's son and now manager, and he had to play both roles, trying to make sure he didn't overextend his dad.

Linda heard the sound of Tony's car pull up as she ran to open the door. A blast of August heat filled the foyer as he hugged his stepmother and walked into the living room. Anthony stood up, hugging his son, and they returned to a comfy position on the sofa. The color had returned to his face, his protruding stomach was now flat, and most importantly of all, his voice was exactly as before – not a note out of place. While chitchatting over iced tea, Tony was overly concerned with the upcoming date. "Dad, it's only five weeks away, are you sure you will be up for an hour and half show in front of thousands? I called the ticket agent yesterday and sales are eighty percent sold out. By show time, we will be sold out, I have no doubt.

Just say the word and we will cancel. I can't and won't put your health in jeopardy," Tony cried as he grabbed his father and held him gently. "I have my voice back, and if I have that, that's all I need."

"I'm going to stick around a few days a week and help you gain back your strength. From the looks of Linda, I think she could use some assistance. I heard you are not the best patient around," Tony joked. He stayed a few days, pushing his dad to walk, and recover his energy. Although he practiced singing and moving around his home, the group never rehearsed for the performance. "Rehearse? We have been singing these songs for decades, we don't need to rehearse."

When Anthony showed up backstage, he got several slaps on the back. "Now that our lead singer is here, the show can go on," jested Robert. The wide stage had ample room for a full band and elaborate choreography. Anthony's microphone was ten feet away from the others', but they wouldn't need practice to stay in sync: they followed their leader; that was all they ever needed to do to stay in sync. Watching Anthony's head bopping to the beat of the drummer provided all the direction the singers needed to keep in touch with the rhythm. Scanning the audience, Anthony felt a warm glow. The house was packed, every seat had been sold, and even the makeshift additional rows of miserably uncomfortable metal folding chairs at the very back were filled.

"I can't believe these seats," screamed Holly as the six friends and ardent fans found their way past the ticket takers and security, and were then ushered to the very last row in the entire auditorium. "You see Ron had to have an aisle seat, and we needed six tickets, and I will admit I waited until two weeks before," said Louise.

"Let's just face facts, you are cheap, just bloody cheap, and this is where we end up, the very last row!"

"But I promise you, the show will be great no matter where we sit," Louise responded. In a huff, Holly began walking up and down the endless rows of seats trying to find just one empty spot. With three minutes to show time, she finally gave up, and begrudgingly took her assigned seat. The music streamed throughout the hall, and it was beautiful, as beautiful as they had imagined, as beautiful as when they had all remembered when they first spin the 45s.

"He is so little, Anthony is so little," said Ron, "But I guess the fact that he is a hundred rows away doesn't help matters." When the performance had ended and the six friends filed out, all they could remember was the perfect sound of Anthony's voice and the way he had moved them to tears. "You guys now know why I love him so much, it doesn't matter where I sit, or where he sings, I'll be there."

"Speak for yourself; next time I'm buying the tickets, and they will be front row. With a voice like that I don't want to miss a note," announced Holly. The sold-out evening was a testimony of the fans' loyalty, and the fact that so many seated in the audience had become curmudgeons. But when Tony walked through the crowd, there were lots of second and third generation fans. Maybe that back row was filled with first generation retirees, but almost every age from six to ninety was represented. Parents brought their kids, and in turn, they brought their kids. That night was a night of creating and resurrecting fond memories; that was a night no one would ever forget.

"What a crowd! Every single seat sold out. I'm thankful I'm alive and to see so many fans here, I think that God wanted me to be alive, to see all this," reflected Anthony while Tony escorted his dad from behind the curtains to the dressing room, handing him a bottle of water and making sure he was feeling fine. "I feel so alive, so blessed and so happy to be singing." Tears swelled up as Tony and Anthony hugged.

"You did it, Dad, you were great! After all you have gone through, between the operation and infection, you were electric. Like the lyrics to a song you don't sing 'I'm still standing…after all these years, yea, yea, yea!" That's you, Dad," said Tony. "Every seat was filled, even the very last row! I heard those people were angry when they first walked in, but I'm quite sure they felt they got their money's worth, since no one left. When you closed the show, I was at the back of the auditorium, and they all stayed for your last bow. They love you, Dad!"

Tony knew his dad was exhausted and once he had changed out of his costume, they snuck out the back door and went home quickly. After hugging him goodnight, Tony went to sleep in the guest room. Linda admonished Anthony to get some sleep, since he was still in recovery. Midmorning at the breakfast table, father and son met to discuss the upcoming schedule. Anthony would have one week off, then it was a cross country flight to Atlantic City for a group oldies show and the following week they would all hop on a cruise ship.

Anthony found traveling was often a drag, having to leave the family and go to parts unknown around the globe, but when he got the call to do the "Malt Shop Memories" tour on a Holland American cruise ship, that was too good to pass up. The three-thousand-guest ship was completely booked and the entertainment line-up was legendary. The family met the ship at St. Maarten. Anthony boarded with Linda, Tony, Elizabeth, and grandchildren Caleb and Brianna, onto a luxurious the ocean liner and were escorted to their VIP suite complete with chilled champagne and gourmet snacks.

"They really treated us entertainers first class all the way, from the beginning until we left the ship. It was the best experience." The list of artists were at the top of their game in the fifties and sixties:

Bill Medley, Neil Sedaka, Gary Bonds, The Four Tops, and Bobby Rydell.

Before his luggage arrived, Anthony was already out of the room, scouring the pool area for old colleagues. Dressed in shorts and a simple tee-shirt, he wanted to make sure he did appear as the average tourist. He spotted The Four Tops at the bar near at the upper deck. Duke was the only original member still alive.

"They used to call me Little Agony because we always hung around them, especially when we traveled into Detroit and visited Motown. They just couldn't get rid of us. The guys were a little older and we envied and emulated them, so we loved to be around them." He ordered a Coke and sat with them for hours until Linda finally caught up with him and insisted he take her for a walk around the ship. Although the roster was filled, the ship didn't feel that crowded: there were so many venues for entertainment, places to exercise, and a wide variety of activities.

"There was music all day long, always some live group playing somewhere and it was all the oldies music. They saved the bigger guys for the headliner shows in the evening, but as I walked around and heard the different acts, they all sounded great. I found out that the cruise company puts this themed trip once a year and it gets sold out in a day."

Even though Anthony's only assigned job was to sing on the last night of the trip, he renewed couples' vows during the day. He performed nuptials, not actually marrying the couple, but doing a spoof renewal. "I became known for this and the chapel was filled with people who wanted to renew their vows, but in a funny way." He also did in-house television interviews and walked around the ship, talking to the passengers. "I met people from all around the world: Scotland, England, Africa, South America, and the States. I would just walk up to them and introduce myself, but they all knew who I was, and then we would talk for a while and they would get to know me as a person."

The evenings were filled with sumptuous dinners. They were seated in a VIP section just for the entertainers. Ernest, Johnny, Robert, and Anthony, with their respective families, made up the Little Anthony and The Imperials table. "I ate so much, I ended up gaining five pounds."

Talking for hours amongst themselves and their colleagues, it was truly a reunion for the performers. No longer on the road in tour buses, it was rare that so many of the groups were gathered together in one place at one time.

The last port of call was Nassau, and that was the night they were scheduled to perform: they were the last headliners on the last night of the trip, an honor unto itself. The group got together for an afternoon sound check and rehearsal. They brought their own drummer, but the horns, two keyboards and guitarist were supplied by the ship. After a couple of rehearsals the musicians had it down pat; this wasn't the first time they had played the music. Sweat sprang from the singer's faces as they rehearsed the dance moves and belted out tunes. "This humidity really gets to me. After so many years in California and Las Vegas, I am used to the dryness. But it's great for the vocal cords. At least we could work off some of the food we ate."

The aging crowd sang along to their ballads, as the music brought back fond memories of their youth. "Looking at the audience and watching all those people having a great time while we sang made me feel good. I knew we were making them happy, and that they would remember us long after the cruise was over. That is one of the reasons why I love to perform: I get to bring joy into so many people's lives." As they made their way off the gangplank, waving good-bye to the crew, Anthony was filled with happy memories – and there were more to be had: the group had been invited back the following year. Little Anthony and The Imperials were the hit of the trip and the entertainment director had received so many requests, she asked them to return.

The cruise was just what Anthony needed to get back his stamina, because once home, he would have another series of cross country concerts on the Eastern Seaboard. Taking advantage of the warm, lazy afternoons, he closed his eyes and dreamed of the next new play sets. After Tony had made the decision to become his manager, his plate was filled. Gigs were coming in constantly, and even at seventy, his career was in an upswing. It was one of the best decisions Anthony had made, and when Tony agreed, it was one of Tony's best decisions.

The limousine was on time picking up the foursome from the airport; they were already discussing the return gig. It was an amazing cruise ship and the passengers were so forthcoming with their loyalty and support. Everyone agreed they would definitely block out the week the following year. Hearing the familiar ring of his cell, Tony slid it out of his pocket, pleased with the sound of the voice of their publicist on the other end. George was calling with a most unusual and exciting proposal.

Too busy with his own call, Anthony didn't pay attention until Tony hung up and a wide smile was cemented across his face. "Dad, George has just made a fantastic offer, one too good to pass. How you would like to sing a Beatles song on an album with several icons like yourself? It's to be a benefit record for Paul McCartney in memory of the cancer fund set up in Linda McCartney's name. Robert Johnson is producing the CD and wants you to be a part of this historic album." Anthony's smile copied his son's as they both shook their heads in unison. Placing a call back to George, they immediately agreed with the offer.

Early Friday night, Anthony eased the Lincoln up to the valet at the Palms Casino, just west of the Las Vegas Strip. Emerging into the crisp, cool, winter air, he and Tony were both invigorated and anxious for the recording. They knew this CD would be historic, a never-been-done-before recording of Beatles songs.

Even though the security guard recognized Anthony, he personally escorted the two of them into the elevator, punched a few buttons, and walked them into the reception area of the studio. Stark and ultramodern, with its blond oak floors, chrome bar, and plush walls, it was completely soundproof. It appeared as if it were the cockpit of a spaceship readied for intergalactic travel. There was one deep, black leather sofa for guests, the ceiling and walls were covered with speakers, and there was an array of sound equipment in a tripod console, with another bank of speakers set above the console, and one technician at the helm. Another glass-enclosed room, with a series of microphones, was prepared for Anthony. The tracks began to permeate the studio into the soundproof booth. There were two chairs: one for the technician and the other for the producer who were moving silently on steel ball bearings as they maneuvered the state-of-the-art sound equipment, taping the song.

Robert Johnson, a writer/producer, who had just flown in from Memphis, emulated the décor of the room. Sporting rose colored glasses with thick black rims, he appeared futuristic. His perpetual smile reflected the way he lived his life through rose colored glasses. Coaxing and encouraging Anthony, Robert fed him tidbits of instruction as his acutely attuned ear listened, nudging the singer into various directions. "I Won't Stay In A World Without Love," co-written by Paul McCartney, was brought to light through the beauty of Anthony's voice, and the technical nuances of Robert's nurturing. "Clever, cool, coming together, ninety-nine percent there," he said. "That take was devastating awesome, but let's try another pass."

Robert has spent his entire life wrapped up in music, beginning as a guitarist, and working his way up the industry. He became a technician, a song writer, and a producer. "The first time I heard Anthony's voice was on the local radio. The song was "Shimmy Shimmy Ko Ko Bop," and I begged my parents to buy me that record. My mom went to Woolworth's and, for 25 cents, she purchased the 45 that I played over and over again. Anthony was my idol and my hero and as I got older, when I went on a date, Little Anthony was the ammunition I used to get closer to my girlfriends. I knew it was my destiny to meet him and the day had finally arrived."

Robert has played his guitar with the most famous bands in the world, including the Rolling Stones. His first recording gig was with Stax Records, and from there he continued to perform, learning the fine art of a recording technician. As he moved up the East Coast to Manhattan, he was exposed to a wide range of music genres, and then one day he hopped on a plane and spent two years in London playing with the best bands the UK had to offer. "I have a rounded sensibility. I love producing, and it's a thrill to hear the music I produced played on the radio. That Friday evening when I recorded Anthony's voice to the Beatles song was a dream come true. He sings like an angel."

After two hours, Anthony walked out of the confined booth, wiping his temple with a towel; they called it a wrap. Playing back his soulful voice conjoined with the Beatles tune, it not only sounded unique, but completely fresh and new; he had breathed life into a classic song, truly making it his very own. That was what a star of such rare talent can do.

After playing back the final take, the production staff was joyful, they all knew this album was history in the making; it was a one-of-a-kind matching of iconic singers with the tunes that would be sold around the world, all through the foresight and genius of Paul McCartney. George, Anthony's publicist, handed him a bottle of water, congratulating his client for a job well done. He was both exhausted and exhilarated, feeling an unbridled passion for the music that was imbued in his heart and soul.

While riding up the glass elevator to the penthouse, he unleashed all that was weighing on his mind: "I don't sing; God just uses my body. It is through God's spirit that I sing. It is Him who you hear through my voice. When I woke up this morning, I sounded like Kermit the Frog, but the moment the track came through the speakers, I could sing. Oh how I love that song. I want to thank all of you for your patience and for this great opportunity. The studio is where I want to be, it feels like home." The others were surprised to hear such a metaphysical confession on the essence of Anthony's voice, and they rode in silence until the elevator doors opened into a spacious, dimly lit restaurant. Seated by the window, the group of men began conversing about music, common friends, and their favorite sports. All civil, but all the while knowing they had just created music that would become moored into the fabric of legendary musical recordings. Not bad for an evening's work.

Anthony drove the Lincoln into a small parking spot, honked the horn, and waited for Skip to emerge from apartment. While his friend of over fifty years slowly rolled his clubs to the trunk of the car, Anthony was happy he had been blessed with a litany of friends who would stay that way forever. It was late February, and the thermometer read seventy-two degrees: it was a perfect day for being on the golf course. "Good morning, Mr. Trenier," kidded Anthony, "And how is my senior friend doing?"

"You know, I'm only five years older than you. I'm not that ancient, I just feel that ancient," he answered. "Man, I can't believe you are still out there globetrotting as if you were in your early twenties. I say it's thanks to your son Tony, who has reinvented you. One week you're here and the next, you're off to England and crisscrossing the States like it's a trip to the grocery store. This is what I think and what I believe to be true.

"Your music and your original fans are taking their kids and their grandkids to hear your music, and it looks like, from reviewing the charts, the music is selling again. Looks like people can't get enough of you and all that great music that Teddy wrote for your group. I'm happy. You deserve the success, but most importantly, those great tunes are being enjoyed as new music by a whole new generation of people; your voice just goes on and on. My family had its run and we passed the baton and retired, but you just keep on going. I swear you will end up singing at your own funeral!" Skip joked.

"Now how much do you want to wager on this mess of a game we are about to play today? I am stating now that I will take a handicap of twenty and everything after that is gravy."

Laughing, Anthony agreed, but confirmed he was a bit rusty, what with being on the road and all. "Thanks for all of your good thoughts, Skip. I know I'm lucky. I am blessed in so many ways, especially when it comes to having friends like you." When they pulled into the golf course, Anthony turned to Skip and said, "Remember when we first moved here? There was no way they would allow us to play these courses. Thank God America has changed. We are all better for it." The two men dragged their clubs into the clubhouse, and sat sipping orange juice until the other half of their foursome arrived. With a perfectly azure sky, and a slight wind blowing from the north, this was going to be an excellent day, yes it was.

Anthony took to heart at what Skip had said: in his early seventies and traveling around the world like a young rock star, his life was full and vibrant. Rubbing his chin, Anthony pondered how fortunate he was to be doing what he loved doing, but how was it possible? There was an answer. Yes, the Lord had blessed him with talent and sustained his health. It was Linda who held it all together providing him with unabashed, unconditional love that gave him the strength and the ability to continue his career. She was always there for him, taking care of him, watching out for him. She always had his back. When at home with the children, Linda maintained her four decade career as a gymnastic teacher, spilling that love for athletics over to their children, each who came to love sports in their own way. Handling the ups and downs with the kids, she always put forth a strong smile and never fretted when Anthony's hand was on the suitcase. A kiss and hug good-bye, she always left him with a smile. When he was on the road and called home, she never complained, it was all about supporting her husband. She knew entertaining was hard work. She had seen him perform hundreds of times: it was taxing, physically exhausting, exhilarating, and sometimes even dangerous. Entertaining was not a simple job; it was fraught with worries, insecurities, and uncertainties. Things could and did go wrong, and he had to make sure that regardless, the show went on. The one thing that Anthony could always count on was Linda's love: it never tired, nor waned, it was as strong as the day the two were married.

Unassuming in every way, Linda epitomizes the classic yet

elusive doting wife. Her first concern is her husband, before herself and the children. "I married Anthony. That's who I fell in love with, and all the rest of this wonderful fantastic ride has been heavenly. I miss him horribly when he is away. I try to go with him on as many trips as possible but between the kids, grandkids, and my job, it's not so easy to pick up and go, but when he returns it's like a honeymoon. We are planning on going on a cruise together, one that he isn't working on. You would think that he could relax a bit when he performs on cruises, but it's just the opposite. He has to watch what he eats, drinks, that he gets plenty of exercise, that he protects his throat from illness, and then he is kept busy during the day with activities intermingling with the passengers, and at night performing. There are no down days on a luxury trip. Sometimes he comes home exhausted, ironically."

Having chosen the entertainment profession, which is unpredictable, fickle, and at times harsh and sporadic, the one thing Anthony can count on is his wife and the love they share. Being a performing artist is one of the most precarious ways to earn a living: he never knows when his next gig will be, or when that next royalty check will be deposited into his bank account. It is a feast or famine life style. With Linda, stalwartly steering an ever-steady course in his life, she smooths out the rough edges, providing the love, security, and emotional strength to get him through the tough times. Taking on much of the heavy burdens of family life, she frees up his mind to allow him the space, freedom, and time he needs to spur on his creative juices. That is what makes this marriage work, and this is one of the secrets that has kept Anthony in front of the spotlight for over fifty years.

Anthony continued to make music history. A tour in the UK was scheduled for February 2014, which was to bring together several groups for their British premier. It was the opposite of the British invasion: it was now America's turn to showcase their best singers and musicians selling their CDs to a new generation of music lovers.

Anthony replaced the cell phone back on the kitchen table, where the glass top still seemed to be rattling from call; it had been David Gest on the phone, world-famous star, producer, and entertainer, asking him to be part of a tour in the UK. The last time he had seen David was when he had sung at his wedding to Liza Minnelli and the entire world knew how that ended up. Apparently David held no grudge and welcomed him to be part of the show, touring a month throughout the country. He named the tour Legends of Soul, and hosted the production with the following star studded line-up: Candi Staton, Percy Sledge, Jody Watley, Gwen Dickey, Cece Peniston, Eddie Floyd, Eddie Holman, and Little Anthony.

Thrilled, Anthony called up his son Tony, now his manager and a consummate businessman, giving him the exciting news. The two would be leaving at the end of January and there were endless details, rehearsals, costumes, press releases, and photos to be taken care of before lift-off over the pond. Anthony wouldn't be taking any of the Imperials, which saddened and worried him. Promised a full orchestra and two back-up singers, his presentation would be strong and full, but he fretted over the ability of the singers to carry the right pitch and resonance needed to sing those intricate ballads. "Dad, that's what I am here to do," reminded Tony. "You just get yourself ready, and I will make sure everything else is taken care of."

The eight hour flight departed JFK airport in overcast skies threatening the tenth heavy snowfall of the winter season. A couple of the entertainers scheduled on the same tour were on board but the plane was so large, none of them connected until they landed.

Flipping on the individual miniature television set, Anthony munched on some snacks until his eyes finally closed and he dozed off. He was traveling alone; Tony would be on the next flight leaving Los Angeles later the same day. Eight hours was a long time to be stuck in a seat, even a comfortable seat.

The grinding sound of the engine combined with a "Welcome to Heathrow Airport" from the cabin crew meant the end of the long journey. As he walked down the long corridors, the sky was as gray and dark as the one he had left in New York. The chauffeur approached Anthony, tossed his bags onto the luggage cart, and meandered around, locating the other two singers on the flight.

Between the time difference and the long trip, the usually talkative performers sat quietly as they were driven to the southern tip of England, finally arriving at the Butlins Resort. Built right on the ocean, it was a complete resort with mid-way rides, water activities, a plethora of restaurants, and of course, a large venue for live entertainment. The only thing that appeared to be missing, at least to Anthony who had been residing in Las Vegas for years, was the promise of sunshine. The grounds were beautiful, quaint, family oriented, everything anyone could hope to find in a tourist destination except for the warm glow of the sun. Yet people came in droves, in the midst of their cold and damp winter, filling the auditoriums every night.

Tony arrived later that day, finding his way to Anthony's room. He held an itinerary and a list of instructions, and they began preparing for the show that evening. Even though so many things seemed the same, so many things were different in the UK. Each room had the ubiquitous flat screen television, but the rooms were much smaller than those in the States, especially the closets and the bathrooms. Did they think everyone was skinny?

Because there were so many artists on the tour, David had arranged regimented eating times with limited menus: the bottom line was tantamount to the success of this tour. If all went well, another one would surely be on the horizon. So they kept to the schedule, and learned to eat as the British.

Tony met with the orchestra director to review the music, and later with the two back-up singers. After several rehearsals, he was confident the three songs Anthony was to sing would go as expected. The two-hour performance began after the later dinner hour, with an intermission and lasted until after midnight. Most nights the troupe didn't arrive back into their hotel rooms until two or three in the morning. As the weeks progressed, they traveled to another Butlins Resort near Wales, a hundred miles north of London. The five hour drive took them through the lush countryside. They had never seen such deep emerald green grassland, or rustic stone homes built decades before. In spite of the constant gray clouds perpetually raining down, the land was beautiful.

Once they were situated in their new rooms, the performers met for an early dinner, dressed and bundled up for the one hour drive to the Manchester Theatre. The turn of the century architecture, with a richly appointed interior, made this stately place an honor to perform in. The plush red velvet seats, deep blue carpets, and soft chandelier lighting affected a sophistication few places offer in America. It was as if the building was dignifying and honoring the artists who graced its stage. The performers took their final bows, always to sold-out audiences, boarded the vans, and returned to the resort. A midnight meal was prepared and waiting for the two busloads of entertainers as they ran in between the raindrops from the parking lot to the lobby. Tony and Anthony took plates, sampled the local English fare of appetizers, chatted with the singers, and then at three in the morning collapsed into bed.

In the morning, they met at the set in time for breakfast, but damn if Anthony wasn't really hungry, specifically for an American breakfast. It seemed as though the English poached just about everything, rarely used seasoning, and clung to the bland palette handed down from generations lacking world class grocery stores. It just wasn't that difficult to cook eggs. Summoning up a bit of courage, he asked the waitress for an egg salad sandwich. In a polite way, she nodded her head in an agreeable manner and later returned with his request. It was two poached eggs atop a mound of iceberg lettuce. Laughing, Anthony put his hands in the air, and said, "I give up. Pass me the beans."

For the remainder of the four weeks, the artists remained at the Radisson Hotel in Liverpool. If they weren't scheduled to perform at the resort, they were bused one to three hours away to various smaller townships, performing at the finest theaters. While driving to the Queens Theatre in downtown Liverpool, they couldn't help but notice they hadn't seen a trace of sun since the moment they landed. The clouds were raging with a heavy downpour, and the streets began to flood. In spite of the inclement weather, the audience was filled; the women were dressed in stunning cocktail dresses, and the men in finely cut Italian and English worsted wool suits.

A standing ovation marked the end of the show as drivers opened up the vans and assisted the singers to their seats. The drive back to the hotel was slow and treacherous; the roadways were overflowing with wide streams of rushing water, and there was flooding everywhere. When they finally arrived safe and sound, it was announced that the next two evening shows were cancelled due to flooding. Breathing a sigh of relief, the performers partied at a small restaurant near the lobby until three in the morning. "Why not have a great time? They had two days of vacation, not a care in the world, and no place to go," said Tony.

The morning news concurred that it had been horrific flooding, reporting it had been 100 years since the country had seen such foul weather. Photos of the Thames River overflowing flashed on the television screens, accompanied by an array of tragedies: people stuck in cars, dogs caught in flowing waters, even cows stuck in drenched fields. The entire country was under siege from the tempest of the relentless rain.

The final two days of the tour were spent in the heart of Liverpool at the Radisson Blu, an Americanized hotel. The sun finally appeared, so Anthony and Tony took a walk through the downtown without holding up a large umbrella. Snapping pictures, Tony captured glimpses of the history of the town: bronze statues, historic buildings, clock towers, plaques commemorating heroes and event.

Following a double-decker bus brimming with tourists, they turned a corner and saw a large outdoor shopping mall. As they walked through the shops and stalls, they were impressed by the quality and cheap prices of the clothing. "It was the shoes that I fell in love with; they were sleek, the leather was so soft, but the heels and the soles were made out of a tough waterproof rubber. I tried a pair on and they were the most comfortable shoes I had ever worn. I was sold." The winds began picking up and they walked back to the hotel. By the time they had reached the lobby, the winds had been clocked at 70 miles an hour. They were done shopping for the day, that was for sure.

The last item on their itinerary was at a charity event at the famed Gilgamesh Restaurant on the outskirts of London. The second floor houses a supper club where David Gest hosted the event to a crowd of celebrities. There appeared to be as many photographers and paparazzi as patrons attending the well-publicized event. In the dead of winter, with the looming fear of more flooding, Londoners took advantage of the break in weather, put on their finest evening clothes, and partied with the performers. The historic structure had been updated on the second floor, turning it into futuristic nightclub décor, with deep purple lighting slanting across the stage, cozy cocktail tables, a sleek oak dance floor, and subdued coral lighting behind the shiny granite bar. Anthony took the stage, singing "Tears on My Pillow" and "Going Out Of My Head," the song he had sung at David's wedding. Leaving the stage, he was overwhelmed by the huge round of applause that the esteemed audience gave.

When his plane departed Heathrow early the next morning, he could still hear the applause ringing in his ears. David thanked him for coming and said he hoped if they reran this tour, Anthony would return. Smiling, Anthony thought of all those bad meals, the beans at breakfast, the dark dank clouds looming in the skies every day. Sure, he would return! England was a beautiful country and the people who lived there were kind, smart, caring, thoughtful, and polite people. What more could a performer ask for?

CHAPTER 26

Back one week in Las Vegas, his body still in jet lag mode, Anthony prepared for an illustrious event: he would be attending the 8th Annual Music and Entertainment Industry Group Taste of Hope Fundraiser at the special events venue, in New York City. Anthony was donating an outfit worn during one of his performances, an advance copy of his biography, dinner for two with him in Las Vegas, tickets to a concert including a meet and greet. After another cross-country flight, he had officially become a member of the Million Mile Club, just another routine flight, but the charity event wasn't routine. There were lots of wealthy people attending and the stakes were high. They needed to raise money for research that would be saving lives around the world. He didn't take this event lightly.

As he walked into the catered affair, accompanied by Reviver CEO David Ross, publicist George Dassinger, and Promotional Executive Jerry Lembo, they were escorted to their table set elaborately with crystal stemware, fine china, and white linens. George introduced Anthony to numerous celebrities and then went over the details of the program. Holding plates piled high with gourmet hors d'oeuvres while a small band played background music, he noticed an unusual hush in the crowded room. There were no sudden laughs or boisterous outbursts, just a sense of prevailing earnestness. The trappings of the refined setting didn't camouflage the purpose for the evening; money had to be raised.

As the evening grew late, Anthony felt compelled to tell George how much he appreciated his work. "I knew if I stuck around with you, you would push me into greater heights and you have."

Next, Taylor Swift, the sweetheart of the country music world, approached. "Anthony I need to talk to you. Just how have you survived fifty years?"

"Taylor, we don't work, we entertain people. It's not work," he replied.

"At times I don't know what to do. I get pulled in so many directions. I need to know how to survive."

Anthony took this as a moment to offer his advice. "It's important to take time off and do something normal like grocery shopping, or reading a book."

"Come to Nashville and spend the day with me," she said.

As she departed, Anthony turned to George, and said, "She is so skinny I could wrap my arms around her, twice!"

Since men don't kiss or get weepy eyed, George twisted around, cocked his head, and said, "Come with me, there are some more people who want to meet you." They walked over to L.A. Reid, and Anthony was taken aback when L.A. bowed and said, "I wouldn't have my job without people like you."

Graciously, Anthony simply said, "I'm so glad I had that effect on you."

When the event was over, Jerry escorted Anthony into the packed elevator. Always quick on his feet, Jerry announced, "A Hall of Fame singer is onboard." And he prompted Little Anthony to sing "It Hurts So Bad." With that, Anthony began singing and when the doors opened and people stepped out into the lobby, there was a spontaneous round of applause as once again, Anthony created memories for his fans.

The next day Anthony was interviewed on Sirius XM Radio by a blast from the past, namely Cousin Brucie (Bruce Morrow), a beloved deejay from the 1960s who drove rock and roll into the national scene. Each week teens would sit glued to their transistor radios as he spun the top forty sounds. He was truly the king of the airways when it came to pop music.

Cousin Brucie's shows have eluded time, transferring from regular AM/FM broadcasting into satellite radio, where his voice and the music he plays can be heard around the globe. Gone are the days when his show could only be heard throughout the five boroughs of New York City; now, the entire planet has become the listening audience. At 78 years old, the deejay has three major programs on Sirius XM Radio: *Cousin Brucie Presents, Cruisin with the Cuz,* and *Cousin Brucie Saturday Rock and Roll Party.*

"I met Anthony when we were both kids. I was a deejay on WINS and he was with The Imperials. Every weekend, at the famed Palisades Park in New Jersey, there was a live show with the hottest rock and roll singers in the country. I was the emcee and I met Anthony backstage, right before he was to go on.

"Thousands of parents would drop off their kids at the park, where they spent the day on the rides, eating junk food and listening to our show. I felt like the busiest babysitter in the world: the parents trusted us, and the park was completely safe. The place was like a magical kingdom, a refuge and a wholesome environment for young kids to escape from family and school. I would walk around on stage in a leopard-print suit, and that became my trademark. All those fans who came to the free shows have followed me through several decades and now their children listen to the music. Palisades Park no longer exists, but I am presenting a reunion show at the Meadowlands in June 2014 and bringing onto the stage several of the artists from the 1950s and 1960s. I hope to have Little Anthony headline the reunion show in 2015. For some reason, my leopard print suit has shrunk, but I still plan to wear it – otherwise my fans wouldn't recognize me.

"Throughout the years, I have really gotten to know Anthony; he exudes a charismatic energy and confidence. When he walks into a room, people are drawn to him, yet he is the most approachable guy I've ever known. He is genuinely sweet. He has this God-given gift. I would say he has one of the most beautiful voices ever recorded; his staying power is absolute because of this great gift. His music has no time limit, and now belongs to multiple generations. When he walks out onto the stage he endears himself to the audience: he is real, and has a rapport. I could feel his contact with the fans. Anthony has an extreme talent, yet he is lovable and touchable and he makes you feel appreciated. He is aware of what is happening today and has a contemporary style; you never feel like you are listening to a song that was written in the 1950s.

"My musical philosophy is that society, as reflected by and through its poets, changes music. The poets write the lyrics that reflect the streets, the times, and the feelings of the people, and this is transcribed into music. In the 1950s, society changed, and teens wanted freedom. Rock and roll was born out of this need, and it is here to stay. Anthony's music is as relevant today as it was when he first sang the songs. New generations of artists are picking up his music: a great example is Bruno Mars. Thanks to Anthony, this entire genre of music keeps being played around the world."

George picked up Anthony early in the morning and they got off at 49th Street and 6th Avenue, in the heart of Manhattan. The elevator silently opened on the 36th floor and they were escorted to a small broadcasting room at the end of a short corridor. The town hall setting for fifty people was filled with ardent fans. The only props were a microphone and a shiny black baby grand piano with a professional at the keys. While joking and singing a few bars of several of his recorded top hits, Anthony interacted with the small audience. By allowing him to take requests, or answer questions, the intimate setting allowed the fans a chance to get reacquainted with their idol. They shook hands, and Bruce invited his guest to return; there was so much more to talk about and to sing.

On his way out of the studio, Anthony ran into his cousin, Noel Gourdin, a well-known R & B artist. "Just what are the chances this should happen? Meeting a member of my family, at a radio station in New York? It was preordained." Surprised, they chatted, hugged, and exchanged phone numbers, promising to meet again. George stood by watching the two men, while the wheels in his mind kept turning. Definitely, this was an auspicious meeting, two great talents. *Hmmm,* he thought.

The last scheduled meeting was with Mike McCann, another legendary deejay, and Anthony was only too happy to share his plans with a friend he had known for over three decades. Mike's office at Premiere Networks, a subsidiary of Clear Channel, was located at the southern tip of Manhattan. With cheaper rent, and a closer view of the harbor, it was a picturesque place to work. "I've interviewed Anthony at least ten times over the years, and his talent and longevity is one of the top in the music industry, said Mike. "We first met in 1971 backstage at the Benedum Theater in Pittsburgh, and immediately hit it off. I loved his music, but we both shared an obsession for baseball that was our common bond throughout the decades."

Born in Manhattan, Mike was shuffled out of the city into the suburbs of Westchester where he spent his youth listening to the radio, dreaming of becoming a deejay. Upon obtaining his long-sought after position as a deejay in St. Louis, he promptly dropped out of college his senior and never looked back. Cutting his teeth spinning the top 40s on AM stations, he only played new rock and roll sounds. "The songs would be on the airwaves for a few weeks and when they dropped off the charts, no one ever heard the music again. The artists always had to be singing something new if they wanted to sell their records. And then two things happened to change the course of radio and the music industry: FM stations, which allowed the listener many more choices and the infiltration of UK music like The Beatles of course.

"Those of us who grew up in the 1960s lived at the cutting edge as society redefined itself," remarked Mike "More changed occurred between 1960 and 1970 than in any other time. It was music that served to bond us all together as a unified nation, and all this took place in just one year, 1963-1964. Society changed and so did music. Music began to challenge our senses; everything was new and fresh, all the old formulas were tossed out. If the performers didn't innovate, their music was no longer in demand. Groups became old relics in a short period of time, and few survived this transition."

"Anthony's group had plenty of hits and got great material. His body of work grew and matured, and his music evolved away from the 1950s image. With producer Don Costa, and Teddy Randazzo's fresh new songs, the group stayed at the top of the charts, and their music never became stale. When a record was released, it was surprising and it became cutting edge.

"Very few American groups could withstand the competition; they had to rev up their creative side to answer the English call; The Beach Boys and Anthony's group were some of the few who withstood the competition. I came to realize that great tunes were only heard for a brief period of time and once they dropped off the charts, there were no other stations that picked up the music. New FM stations began popping up with unique sounds, creating niche markets. I began playing what was considered Classic Rock: hit songs that were familiar but once off the pop charts had no air time. Anthony and The Imperials was one of my favorite groups and I played their music a lot.

"I love my job: interviewing famous stars, seeing the live shows, and watching them perform on the various new medias. Unlike the typical top 40 deejays, the artists I interview have been around for decades, and they have become my friends. As I spin these classic sounds, a new generation has come to love the songs and the demand for live bookings began to jump. The movie *American Graffiti* and the television show *Happy Days* reintroduced a younger generation to the music, and resurrected the demand for the music. Yes, I do love my job; and it's because of great entertainers like Anthony that I will always love my job."

When George dropped Anthony off at the airport, and watched him wheel his suitcase into the glass-enclosed building, all he could think was that Anthony hadn't a clue as to how many people truly loved him and supported his talents. Humble, and naïve to a fault, this talented man would see a lot more play in his lifetime and George was the man for that job.

On the serene plane ride home, Anthony felt a sense of calm and joy. When all the money had been counted from the charity, it had been a hugely successful event and the ratings from Cousin Brucie's show were high; all in all, a very good trip. With George, and his son, Tony in his corner, his career continued to escalate. Closing his eyes, he thanked God for all that he had been given. This great ride of life, so full of love and joy, was something he never took for granted. His voice, his talent, his family, his friends, and his career, were a precious gift from above, and he was determined to help others achieve what he had been so blessed to be given.

Flipping open his cell phone, Anthony saw a series of messages from Tony. They all said "Call me." Anxious, Anthony punched in his son's phone number, who picked up immediately. "Dad, how are you?" he said breathlessly. "Because we have a lot to talk about. There are so many things coming your way, I don't know where to begin."

"Great, I'm thrilled, but I could sure use a day to get back into my time zone," Anthony laughed. Spying Linda patiently waiting at the luggage turn-style, he waved his arm, and ten minutes later he was standing at the front of his home. She rolled the suitcase into the wide foyer, took his jacket, and made him sit in the backyard. She poured him a glass of chilled iced-tea; he sipped it and stretched out on a lounge chair, and ten minutes later he was sound asleep.

Before Anthony's plane had penetrated the second layer of cumulous clouds, George was on the phone to his number one client, Reviver Records, with an idea he knew would sell. After he called David Ross, President and CEO, the two met later that day, discussing the possibilities of Anthony and how they could use his rare talent.

David grew up in New York, exposed at an early age to the hottest rock stars in the business through his father's profession. That passion and love for music stayed with him his entire life as he laid down his own set of tracks in the music recording industry. He worked at Alpha Distributors and several other music companies, expanding his horizons, meeting with agents, singers, and musicians; he literally knew thousands in the tight-knit industry.

He ingested every aspect of the music industry, and became familiar with every step needed to make an artist successful. Taking a leap of faith he, along with his business partners, Mark and Virginia, and his producer, Dennis D'Amico, launched Reviver. David's talent lay in his ability to understand and act upon a complete marketing package; he has an in-depth understanding of discovering, molding, and launching successful careers. Early on, he had learned that even though an artist had talent, the key was packaging this talent to appeal to the world. The company has been collecting performing artists, some just starting their careers, and others, like Anthony, who are seeking a change of management. What has made David's distribution company, Brody Distribution Group/SONY RED unusual is that they offer the entire package, from recording, to managing, to promoting, to booking: it is a one stop firm.

As an example of the prestige Reviver commands, they were given Paul McCartney's blessing to release the Limited Edited Alan Aldridge Beatles Illustrated Collective Set, Music For Linda, solely for the purpose of benefiting The Women and Cancer Fund. Using five of the classic Beatles tunes, recording artists sang their own version of the hit songs; Anthony sang the third song on the album, "A World Without Love," which was a soulful R & B rendition. With the assistance of Sony Red distribution, the music recorded by

Reviver has the ability to be heard around the globe.

Ideas are either born alone, or born with the intervention of many creative minds. George Dassinger who is publicist for both Reviver and Little Anthony, put the two together, and with David Ross' insight, a series of records will be forthcoming, the first of which is a duets album. "I want to record this in New York City," said Anthony, as he envisioned the songs he would sing and the artists he would be singing with.

David Ross, who had been following Anthony for decades, proposed a rejuvenation of the singer's career. And after a meeting of the minds, Reviver signed Anthony on as one of their artists. They laid out a plan of gigs, recordings, and marketing presentations to make Anthony's face and voice extremely recognizable to an entire new generation of music lovers. The planning for the first of a series of albums was soundly sealed in place: *Duets* was a record that would combine Anthony's voice with a cross-section of superstars in the music industry. David flew to Las Vegas, and hired the finest photographer, Bobby Black, who set up a photo shoot for the impending album. Not only is Bobby Black a topnotch photographer, but he is also a singer with the Las Vegas Tenors.

Another prong to David's grand design team was hiring the perfect promotion manager, which he found in Jerry Lembo. The art of masterminding the excitement and anticipation of new music was what Jerry is all about. "I'm not a singer, nor do I know how to play a musical instrument, I just love music. It is my passion and I couldn't live a day without hearing music," he said. He too, lives on the East Coast in northern New Jersey, hidden away from the tumult of Manhattan; it is a twenty minute ride from his placid township into the heart of the city, where he meets with the head honchos of various media. It's often said that those who have the ear of the media have the power to make things happen, and that is precisely what Jerry does. He is one of the most personable men you will ever meet; he has more than a gift of gab – with him comes decades of experience with numerous companies, including Columbia Records.

One of his first memories was unscrewing the top to his four poster bed and using the knob as a microphone, mimicking the voices of deejays on the various radio stations. As he pretended to slide another record onto the turntable, he fell in love with music, the artists, the rhetoric of the deejays, and how it all came together. He pondered the mystery of how music moved from the recording studios into the airwaves. In elementary school, he was always the emcee of the talent shows and his job was procuring the talent. When none could be found, he stood up and entertained his classmates with jokes.

"I learned to be a ham, and I found I could entertain my friends. From that moment on, I took every opportunity to put together talent with gigs. I was the go-to person whenever anyone wanted or needed entertainers. I had an insatiable thirst for new singers and performing artists, and spent my time learning as much as I could about them and the music industry. Since they didn't teach about the music industry in school, I made a huge mistake dropping out my senior year. With a minimum wage job, I retraced my steps, went back the following fall, and got my diploma. I took every dime I had and went to broadcast school in Manhattan, with big dreams of becoming a famous deejay after only two months of classes. Reality hit me in the face when the only job I could land was in a small market in some tiny suburban town. I knew I would suffer withdrawal if I couldn't see the Big Apple, so I remained at home, got married, and had three kids."

Like a burning comet shooting across the sky, live entertainment was eviscerated, replaced with deejays who spun everyone's lives into Disco Fever. Jerry obtained a seven day a week gig: a radio spot where he worked his butt off for years. During the course of his work, he continued brokering deals between talent and venues; it came naturally to him, it simply made him feel great. "Record labels began approaching me to promote their releases to radio. After running my independent firm Platinum Promotions, I had executive positions at Chrysalis Records and Columbia Records from 1984 to 1997, before returning to my entrepreneurial roots, establishing the Jerry Lembo Entertainment Group. A lunch meeting with Reviver CEO David Ross led to the current collaborative efforts to execute a Little Anthony career extension plan.

After decades at Columbia, Jerry began his own business and was quickly sought after by Reviver Records. Now, boss of his own firm, he can pick and choose his clients, the hours he works, and how he will promote his clients. His list of clients is a promoter's dream, but then, Jerry has the background, the ability, and the connections to make it all happen. Just open up his website and the list of accolades is all any artist would need to know when seeking the preeminent promoter in the music business.

As he boarded the plane for his cross-country flight, David Ross took in a long, easy breath anticipating the next few days in Las Vegas: he had his superstar artist, the best promoter in the business, a worldwide public relations firm on the East Coast, and had hired one of the top photographers. Everything was set for the historic roll-out of Little Anthony's new album.

A day in the life of a superstar; this was not how the rest of the society got to spend their days. Those extraordinary days are spent by extraordinary people whose musical talent becomes further nourished, enriched, and later exposed to the world. Through David Ross' eyes, the rolling out of Anthony's first album with Reviver was born with a precise vision of how David understood the singer's genius and how his vision would be presented to the world.

Early Friday morning, sporting a broad smile, Anthony plunked bags of costumes and accessories into the trunk of the car. The driver would see to it that his every need was met, but first a stop at the local bank. A house filled with children and grandchildren often left his pockets empty, and so not to be embarrassed, he replaced the missing cash in his worn leather wallet.

The spring air was cool, the skies veiled with a thin layer of clouds, the temperature in the high sixties, a perfect day for shooting. Holding the computer printout, Anthony dictated directions as the driver cruised through the streets of Henderson. The first stop was a recording studio, tucked in an older residential neighborhood. Unusual, yes, but secure and serenely quiet, this was Joey Melotti's private recording studio. Cloistered by the tallest trees in the desert valley, a constant cool breeze filtered throughout the one-story home; this was his safe haven, the place where his musical genius was nourished, written, and recorded.

Bobby Black, a tall, hefty, thirty-something, balding man, took his time meticulously setting up the trappings of a photographer's paraphernalia, while David Ross fluttered over Anthony like a mother hen. He set out a spread of food and drinks, aiming to make his superstar feel comfortable. The living room had been transformed into a small stage that captured and trapped sounds exuding from the Yamaha baby grand and the voices on a series of adjustable microphones. Joey, an expert piano player, keyboardist, arranger, writer, and producer, began jamming with Anthony, each showing off their talents. An impromptu concert took place inside the studio that morning: Anthony sang "God Bless the Child" and "What Are You Doing the Rest of Your Life," bringing tears to eyes of the audience of the four handlers. "I'm warming up for the photographs," laughed Anthony. Dressed in a black tuxedo, with a matching black fedora atop his head, with a single spotlight bathing his face, was the image David wanted to capture. Anthony was an artist whose music was so well-defined, that simplicity in design was warranted.

While Bobby was busy resetting the cameras for another series of shots, Joey began talking about his years spent with Michael Bolton as his music director and later with Barry Manilow as his keyboardist, arranger, and writer. In 1988 Joey had written a couple of songs with Barry, and he now played "Be Mine Tonight" for Anthony. That song was never recorded. Anthony was listening very carefully: what a song, what a melody line. "It never got recorded?" asked Anthony. Joey shook his head no, and then took Anthony into an adjacent room, flipped on a couple of switches, and played the track recorded by a back-up singer. As he stared at the floor, the intensity of Anthony's concentration was evident.

At the end of the last note, he pronounced, "Yes, I think I can do that song." He never learned to read music. "It's all up here," he said as he pointed to his brain. One listen to the song and it became embedded in his mind; he would make it his own. Turning to Joey, Anthony began a fondly remembered anecdote about his inability to read notes: "I was singing with the San Francisco Philharmonic Orchestra and I suggested to the maestro that there were problems, the tone wasn't right; it was coming from the violins. When the maestro carefully listened, he discovered the violins were playing in the wrong octave. He looked over to me and said I was right, that I had some set of ears, and then blasted out instructions to the string players. I can hear a rat pissing on cotton," Anthony joked. "I hear the music inside my brain and when the sounds come out, I know if there is something off-key."

While reviewing some of the preliminary pictures, the photographer noticed an animation in his subject's face after the short concert; Anthony had to sing to wake up his facial muscles, to get that glint in his eyes, and a rise in his cheeks. "The camera knows when you are having a good or bad day; the camera never lies," said Bobby.

After two hours of constant shooting, it was time to move to another studio, an actual photo studio. After he changed into jeans and a navy tee-shirt, everyone packed-up and caravanned to the southern tip of Henderson. Again the studio was enmeshed inside a community of residential homes, but the neighborhood was new, with fewer trees and smaller backyards. The stark white living room had a thirty foot ceiling, with two high rectangular windows to allow the sun to filter in. A white cloth was strewn on the floor, and a white backdrop hung from the walls, which allowed for the introduction of any background colors and images. Changing his clothing for a third time, Anthony did the requisite series of poses of the typical model: hands in pockets and out, smiles, no smiles, standing, sitting, adding props, moving in different directions, silhouettes, or full face; it was another two hours of capturing the soul of the artist.

Anthony and Bobby talked about their morning frog throats, especially in the dry desert climate. "I remember I was to sing on one of those early talk shows – actually, it was the *Today Show*, and I had to be at the station by five in the morning. One of my friends said, 'Hey man, just fake it.'

"I turned to him and said 'Fake it? I don't think so, especially with my falsetto.' So the night before, I sat up in a chair, I never went to sleep. And when I arrived at the television station and they handed me the microphone, my voice was ready to go."

Bobby had arrived in Las Vegas via Nashville, a town filled with recording artists and lots of humidity. "I loved Nashville, but Las Vegas offered so many venues to perform in. There are only so many recordings I could make and then it was time to go out and perform. I packed my bags and have never looked back." Bobby and Anthony then began making a series of dissonant noises as they described how they warmed up their vocal muscles, which put the rest of the team in stitches.

The afternoon quickly drifted by as the caravan drove to the last stop of the day: New York, New York Hotel and Casino, filled with the essence of Anthony's hometown, Brooklyn. Taking the two-story escalator to the second level, they camped out at Nathan's for the rest of the shoot. After a lunch of their world famous hotdogs and fries, Bobby removed the cameras from his cushioned case and began snapping away. Because Las Vegas is the heart of tourism, nobody bothered with the celebrity; the town was filled with celebrities and visitors, all doing the same thing. Anthony was as anonymous as anyone could get. After chugging down two hotdogs, the photographer led the group out to the street taking a series of photos underneath the Brooklyn Bridge, albeit the one constructed framing the entrance to the casino. With a few touch-ups, it looked as though Anthony was above the Hudson River, smiling in his camouflage jacket. Traipsing back to their cars, the men shook hands, congratulating each other on the fine work they had produced that day.

When the driver finally dropped off Anthony at his home, the driver could see the lasting vestige of his smile still cemented on his face. "Aren't you tired? And if you say you're not then you should be. Eight hours on your feet, several changes of clothing, taking commands from the photographer, you should be tired. I'm tired just looking at you."

"I love it all. This isn't work, it's what I love doing, it's what I'm blessed to do, so no, I'm not tired."

CHAPTER 27

"Redemption: that is my life. I know I wasn't always that good of a person; I did a lot of bad things in my life. I drank, womanized, cheated on my first wife, ignored my kids, and took way too many drugs, but here I stand by the grace of God. When I almost lost my voice, it was God who returned it to me when I went down that dark path of drug addiction, it was God who pulled me out; when I landed in the hospital, it was God who turned the tide and allowed me to walk out a healthy man. That day, that one singular day in my life at Redondo Beach, when I had cried a river a tears and felt the warmth of God's love embrace me, did I become another human being. His shroud of unconditional love overtook my being: God forgave me, God accepted me, God loved me. All God asked in return was for me to love him too. I would say I believe in God, but I believe God. I can't explain it, I wouldn't attempt to explain this real sense of love, but it's there and I have felt this every day of my life since that moment.

"We go to church, The Word of Life, Pastor David and Vicky Shearin, and pray with the congregation. For me, it's more than uttering words from the Bible or singing classic psalms, it's a way of life. I know the power of God. I have witnessed it in my life. I find my truth and the essence of love through His omnipotent powers. When I am standing on stage and my voice sings, I feel as though I am simply a vessel through which God's will works.

"I look around and see others, many who have died, and I wonder why I am still here, still singing with the same voice I had when I was in my twenties and there is only one answer: God. Many mornings I woke up barely able to talk, yet when the microphone was handed to me, all of a sudden my voice rang through; it's supernatural and can only be explained by God.

"With a deep love for my family, I have a complete life. Now with a stream of grandchildren, my name and legacy lives on. Perhaps none of my family will be blessed with the gift of voice, but in so many other ways, their lives are blessed: with health, intelligence, and the ability to love and be loved."

"My best years are still ahead of me. There are songs to be sung, movies to be made, Broadway shows to be produced, albums to be cut, concerts to be played and charity events to be attended. I know I'm no longer the life of the party, nor is that what I seek to do. The legacy of my music, all those melodies created by the most brilliant lyricists, the conductors' talents of creative orchestrations, the sewers of all those one-of-a kind costumes, the genius of the recording technicians, the lighting and film directors, have made my career the success that it stands for today and I thank them all."

"On the horizon I hear the noise of children's laughter, the loud sound of applause, the warm glow of the spotlight beaming down on my head. I know I'm not on that stage alone: I carry with me a lifetime of memories, and a future filled with the unconditional love of God. I am redeemed as each day of my life I come closer to the meaning of love and life.

"When I think back to all the music I have sung, to the millions of people around the globe who I have been privileged to entertain, I consider myself blessed. This life as an entertainer is a life I have loved since my earliest memories. I remember singing in my crib, those Saturday evening get-togethers with my aunts, the school dances, the harmonizing around the streetlamps in Brooklyn. I loved it all, every moment, every note, and every sound. I saw both my parents working hard in jobs that held no promise for their dreams. I have never taken for granted the luxury to be able to make a living doing what I love to do: make music.

"On the plane ride home from New York, after performing at the City of Hope event, it made me both humble and thankful that the gift God has given me can be used to help others. As long as I can continue to sing, I will continue to share my joy by helping to raise money for great causes. My initial passion for singing pleased myself, later my family, my friends, and audiences, and now I can use this passion to help others have a better life. I could ask for no more; this is my legacy and for as long as God sees fit, I will sing my heart out."

Grabbing the ringing cell phone, tireless Anthony listened to Tony conveying the next set of gigs. "Yes son, yes son, sure, tell them we will be there. A gig in Las Vegas, sure, a charity event in downtown Los Angeles, yes of course. Yep, this legacy just keeps rolling along. Thank you, Lord!"

To be continued…

GREATEST SINGLES

Tears on My Pillow
Two People in the World
So Much
Diary
It's Not For Me
Wishful Thinking
A Prayer and A Juke Box
I'm Alright
Shinny Shimmy Ko-ko Bop
My Empty Room
I'm Taking a Vacation From Love
Please Say You Want Me
Traveling Stranger
I Miss You So
Out of Sight Out of Mind
Hurt
Ten Commandments of Love

Teddy Randazzo wrote and co-wrote the following songs:
I'm on the Outside Looking In
Going Out of My Head
Hurt So Bad
Take Me Back
Out of Sight Out of Mind

Better Use Your Head
Gonna Fix You Good
I'm Hypnotized
Yesterday Has Gone

TOP SELLING ALBUMS

Little Anthony and The Imperial's Greatest Hits
The Best of Little Anthony and the Imperials
Tears on My Pillow and All Their Greatest Recordings
Hot Pastrami
Two Kinds of People in the World
On a New Street/Hold On
Little Anthony and The Imperials The Diary
Going Out of My Head
25 Greatest Hits
Better Use Your Head/The Wonder of it All
Hurst So Bad/ Reputation
Shades of the 40's
Shimmy Shimmy Ko-Ko Bop
Take Me Back/Our Song